COLLECTIVE YEARNING

COLLECTIVE YEARNING

BLACK WOMEN ARTISTS FROM THE ZIMMERLI ART MUSEUM

Edited by Amber N. Wiley
Foreword by Nicole Simpson

Rutgers University Press
New Brunswick, Camden, and Newark, New Jersey
London

Rutgers University Press is a department of Rutgers, The State University of New Jersey, one of the leading public research universities in the nation. By publishing worldwide, it furthers the University's mission of dedication to excellence in teaching, scholarship, research, and clinical care.

978-1-9788-4284-7 (cloth)
978-1-9788-4285-4 (epub)

Cataloging-in-publication data is available from the Library of Congress.
LCCN 2025041049

A British Cataloging-in-Publication record for this book is available from the British Library.

Publication of this book was supported by the following organizations:

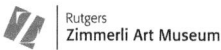 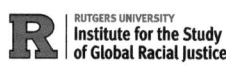 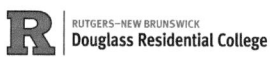

References to internet websites (URLs) were accurate at the time of writing. Neither the author nor Rutgers University Press is responsible for URLs that may have expired or changed since the manuscript was prepared.

♾ The paper used in this publication meets the requirements of the American National Standard for Information Sciences—Permanence of Paper for Printed Library Materials, ANSI Z39.48-1992.

rutgersuniversitypress.org

For my Momma(s), grandmas, all my aunties,
sisters, girl cousins, and nieces

Contents

Illustrations

Foreword

IN THE SPRING OF 2021, a group of students at Rutgers University embarked on an ambitious, collaborative project to organize the first exhibition devoted to works by Black women artists from the collection of the Zimmerli Art Museum. Expertly led by Amber N. Wiley, then an assistant professor of art history, students in her upper-level exhibition seminar spent the semester learning and implementing curatorial practice. The class worked under extraordinary circumstances, coming together during the global COVID-19 pandemic and the widespread Black Lives Matter movement, to collectively curate an insightful and inspiring exhibition that celebrated the excellence of twenty-four Black women artists and their prints, photographs, and multimedia works.

Curatorial projects often present problems that require creative solutions, and this project posed some new and unprecedented challenges. The first step was creating a list of works by Black women artists in the permanent collection. The Zimmerli, like many museums, does not historically indicate the artist's race or gender in its cataloging (typically including only nationality and life dates). In my role as associate curator of prints and drawings, I searched through any existing information, consulted with my curatorial colleagues, and spent time going through our database and historical records to generate a list of potential candidates for the exhibition. While normally the students would then come to the museum to view the artworks in person, Rutgers had shifted to online learning and the Zimmerli was closed, with staff working off-site. I gathered any existing digital images, students searched for comparable works online, and we benefited from the gracious assistance of Christine Giviskos, curator of prints, drawings, and European art, who visited the museum during its closure to photograph several works. Although an inferior substitute to hands-on experience, the use of these lists and digital images provided the basis for students to begin to review the works and research them online. With her customary skill and sensitivity, Professor Wiley guided them through this complex process via class Zoom sessions and online conversations. The students, coming from diverse and interdisciplinary backgrounds, wove together their research and interpretations to tell multilayered stories about these women artists. They discovered threads of thematic connections about how these artists explored identity and self-narratives and spirituality and religion, and, given that the majority of the works were prints, they examined the communal nature of printmaking and the importance of the Brodsky Center (active at Rutgers 1986–2017) in publishing work by women and artists of color.

The exhibition *Collective Yearning: Black Women Artists from the Zimmerli Art Museum* opened in fall 2022 at two venues: the main show at the Mary H. Dana Women Artists Series galleries at the Mabel Smith Douglass Library and a smaller, satellite show at the Focus Gallery at the Zimmerli Art Museum. Located on two separate campuses within New Brunswick, these venues engaged a wide community at Rutgers, including those who wouldn't traditionally visit an art museum. Throughout the run of the exhibition, visitors to the Douglass Library venue were welcomed daily by student guides who had been trained by Kyle b. co., one of the exhibition's curators and a master of fine arts student at Mason Gross School of the Arts, through the Douglass Faculty Fellows Program. Accompanying the exhibition was a series of engaging public programs, both virtual and in-person, that featured student curators, contemporary artists and scholars, and cultural organizers, who expanded on the themes of the exhibition and brought it to an even wider audience. This catalog is a significant record of the exhibition and the transformative power of inviting students to become curators. Their voices are a testament to the importance of engaging the wider community in museum work and vital in reimaging the museum as an active and engaging space for all.

The exhibition and catalog were made possible through the mutual support of the Art History Department, the Center for Women in the Arts and Humanities (CWAH), and the Zimmerli Art Museum and the assistance of its staff throughout the various stages of this project. An important note of gratitude for Nicole Ianuzelli at CWAH, who was indispensable in every aspect of the exhibition and the related programming. The exhibition opened soon after the Zimmerli welcomed its new director, Maura

Reilly, a longtime advocate for women and diversity in the arts, who embraced this show with great enthusiasm and support. The largest thank-you, for their perseverance, creativity, and hard work, goes to Professor Wiley and her students: Jasmine Daria Cannon, Kyle b. co., Helen Gao, Grace Lynne Haynes, Emily Hu, Grace Kim, Desiree Morales, Michael Randall, and Audrey Roclore. At a time when we collectively and individually experienced feelings of isolation, fear, and uncertainty, this project fostered a spirit of community and of shared hope and brought us together to create an exhibition with lasting impact.

—NICOLE SIMPSON, PhD
ASSOCIATE CURATOR
OF PRINTS AND DRAWINGS
ZIMMERLI ART MUSEUM

COLLECTIVE YEARNING

I can't do anything outside of my experience.

I am Black and I am a woman.

There it is! Right there.

And I can't be one without the other

because it just can't happen.

—FAITH RINGGOLD,
2008

Introduction
Pedagogical Yearning

AMBER N. WILEY

IN THE WINTER OF 2022, the students in my African American Art survey class at Rutgers University authored a final paper responding to the following prompt: *Do we need an exhibition on Black women artists in 2022? Why or why not? What are the advantages or disadvantages of organizing an exhibition around a group of artists on the basis of race, gender, and nationality?* I tasked them with engaging the exhibition *Collective Yearning: Black Women Artists from the Zimmerli Art Museum* on display at the Mary H. Dana Women Artists Series and the Zimmerli Art Museum (ZAM) that semester. The exhibition would serve as a case study to explore the tenets of critical race art history as well as what it means to challenge the artistic canon and the museum as an institution.

Back to the question at hand—did we need an exhibition on Black women artists in contemporary times? Indeed, on the surface the query smacked of 1990s tokenism by race and gender, or an outdated version of "diversity and inclusion." I had heard as much from informants who had an ear to the ground as I prepared to launch the exhibition. People were tired of run-of-the-mill "identity politics." In my classes, we understand both race and gender to be social constructs and challenge the notion of who qualifies as Black and woman.[1] Even legal scholar and activist Kimberlé Crenshaw, originator of the term *intersectionality*, warned in the early 1990s that "the problem with identity politics is not that it fails to transcend difference, as some critics charge, but rather the opposite—that it frequently conflates or ignores intragroup differences."[2] I had hoped (overly optimistically and with a bit of naïveté) that the students would not be influenced by my imprint on the show. I encouraged them to say, "No, we don't need this type of exhibition, and I'll tell you why" or even "I wish we didn't, but we do, for these reasons." Their grades were determined not by whether they answered in the affirmative or negative, but by the well-reasoned arguments they made, based on the readings we had consulted that semester, backed up with evidence from the research they conducted as well as their own experience of the exhibition.

The forty students in the class reflected the wide range of backgrounds of Rutgers's student body—from first- and second-generation students of Chinese, Ghanaian, Haitian, Indian, Korean, Nigerian, and Puerto Rican descent to generational African Americans and white Americans of Greek, Irish, and Italian lineages. Students embodied a variety of gender identities, sexual orientations, and socioeconomic and political backgrounds.[3] As the historian and artist Nell Irvin Painter has said of her graduate experience at Rutgers, "[The] students were black and brown; they wore T-shirts, shorts, tiny little skirts, the hijab, or preprofessional uniforms. Rutgers isn't like those lame midwestern universities that need Photoshop to multiculturalize their image. Rutgers in its multifariousness is lovable, multicultural New Jersey. Rutgers is in New Jersey, with everyone from everywhere."[4] The vast majority of students in my class were not art history majors. Their chosen academic specializations included actuarial science, business analytics, communication and media studies, comparative literature, health administration, information technology, labor studies, lighting design, photography, and political science. The class thrived on these distinctions. "Difference," the poet and critical theorist Audre Lorde argued, "is that raw and powerful connection from which our personal power is forged."[5] This was true for my students as well. So, despite these differences, they came to the same conclusion: an exhibition on Black women artists is still needed in this day and time.

These students, turned art and culture critics, based their arguments in deep theoretical and interdisciplinary dialogues in art history, Black feminist thought, critical race theory, and museology. They spoke of the intersectional challenges Black women faced in the art world and society. Students argued that the women in the show offered counternarratives to mainstream depictions of the Black experience, and of Black women in particular. One student cited historical stereotypical portrayals of Black women as mammies and wenches, quoting Frederick Douglass: "Negroes can never have impartial portraits, at the hands of white artists."[6] Another scholar offered the advantages of organizing an exhibition around an identity to build community among artists and to connect museums and galleries to a more diverse audience. Yet another undergraduate contended that "social stratification and intersectionality are critical factors affecting the consumption and production of art," such that ignoring these facts would be detrimental to the art world and especially the quality and quantity of art produced by Black women.[7] Many students returned to a 2019 study that found that among the holdings of eighteen major art museums in the United States, 85 percent of the artists were white and 87 percent were men.[8] That study further revealed, "The four largest groups represented . . . in terms of gender and ethnicity are white men (75.7%), white women (10.8%), Asian men (7.5%), and Hispanic/Latinx men (2.6%). All other groups are represented in proportions less than 1%."[9] Those statistics alone, the students argued, necessitated initiatives to inspire U.S. museums to more accurately reflect the demographics of the communities they serve.

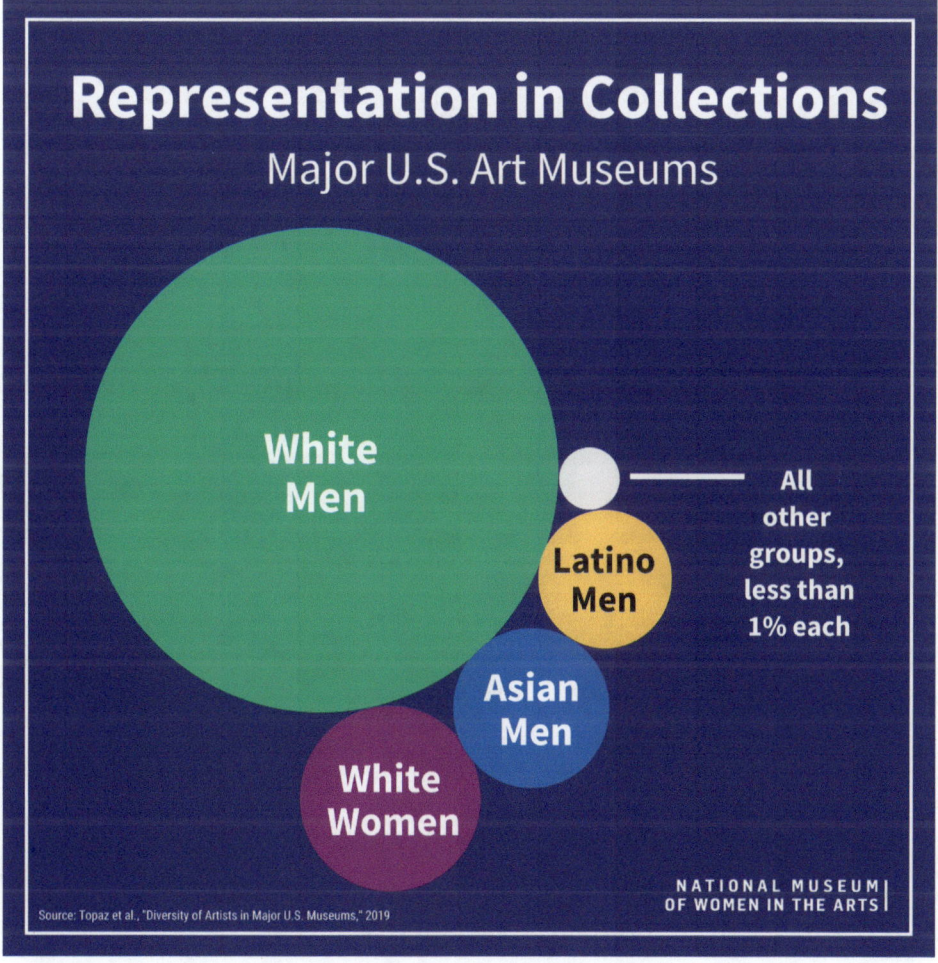

Fig. I.1. Demographic representation in collections of major U.S. art museums. Data from Chad M. Topaz et al., "Diversity of Artists in Major U.S. Museums," *PLoS One* 14, no. 3 (2019): e0212852. National Museum of Women in the Arts.

Moreover, the art pieces in the exhibition served as source material for these student critics' arguments. As one student critic contended, the art highlighted themes "regarding the essence of creative freedom, consumerism, identity, and disappearing and s[ought] to redefine binary constructs of being." This was certainly the case for a student who compared Emma Amos's self-portrait *Identity* with student curator Helen Gao's comprehensive portrait *Faces of Collective Yearning*, maintaining that all artists in the exhibition wished to be known by their art *and* their individual personhood. The exhibition as well as Gao's artwork, the student argued, rectified the erasure of these women in the art world. Still other student critics found varying, sometimes conflicting, messages about Black women's ability to reclaim their power, contrasting Nona Faustine's *Scarlet and Black* with Nell Irvin Painter's *Wise Woman Disappears* as examples in which power is contradictory and even ephemeral.[10]

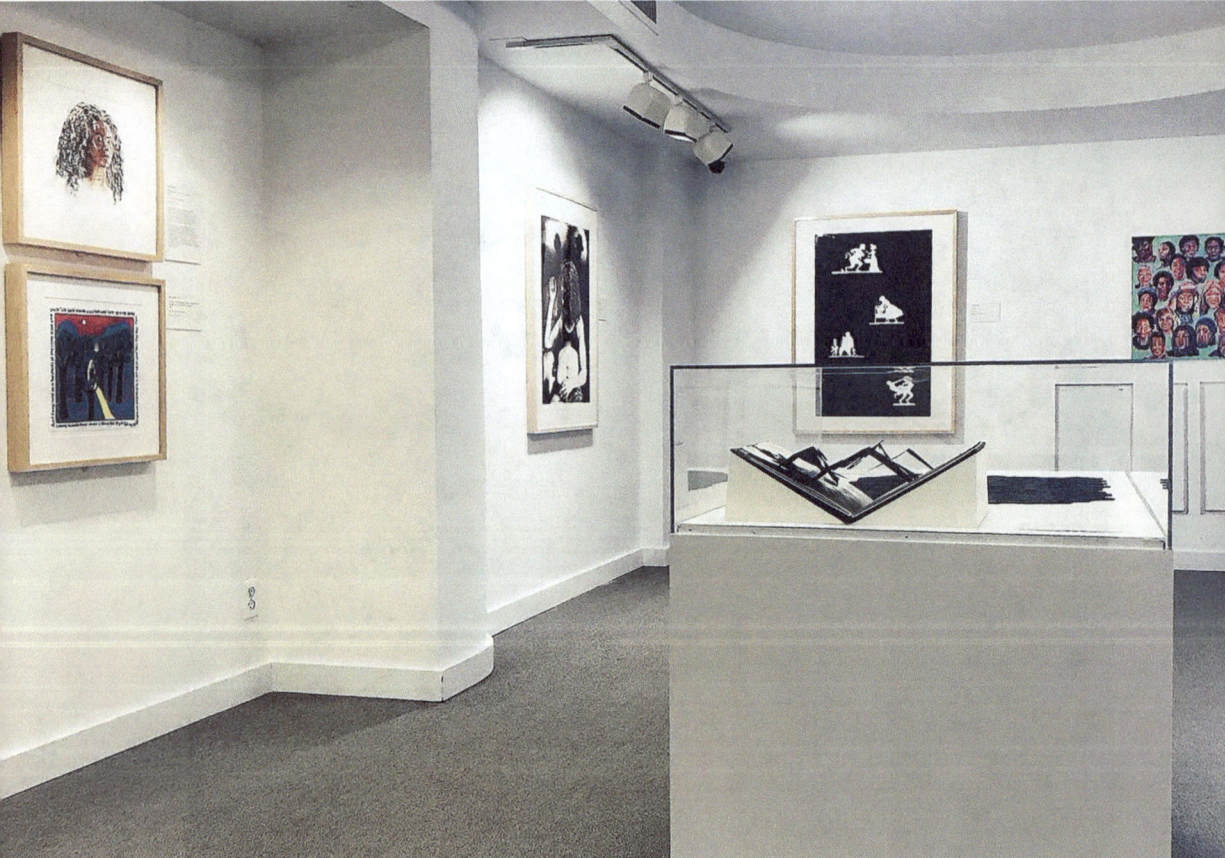

Fig. I.2. Installation in the Focus Gallery at the Zimmerli Art Museum (ZAM). Emma Amos's *Identity* is at the top left of the photograph; Helen Gao's *Faces of Collective Yearning* is on the far right. 2022. Nicole Simpson, photographer.

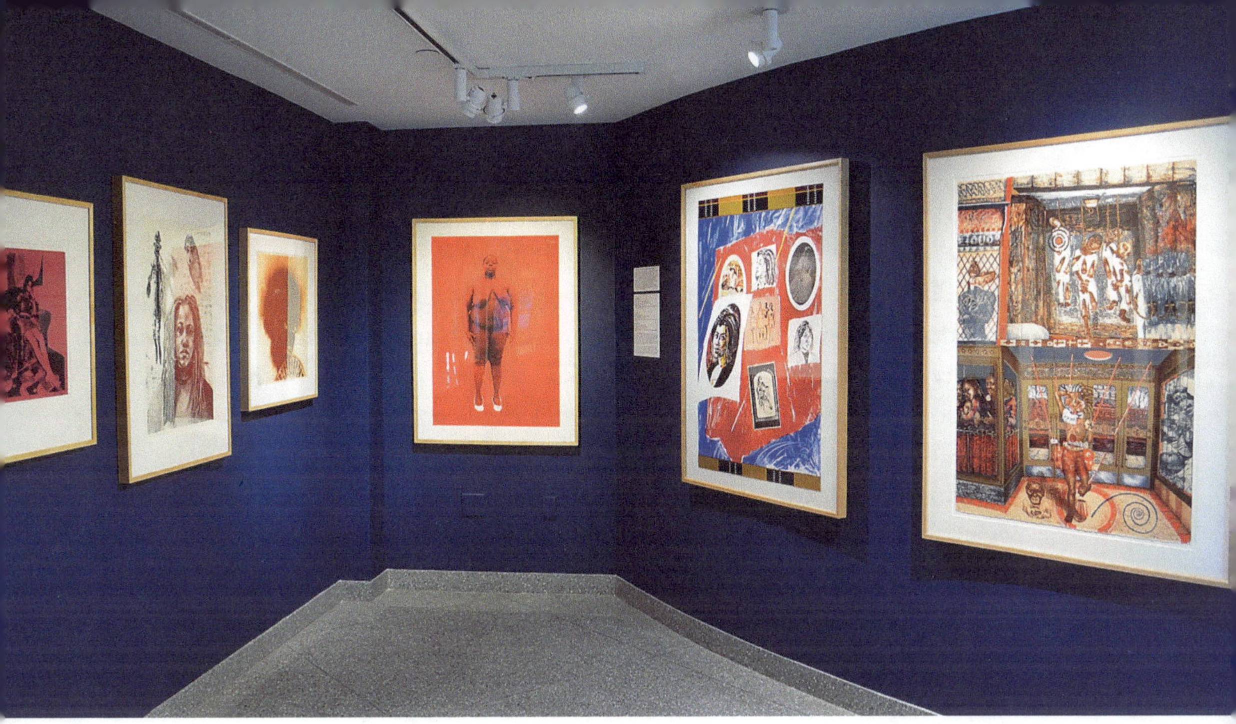

Fig. I.3. Installation in Gallery 104A at the Mary H. Dana Women Artists Series (DWAS) in the Mabel Smith Douglass Library. Nona Faustine's *Scarlet and Black* is in the center. 2022. Nicole Ianuzelli, photographer.

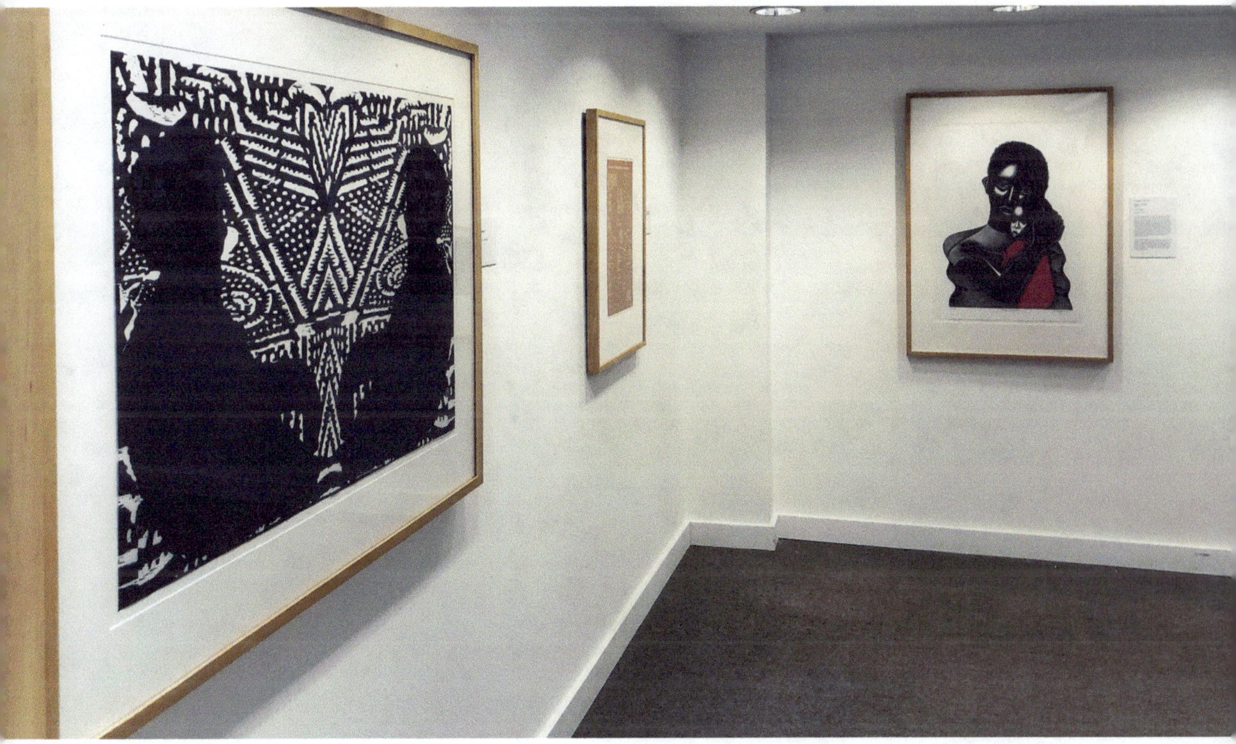

Fig. I.4. Nell Irvin Painter's *Wise Woman Disappears* installed on the left wall. Focus Gallery of the ZAM. 2022. Nicole Simpson, photographer.

These budding art critics were sensitive to the potential negative messages that an exhibition centered on identity might send to the world. They warned against the risks of tokenization, referencing Crenshaw, who cautioned that "tokenistic, objectifying, voyeuristic inclusion is at least as disempowering as complete exclusion."[11] Students were concerned that identity-based shows could reinforce a sense of otherness and marginalization for the artists, and they were wary of the potential such exhibitions had to create the impression that Black women were a monolith.

To combat simplistic, essentialist notions that threatened to unilaterally flatten the experiences of Black women artists in the United States, students observed "the mixture of compositions and subject matter," from the figurative to the abstract, which "demonstrate that the current space for female African American artists is too small."[12] Indeed, one student argued that the gallery space was not big enough to hold all the talent in the room, and, as a result, the show seemed lackluster. The artworks needed to breathe. The artists needed more space to shine. There were also personal reflections on the power of the show and how it changed the students, broadened their horizons,

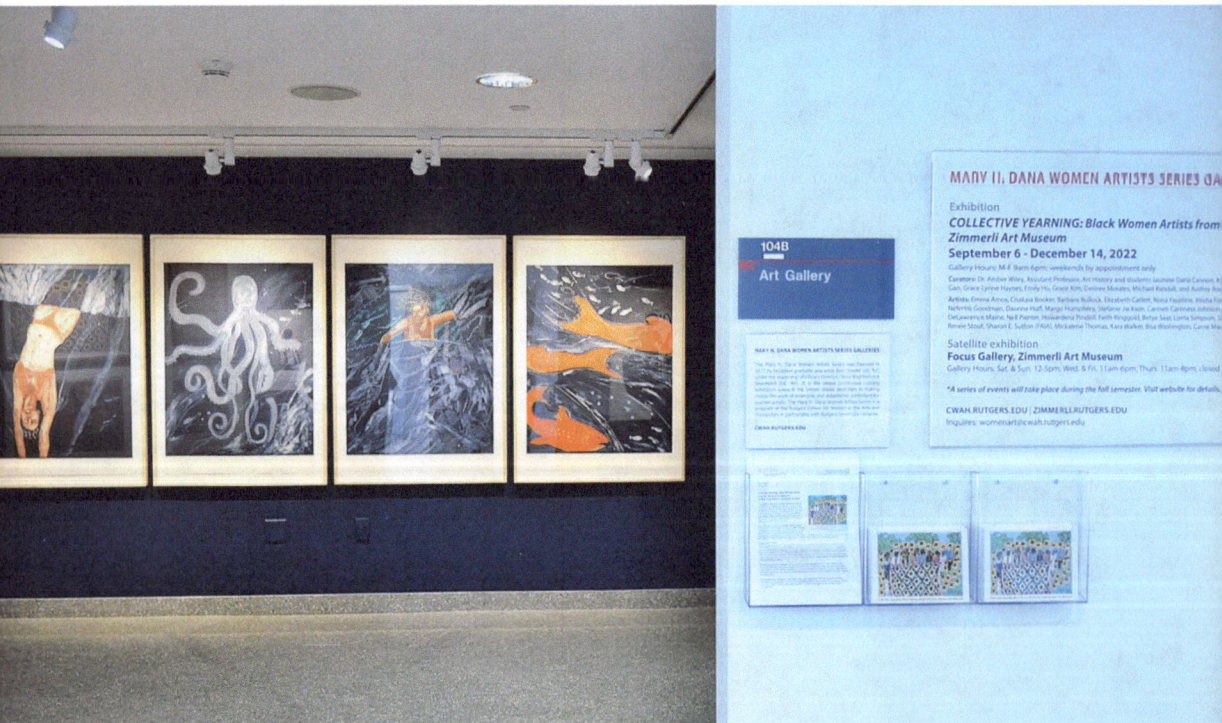

Fig. I.5. Emma Amos's *Aquarium Series* seen from the entrance to Gallery 104B at the DWAS. 2022. Nicole Ianuzelli, photographer.

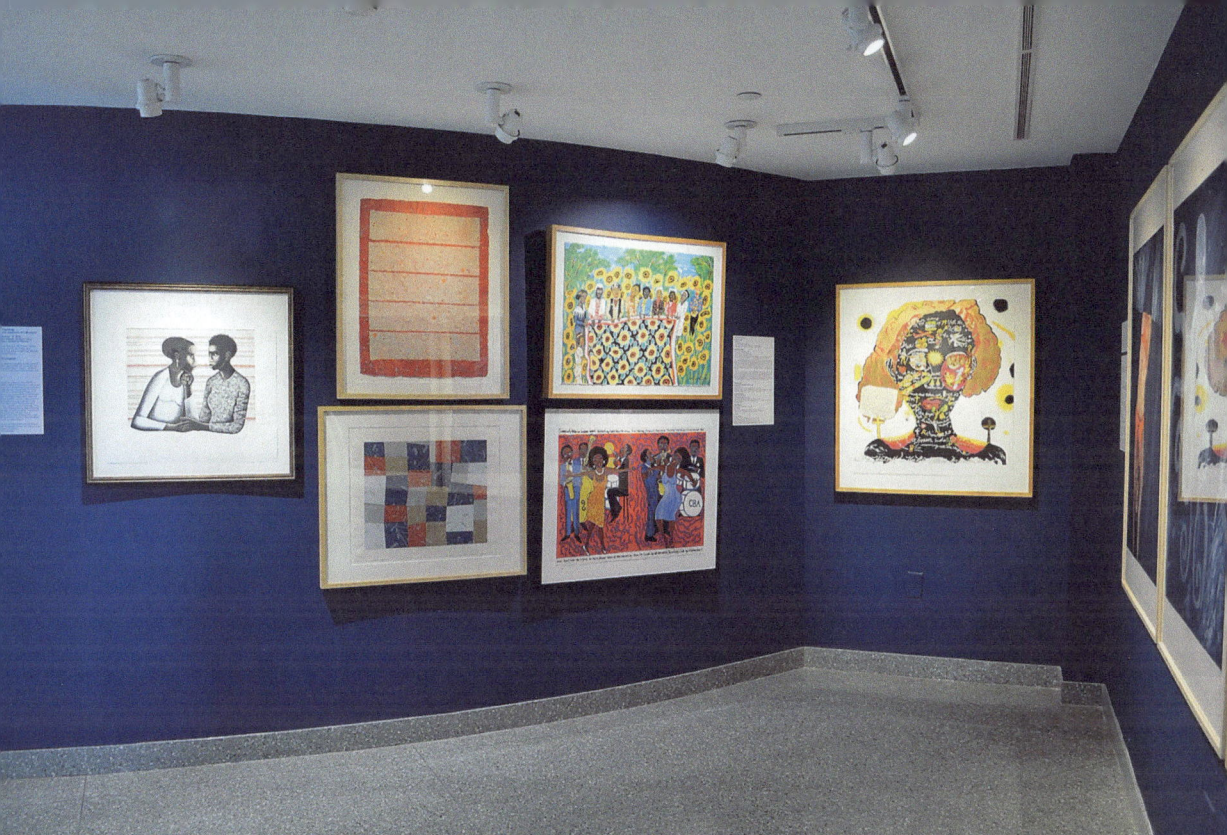

Fig. 1.6. Introductory images and text for the *Collective Yearning* exhibition in Gallery 104B at the DWAS. 2022. Nicole Ianuzelli, photographer.

led them to feel passionately about the place of Black women in the art world. I was moved to tears.

That impact is how I count the success of the show. It was not covered in *The New York Times*, nor was it written up in an art journal. But it left an impression on my students, Rutgers University, and the wider central New Jersey community. I know that from the array of Rutgers classes that visited the show and instructors who incorporated it into their coursework. And from a glowing endorsement by a student reporter in the *Rutgers Review*, who deemed it "the most remarkable art exhibition at the Douglass Library" and a "highlight of this year's art experience on the Rutgers campus."[13] And from the people who showed up for the in-person and virtual programming. I take pride in understanding the pedagogical and communal impact, but there was more work to be done. There needed to be a record. As one young student art critic plainly stated: *"Collective Yearning* is only temporary. By the time this paper is submitted, it'll be closed."[14] Indeed, the exhibition was a moment. This publication is a confirmation of its existence, one that adds to the archive and stands in the silence of critical engagement with Black women artists, and the art world more generally.

This book documents the evolution of the *Collective Yearning: Black Women Artists from the Zimmerli Art Museum* exhibition, from its germination in a class assignment, development into a graduate-level seminar topic, and physical launch as a showcase of artworks in two venues on the Rutgers University–New Brunswick campus. A project of Rutgers University's Center for Women in the Arts and Humanities (now the Center for Women in the Arts at Douglass), the ZAM, and the Department of Art History, the exhibition was accompanied by related public outreach; student guide training; fellowship programs; faculty, student, and alumni engagement; and the creation of original artwork.

The exhibition *Collective Yearning* was publicized as the first time the university had conducted a comprehensive and methodical review of its holdings of art by Black women artists. But it was not the university that did the work—in reality, my students conducted this review. It was their passion, interest, and research that filled in the gaping holes in the university's records. Their investigation was important not just for the educational institution but also for the region, as many of the artists had ties to New Jersey, New York City, and Philadelphia, ranging from canonical figures such as former Rutgers faculty members Emma Amos and Kara Walker to emerging artists Nona Faustine, Atisha Fordyce, and Daonne Huff.

The book *Collective Yearning* offers strategies for addressing gaps in curriculums and strengthening classes to meet university-wide core requirements while also providing student instruction in collections research, visual literacy, object-based analysis, public interpretation, and applied learning. Furthermore, it highlights cross-campus collaborative work, arguing that interdisciplinarity is an essential part of university operations. Finally, the book celebrates the excellent student work that manifested in the exhibition, even with limited resources because of the global COVID-19 pandemic and heightened racial tensions in the wake of the murders of Ahmaud Arbery, Breonna Taylor, and George Floyd, and the subsequent political uprisings of 2020.

At the time of the exhibition's launch, there was increased animosity and acrimony between, toward, and among Asian American communities in the United States. As I worked to get my graduate exhibition seminar off the ground, we were living during a pandemic, lockdown, and social distancing, as well as the rise of social movements such as #BlackLivesMatter, #MuseumsAreNotNeutral, #DecolonizeThisPlace, and #StopAsianHate. It was a time of radical challenges, but also radical opportunity.[15]

Today, state legislators are striking African American history from K–12 and college curriculums and dismantling diversity, equity, and inclusion programs in the workplace. In 2024, a qualified Black and Indian woman, a second-generation American (like so many of my students), ran for president of the United States and lost to a white man, a convicted felon, whose campaign was based on racism, sexism, misogyny, misogynoir, transphobia, homophobia, Islamophobia, xenophobia, bigotry—fearmongering writ large. I posit that an exhibition highlighting the artistic output of Black women is essential to address these issues, even when the connections may seem tenuous. As the sociologist Margaret L. Andersen and the social theorist Patricia Hill Collins argue, not only are race and gender identities, but they are also social constructions and systemic forms of power and inequality. We must all shift our thinking "so that groups who are so often silenced or ignored become heard," enabling us to "imagine ways to transform, rather than reproduce, existing social arrangements."[16] In doing so, we can subvert hegemonic power relationships, acquire fresh knowledge, and battle a poverty of imagination for the future.

The process of putting together the *Collective Yearning* exhibition was a prime example of students and a professor coming together to address an epistemological problem. Knowledge production is at the heart of the purpose of a university. In class, we were not bending to the whims of the moment, what detractors call "political agendas" around race, diversity, and belonging. We were, in fact, creating a more complete learning experience. For my students, to enter the ZAM or any other gallery on campus without exposure to holdings that included Black women artists was a misrepresentation of reality. Andersen and Hill Collins maintain that "reconstructing knowledge about excluded groups matter[s]" because "there are real consequences to having partial or distorted knowledge."[17] Such gaps in awareness lead to ignorance, which influences how one behaves and how one treats others, with the potential to reproduce systems of oppression—sexism, racism, homophobia, classism, and so on. At the heart of the matter was the need to listen to my students and formulate a pedagogical practice in which they journeyed *with me* to develop new insights about our home state, our institution, our community, and ourselves.

The necessity to create new knowledge was born of student demand from an assignment I developed in my undergraduate survey course. From 2018 to 2021, I taught African American Art at Rutgers. I specifically bound the class within the continental United States, though we started with an introduction to the transatlantic slave trade and the Afrodiasporic relationships between Europe, West and Central Africa, and the Americas. We looked at artifacts of all scales, starting from early colonial material culture: walking sticks, clay pots, quilts, Georgian woodwork, such as dressers, mantles, balustrades, and coatracks; art by trained and self-taught artists alike; portraiture, sculpture, daguerreotypes; and structures built by free and enslaved Black Americans, including Creole cottages in Louisiana and Thomas Jefferson's Monticello, in Virginia, to contemporary artistic practices of the twenty-first century.

Over the years, I worked and reworked the curriculum and assignments to satisfy both the Diversities and Social Inequities and Arts and Humanities core requirements for undergraduates in the Rutgers–New Brunswick School of Arts and Sciences.[18] As such, my students had to analyze art and its relation to specific histories, values, and cultures, and demonstrate a fuller understanding of the historical development of Black America. These learning goals shaped the contour of my assignments, the first of which was an art analysis paper based on Black American artists on display at the ZAM. It was from that assignment that students desired more representation of Black artists, and especially Black women artists.

The assignment directed my fledgling art critics to use the permanent collection of the ZAM to source an artwork they would analyze. I wanted them to go into the museum, wander down its halls, get a feel for its scale, and begin to understand the didactic relationship between the various artworks on the walls and pedestals. Given that I offered the course annually, I could not depend on special exhibitions for such an assignment. I relied on what Rutgers had in its permanent collection to utilize the museum as a teaching resource.

The ZAM includes more than seventy thousand artworks. The most well-known of these are Russian and Soviet Nonconformist pieces from the Dodge Collection. In addition, there is American art from the eighteenth century to the present and also six centuries of European art, with a particular strength in nineteenth-century French art.[19] How does the collection correspond to what is taught at Rutgers, and how does it respond to student needs?

The museum's American art collection contains more than 16,500 objects. These include paintings, sculpture, works on paper (prints, drawings, and photographs), and decorative arts. Given that my class focused on African American artists, I was concerned with the American collection. In fall 2018, the first year I taught the course, there were seven artworks on display by Black American artists in the whole of the museum. Only one was by a Black woman—celebrated artist and former Mason Gross School of the Arts faculty member Emma Amos. My students had something to say about that. The next year, that representative number decreased to four artworks by Black artists, none of them Black women.[20] I do not have to explain how that went over with the students in my class. To make up for the deficiency, that year I allowed students to analyze an additional two photographs that featured Black subjects, though their photographers and dates were unknown. I reasoned that since they were not professional portraits, the photographers most likely were family members or friends who knew the subjects intimately. I encouraged students to take on either of the photographs for the assignment in spite of the unknown variables, if they were up for the challenge.[21]

The third year I taught the class was during the pandemic, an experience that was surprisingly freeing. I used the Zimmerli's eMuseum website to curate a selection of artworks from the permanent collection, and, by doing so, I not only increased the total number of artworks for student consideration, but also supplied them with more art by Black women than in my previous two years combined. It was only when I offered the class virtually that we had ten pieces by Black artists, half of them Black women.[22] One of the few advantages of remote learning, it seemed, was that wall and floor space were limitless in our virtual gallery.

My experience during the pandemic only reinforced my desire to work with the Zimmerli collection to highlight artworks by Black artists for my students' benefit, and to leave a record of that work with Rutgers. The following semester I developed a graduate-level exhibition seminar focused on the Black American artists in the permanent collection. I did not know what the students and I would find, but I knew there was a wealth of art in storage that we could somehow turn into a public exhibition, either physical or virtual.

For the graduate seminar, I hoped to take lessons learned from cultural critic bell hooks in her manifesto *Teaching to Transgress* and incorporate them into the classroom. As hooks poignantly argued, "There must be an ongoing recognition that everyone influences the classroom dynamic, that everyone contributes. These contributions are resources."[23] This seminar would be an exploration, and I would not hold all the answers (not that I ever do). My students and I would investigate the Zimmerli collection together. The class would provide space for greater agency across positionalities, so that the students who chose to go on the adventure with me would feel empowered in their learning process. I began to see the classroom, as hooks asserts, "as a communal place [that] enhances the likelihood of collective effort in creating and sustaining a learning community."[24] I can only hope that we succeeded.

Collective Yearning is relevant to a wide audience—fellow academics in the arts and humanities who are interested in pedagogical innovation, applied research, and interdisciplinarity; museum professionals who wish to take deep dives into their own collections and expand their public outreach; art historians and artists inspired by collaborative work with students and the lasting impact it can leave on their university. It is also of interest to those seeking an institutional history of Rutgers that covers various departments, programs, initiatives, and art spaces. Finally, the book offers a richly illustrated blueprint for what hooks calls a "liberatory practice" of applied theory, with broad appeal to people concerned with gender and Afrodiasporic studies, Black feminist theory, and printmaking (prints make up most of the art pieces by Black women in the collection).[25]

When the exhibition was installed, Rutgers professors teaching courses in Africana studies, art history, history, studio art, and women's, gender, and sexuality studies brought their students to see the show.[26] The professors engaged with exhibition content in their courses, assigning response essays and papers. Some classes visited the exhibition multiple times, taking advantage of the student docents who were on hand to speak with visitors. Other classes came to in-person and online programming events. Faculty invited me to speak with their students. Given the elevated level of engagement

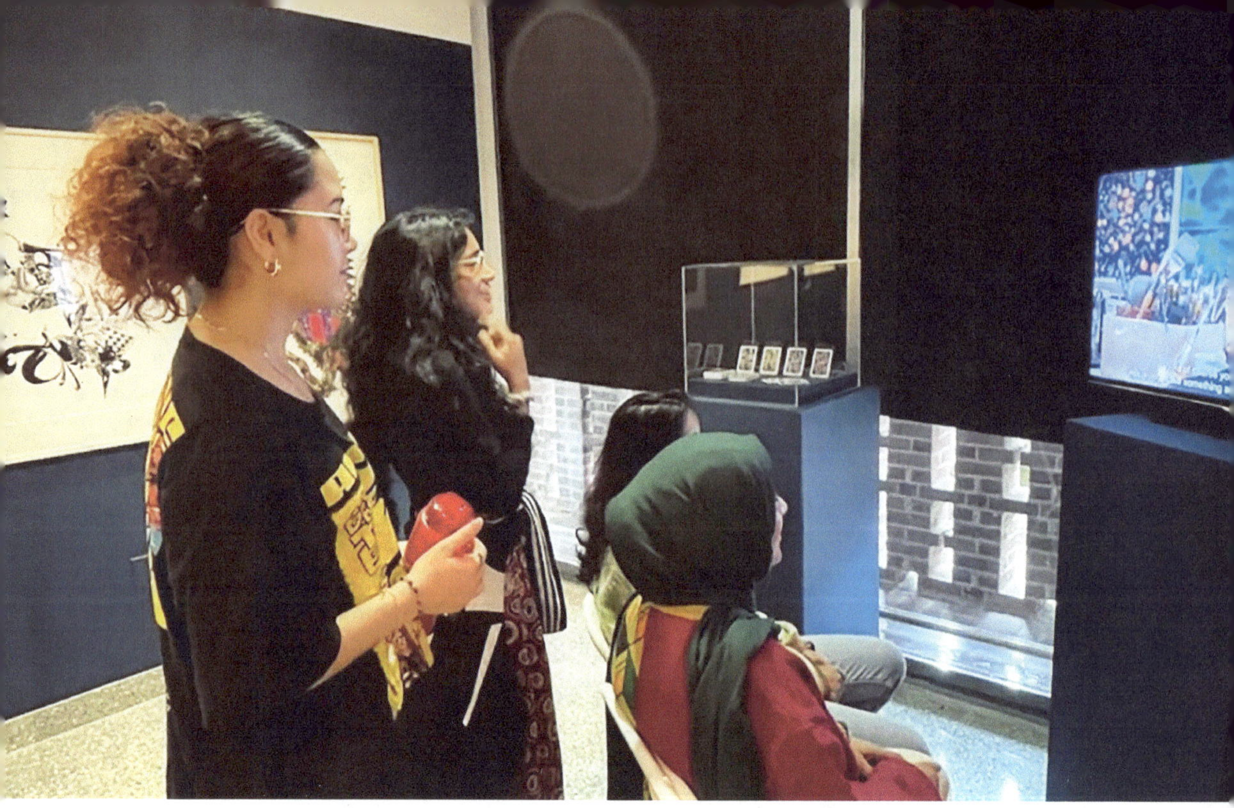

Fig. I.7. First-year Leadership Scholars from Charlotte Bunch's Women and Leadership seminar viewing *Taking Flight: An Interview with Faith Ringgold* by Leadership Scholar alum Karin Zahavi (class of 2010) in the DWAS. 2022.

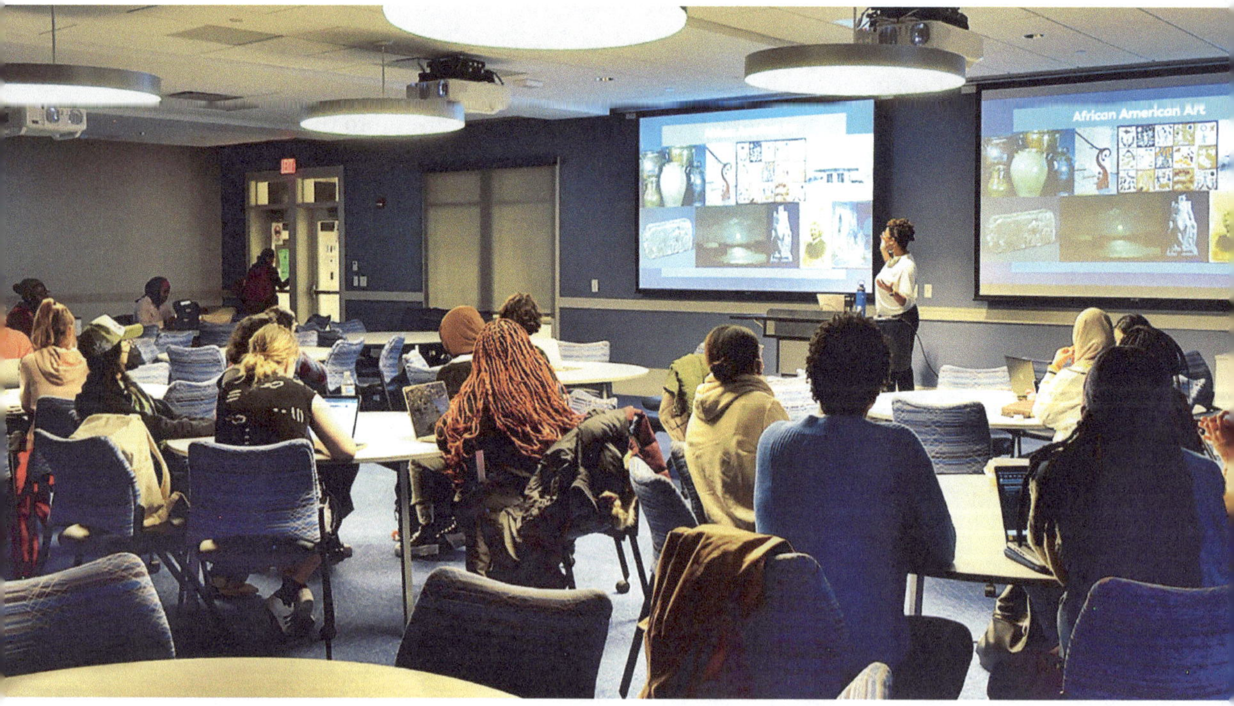

Fig. I.8. Amber N. Wiley giving a lecture for the Art as Activism House of Douglass Residential College's Global Village. 2022. Nicole Ianuzelli, photographer.

with the exhibition, the book can serve as a model for future collaboration across campuses and between different departmental and institutional areas.

The book has significant potential for use in the classroom and as a pedagogical guide for professors, curators, museum educators, and other university and museum staff. Connected as it is to Rutgers's unique history and institutions, there is no other book like it. Yet that same specificity does not limit its utility, as the book is a source whose methods other institutions can replicate. Indeed, *Collective Yearning* is a complement to other academic books, including the three-volume *Scarlet and Black* series, born as it was out of student demand, coalescing with Rutgers's 250th anniversary, and also to other universities' recent publications and committees related to slavery and academic institutions. The first volume of *Scarlet and Black* traced the colonial history of dispossession of Native lands and the relationship of slavery to the founding of Rutgers University, but it also ended with calls for a campus walking tour, historical plaques and widely accessible digital archival material.[27] In 2016, in response to that research, a new student housing complex was named for Sojourner Truth, a self-emancipated abolitionist and activist who had been previously owned by the family of Rutgers's first president, Jacob Hardenbergh. The publication of *Collective Yearning* approaches the 260th anniversary of Rutgers, with significant milestones since the last major anniversary—namely, the centennial of Paul Robeson's 1919 graduation, which Rutgers marked with commemorative events across the campus, and the inauguration of Jonathan Holloway in 2020 as the first Black president of the university. It is useful to consider these significant milestones in contrast to the ways Black women have been traditionally excluded from the historical narrative of the university.

This book also complements publications that highlight the history of women at Rutgers, as well as the creative collaborations that can happen within the classroom. *Collective Yearning* builds on Joan Marter's *Women Artists on the Leading Edge*, in which she documents the emergence of postwar feminist artistic activities at Douglass College. *Collective Yearning* also has a special synchronicity with Jenevieve DeLosSantos's transdisciplinary *Poetries—Politics: A Celebration of Language, Art, and Learning*, which describes a multiyear, project-based learning alliance between humanities and fine arts professors and students.[28] Taking all these publications as foundational blueprints, *Collective Yearning* fills a gap in the historiography of Rutgers, the ZAM, and the Center for Women in the Arts and Humanities, while celebrating curricular innovation and Black women's artistic genius.

The book is divided into two parts. Part 1: "Framing the Question and Creating the Space," focuses on pedagogical intentions and collaborative reflections from artist partners and student curators involved in the *Collective Yearning* exhibition. This segment of the book situates the reader directly in the historical, social, and cultural milieu in which my classes and the exhibition took place. It introduces Black feminist and critical race art theory as two pillars of the classes and the exhibition. It also engages discourse around the notion of knowledge production, specifically what Patricia Hill Collins refers to as "resistant knowledge projects."[29]

Part 2: "Collective Yearning and Curatorial Action," consists of content that student curators created for the exhibition—didactic material researched and developed by students—that stands as a record of the wide range of work they examined over the course of a semester. This student-developed portion of the book includes thematic essays and catalog entries written by Jasmine Daria Cannon, Kyle b. co., Helen Gao, Grace Lynne Haynes, Emily Hu, Grace Kim, Desiree Morales, Michael Randall, Audrey Roclore, and me. Most of the research, analysis, and editing was collaborative. These student curators examined the work of twenty-four Black women represented in the ZAM's permanent collection: Emma Amos, Chakaia Booker, Barbara Bullock, Elizabeth Catlett, Nona Faustine, Atisha Fordyce, Nefertiti Goodman, Daonne Huff, Margo Humphrey, Stefanie Jackson, Carmen Cartiness Johnson, Nadine DeLawrence Maine, Nell Irvin Painter, Howardena Pindell, Faith Ringgold, Betye Saar, Lorna Simpson, Shinique Smith, Renée Stout, Sharon E. Sutton, Mickalene Thomas, Kara Walker, Bisa Washington, and Carrie Mae Weems.

The artworks by Black women in the collection were relatively modern and contemporary, created within the last fifty years. Their dates of production ranged from 1977 to 2018, with the greatest number from the first decade of the 2000s. Our analysis did not include the 2018 Jersey City Museum gift, which significantly expanded the Zimmerli's collection of Black women artists, and artists of color more generally. At the time of our exhibition seminar, the gift pieces were not fully cataloged, nor were they available to us.

From the prints, photographs, and multimedia artworks the student curators researched, they produced the following didactic themes that shaped the exhibition: "Self-Making and Identity," "The Brodsky Center and the Rutgers Print Collaborative," "Process and Materiality," "The Art of Storytelling," and "Alchemy and Spirituality." Chapters 4–8 of the book are based on these themes, with accompanying artwork and catalog entries.

Chapter 1, "Teaching to Transgress," discusses two courses that I offered at Rutgers—the undergraduate survey African American Art and the graduate-level Exhibition Seminar. The chapter consists of a how-to component using the *Collective Yearning* exhibition as its case study. I describe the creation of the Art Analysis assignment that gave birth to the exhibition and detail the construction of the Exhibition Seminar focused on Black women artists in the Zimmerli collection. The chapter highlights the constraints of the pandemic and the virtual classroom, in which students could not view the artworks in person. In fact, most of the student curators met one another and viewed the artwork up close for the first time *during* the exhibition.

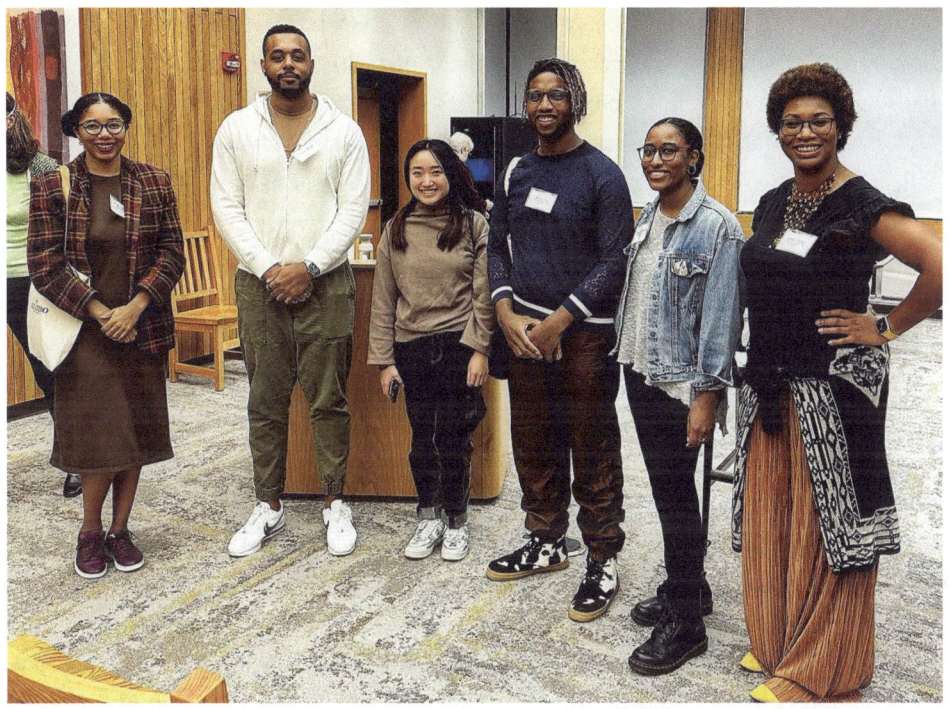

Fig. I.9. Five of the nine student curators with Professor Wiley. Pictured left to right: Grace Lynne Haynes, Michael Randall, Helen Gao, Kyle b. co., and Desiree Morales. Not pictured: Jasmine Daria Cannon, Emily Hu, Grace Kim, and Audrey Roclore. 2022. Nicole Ianuzelli, photographer.

Chapter 1 argues that within the confines of core curriculum and graduation require-ments, one can create assignments, classes, and public-facing work that is groundbreak-ing and critically relevant.

Chapter 2, "Echoes: Speaking from the Threshold," introduces the artist-educator Heather Hart's process as an archivist and art maker. Inspired by her work with the Black Lunch Table, "a radical archiving project" working to build "a more complete understanding of cultural history by illuminating the stories of Black people and our shared stake in the world," I invited Hart to give a guest lecture in the Exhibition Sem-inar.[30] As Hart explains, her artistic and archival practice is part autobiographical, part exploratory, and, most of all, born out of a necessity to fill the void in writing and recording the lives of Black artists. This is a struggle that others have experienced as well. My students undertook rigorous detective work to fill in the silences of cru-cial moments in the lives of our Black women artists. For Black Americans, those silences are particularly daunting, as the process of erasing their humanity was cen-tral to the project of chattel slavery. In Hart's essay, she argues for the importance of both memory and imagination as tools for a liberatory practice of storytelling and artistic method. Citing Saidiya Hartman's process of "critical fabulation," Hart grounds her sculptural practice in an embodied, alternate space of healing.[31]

"'Pass the Mic': A Conversation with Student Curators," chapter 3, documents the reflections of two graduates of Rutgers' Mason Gross School of the Arts, Kyle b. co. and Desiree Morales, on their experiences as curators, incorporating fresh insights on their own teaching methods and the ways curation and teaching influence their artistic processes. They address the importance of collective work within their respective practices and investigate how the exhibition themes have impacted their own work as curators, artists, educators, and activists. b. co. and Morales argue for the importance of "passing the mic," a contemporary spin on the early twentieth-century notion of "lifting as we climb." This step includes making opportunities for others, sharing platforms, and taking part in mentorship activities.

Chapter 4, "Self-Making and Identity," inaugurates part 2 of the book, which highlights student-produced thematic essays accompanied by full-page reproductions of a majority of exhibition artworks and catalog entries. While I was the lead curator of the exhibition, the students were the real intellectual capital behind the art selections, themes, and exhibition design. In this chapter, the student authors build on Audre Lorde's contention that "your silence will not protect you." Faced with historical erasure and misrepresentation—the jezebel, Venus Hottentot, mammy—these Black women artists refuse to be silenced. Women, and Black women in particular, "have been raised to fear the *yes* within ourselves, our deepest cravings."[32] These Black women artists speak for themselves—voicing their own desires, using art as the medium to define themselves, for themselves. Their art amplifies an integrity of nuances and complexities that can neither be ignored nor disregarded.

"The Brodsky Center and the Rutgers Print Collaborative," chapter 5, emphasizes how one woman's initiative positively changed the collecting customs of the Zimmerli. Judith K. Brodsky, Rutgers distinguished professor emerita, is the single most consequential donor of artwork by Black women in the museum collection. At Rutgers she developed a residency for artists whose identities often put them on the margins of the art world. The residency emphasized collaboration between students and these artists. Adding to this tradition was the Rutgers Print Collaborative established by Professor Barbara Madsen, which continued the collaborative nature of artist residencies and the opportunity to donate groundbreaking works to the Zimmerli. The chapter also ties the method and process of printmaking to the longer tradition of communal and radical artmaking within the Black community.

Chapter 6, "Process and Materiality," contemplates the formal qualities of printmaking, as well as the wide assortment of printing processes employed by artists in the exhibition. It is a testament to the collaborative process and to the inventive nature of artists who experiment with material and method. The preponderance of prints also comes at a cost. Paintings and sculpture, two traditionally high-value artistic outputs, have long been the bread and butter of museum collections. Only since the 1970s have art institutions actively collected media such as photography and printworks. And while these newer media have become a mainstay and constitute a significant percentage of U.S. museum collections, there is limited ability to display them. Best practices recommend three-month exhibitions, limiting the possibility for multi-venue traveling shows.[33]

"The Art of Storytelling," chapter 7, emphasizes both the vital role of narrative drama in Black expressive traditions and the serial nature of printmaking. The artists are griots, bringing oral traditions into the visual and textual plane. This storytelling is exemplified by serial prints produced by Amos and Ringgold, as well as Walker's nineteenth-century inspired storybooks. Like the notion of self-making, storytelling grants these Black women room for capacious and inventive redefinitions to counter derogatory fallacies told about them. Storytelling also brings to light underappreciated perspectives to fill the vacuum of the historical record of Black women's lived experiences. Through these stories, we hear their voices in first person.

Chapter 8, "Alchemy and Spirituality," celebrates the wide range of faith-based observations and rituals at the core of the artists' individual and collective well-being. Drawing on a variety of sources—folkloric, ancestral, religious, meditative—these artists conjure up connections to their inner truths, relationships with dearly departed loved ones and inspirational characters of the past, and things known and unknown. The chapter also emphasizes the mystical power of art as a transformative exercise—the spiritual and magical alchemy of combining various media to create new matter.

Finally, the book concludes with a coda reflecting on the learning process, the work produced by the student curators and our collaborators, and the work ahead. The exhibition was a moment in time, and this book is its record. Beyond that, as we look to the future of the art world, interdisciplinary study, the university, and the country, we need to continue to ask ourselves questions like *Do we need an exhibition on Black women artists in 20XX? Why or why not? What are the advantages or disadvantages of organizing an exhibition around a group of artists on the basis of race, gender, and nationality?* Because, regardless of the political moment, there is a lesson to be learned. My students pushed me to ask the questions and worked with me to find the answers. Thankfully, for all of us—and you, gentle reader, included—the learning process is never over, and the answers may change. It is our duty to keep asking the questions and moving forward.

Notes

1. A word on terminology: in all my classes that deal with the topic of race, we affirm that race is a social construct. *Black* as a racial qualifier means different things across time and space. In the African American Art class, however, when we discussed *Blackness*, we confined our definition to the continental United States and residents therein transported through the transatlantic slave trade and those members of the African diaspora who continued to settle in the United States after that trade ended. Our delimitations around what constituted a "woman," or Black woman, relied on more traditional notions of sex, but offered up the possibility of including Black femmes. The difficulty of highlighting work by the more inclusive term *femme*, over *woman*, lies in the narrow ways that gallerists, museums, and collection management software categorize artists and artworks. My students understood the need to push past essentialist notions of Blackness and womanness to be inclusive of femme, trans, queer folk. Moreover, artists have often been cataloged according to nationality, which has also been problematic in our complex contemporary world. Ukrainian art historian Oksana Semenik highlights this issue, in her work to identify Ukrainian artists mislabeled as Russian in museum collections. See Constant Méheut, "'Decolonizing' Ukrainian Art, One Name-and-Shame Post at a Time," *New York Times*, March 8, 2024, https://www.nytimes.com/2024/03/08/world/europe/decolonizing-ukrainian-art-oksana-semenik.html. Closer to home (and the Zimmerli collection), the artist Elizabeth Catlett is listed in many online museum databases as both American and Mexican, since she spent much of her productive years as a Mexican citizen. She is included in the *Collective Yearning* exhibition because she was born and raised in Washington, DC, and her formative years were spent in the United States. In a similar vein, the work of Black American expat artist Henry Ossawa Tanner, who spent much of his career in France, can be found in both the American and European galleries of the Philadelphia Museum of Art. The convention of prescribing a nationality to an artist is being replaced by place of birth or the countries in which they resided and practiced for substantial periods of time.

2. Kimberlé Crenshaw, "Mapping the Margins: Intersectionality, Identity Politics, and Violence Against Women of Color," *Stanford Law Review* 43, no. 6 (1991): 1242.

3. In the fall of 2022, there were 43,850 students enrolled in the flagship New Brunswick campus, not including those in Rutgers Biomedical and Health Sciences programs. Of this number, 34 percent identified as white (non-Hispanic), 27.3 percent as Asian, 14.5 percent as Hispanic/Latino, 11.2 percent as international, 7.3 percent as Black/African American, 3.4 percent as two or more races, and 2.1 percent as other (including American Indian/Alaska Native, Native Hawaiian or Pacific Islander, and unknown). Rutgers University–New Brunswick students hailed from all fifty U.S. states and over one hundred countries. "Fact Book: Student Enrollment," Office of Institutional Research and Decision Support, Rutgers University, 2025, https://oirap.rutgers.edu/StudentEnrollment.html. The source for the fact book's data is the Integrated Postsecondary Education Data System (IPEDS) Enrollment Survey.

4. Nell Painter, *Old in Art School: A Memoir of Starting Over* (Counterpoint Press, 2018), 10–11.

5. Audre Lorde, "The Master's Tools Will Never Dismantle the Master's House," in *Sister Outsider: Essays and Speeches* (Crossing Press, 2007), 112.

6. The student sourced the quotation from an article they read earlier in the semester by the feminist theorist Laura Wexler, "'A More Perfect Likeness:' Frederick Douglass and the Image of the Nation," *Yale Review* 99, no. 4 (October 2011): 148.

7. Undergraduate student paper responses, 2022, pulling from Camara Dia Holloway, "Critical Race Art History," *Art Journal* 75, no. 1 (2016): 89–92.

8. Chad M. Topaz, Bernhard Klingenberg, Daniel Turek, Brianna Heggeseth, Pamela E. Harris, Julie C. Blackwood, C. Ondine Chavoya, Steven Nelson, and Kevin M. Murphy, "Diversity of Artists in Major U.S. Museums," *PLoS One* 14, no. 3 (2019): 9, e0212852.

9. Topaz et al., "Diversity of Artists," 8.

10. Undergraduate student paper responses, 2022.

11. Crenshaw, "Mapping the Margins," 1261. Student papers sourced a wide variety of scholarly perspectives on art education, production, criticism, and collecting as these practices relate to race and gender, including:

Joni Boyd Acuff, "Black Feminist Theory in 21st-Century Art Education Research," *Studies in Art Education* 59, no. 3 (2018): 201–214; Uri McMillan, *Embodied Avatars: Genealogies of Black Feminist Art and Performance* (New York University Press, 2015); Topaz et al., "Diversity of Artists"; Kay Brown, "The Emergence of Black Women Artists: The Founding of 'Where We At,'" *Nka: Journal of Contemporary African Art*, no. 29 (2011): 118–127; bell hooks, *Art on My Mind: Visual Politics* (New Press, 1995); Jordana Moore Saggese, Camara Dia Holloway, T'ai Smith, Tina Takemoto, and Tobias Wofford, "Beyond the Numbers Game: Diversity in Theory and Practice," *Art Journal* 75, no. 1 (Spring 2016): 98–109.

12. Undergraduate student paper responses, 2022.

13. Yvonne Liu, "Collective Yearning," *Rutgers Review* 58, no. 1 (December 2022): 18–19.

14. Undergraduate student paper response, 2022.

15. Erica Lehrer and Shelley Ruth Butler, "Curatorial Dreaming in the Age of COVID-19," Museums and Equity in Times of Crisis, *Alliance Blog*, American Alliance of Museums, May 4, 2020, https://www.aam-us .org/2020/05/04/curatorial-dreaming-in-the-age-of-covid-19/.

16. Margaret L. Andersen and Patricia Hill Collins, "Why Race, Class, and Gender Still Matter," in *Race, Class, and Gender: An Anthology*, 9th ed. (Cengage Learning, 2016), 2; Andersen and Hill Collins, "Systems of Power and Inequality," in *Race, Class, and Gender*, 51–73.

17. Andersen and Hill Collins, "Race, Class, and Gender," 3.

18. Diversity and Social Inequalities is a subset of the Contemporary Challenges requirement, while Arts and Humanities is a subset of the Areas of Inquiry requirement. See "SAS Core Curriculum," Academic and Advising Services, Rutgers–New Brunswick School of Arts and Sciences, accessed December 1, 2025, https://sasundergrad.rutgers.edu/degree-requirements/core.

19. See Zimmerli Art Museum, Rutgers University: "Museum Overview," 2025, https://zimmerli.rutgers.edu /museum-overview; "Art of the Americas," 2025, https://zimmerli.rutgers.edu/collections/art-americas; "European Art," 2025, https://zimmerli.rutgers.edu/collections/european-art.

20. Artworks by Black artists on display at the Zimmerli, by year. In 2018: *The Good Shepherd*, Henry Ossawa Tanner, oil on canvas, 1902; *The Adoration of the Magi*, Romare Bearden, oil on Masonite, ca. 1945; *Three Girls*, Hughie Lee Smith, oil on canvas, ca. 1960; *Breeze*, Sam Gilliam, acrylic on canvas, 1967; *From Home*, Benny Andrews, collage on paper, 1975; *Sand Reflections*, Emma Amos, color lithograph on paper, 1980s; *Untitled*, Richard Hunt, lithograph, 1981. In 2019: *The Adoration of the Magi*; *Three Girls*; *Breeze*; *Workshop*, Jacob Lawrence, lithograph, 1972.

21. The two undated photographs of Black subjects taken by anonymous photographers were on display as part of the 2019 Peter J. Cohen gift to the museum. Due to the casual nature of the photographs, I assumed a close relationship between photographer and sitter, and while there was no artist of record, I allowed my students to conduct art analyses of either of the photographs, if they chose to do so. Only one student accepted the challenge. For our purposes, I added titles to distinguish between the two photographs: *Untitled (Boxers)*, unidentified photographer, undated (twentieth century); *Untitled (Cowboys and Cowgirls)*, unidentified photographer, undated (twentieth century). While the museum did not specify dates, I believe the photographs were produced in the mid-twentieth century, specifically in the 1940s or 1950s, based on the style of dress.

22. The ten artworks were *The Good Shepherd*; *The Adoration of the Magi*; *Warriors*, Barbara Chase-Riboud, bronze, undated; *Freedom Fighter*, Calvin Burnett, lithograph on paper, 1969; *Water Wonder Woman* from the *Aquarium Series*, Emma Amos, color silk collagraph on paper, 1987; *III*, Lorna Simpson, wood box and felt liner with ceramic, rubber, and bronze wishbones, 1992; *Once We Were Warriors*, Juan Sanchez, lithograph, pulp painting, and hand coloring, 1999; *The Right to Vote* from the portfolio *Letter from Birmingham City Jail*, Faith Ringgold, color screen print on paper, 2007; *Components: Left Resonance*, Jennie C. Jones, color screen print on paper, 2012; *How Do You Feel?* from the *Mason Gross School of the Arts MFA Class of 2019 Print Portfolio*, Malcolm Peacock, screen print on paper, 2019.

23. bell hooks, "Introduction: Teaching to Transgress," in *Teaching to Transgress: Education as the Practice of Freedom* (Routledge, 1994), 8.

24. hooks, "Introduction: Teaching to Transgress," 8.

25. hooks, "Theory as Liberatory Practice," in *Teaching to Transgress*, 59–75.

26. The following courses attended the exhibition: Feeling Race: The Emotional Politics of Race; African American Art; Curatorial Training; Women and Art; Black Lives Matter; Black Women's History Colloquium; 4-D Fundamentals: Time and Space; Introduction to Digital Photography; Print: Silkscreen; Art as Activism; Feminist Theory: Contemporary Engagements; Introduction to Social Justice; Global Feminism; Global Leaders; and Women and Leadership.

27. Marisa J. Fuentes and Deborah Gray White, eds., *Slavery and Dispossession in Rutgers History*, vol. 1 of *Scarlet and Black* (Rutgers University Press, 2016).

28. Joan Marter, *Women Artists on the Leading Edge: Visual Arts at Douglass College* (Rutgers University Press, 2019); Jenevieve DeLosSantos, ed., *Poetries—Politics: A Celebration of Language, Art, and Learning* (Rutgers University Press, 2023).

29. Patricia Hill Collins, "Intersectionality and Resistant Knowledge Projects," in *Intersectionality as Critical Social Theory* (Duke University Press, 2019), 87–120.

30. Black Lunch Table, https://www.blacklunchtable.com/.

31. Saidiya Hartman, "Venus in Two Acts," *Small Axe* 12, no. 2 (June 2008): 1–14.

32. Audre Lorde, "Uses of the Erotic: The Erotic as Power," in *Sister Outsider*, 57.

33. When discussing the chronology of collecting prints, it is important to distinguish between ancient and historical illustrated manuscripts and engravings and more contemporary print media of the mid-twentieth century. Independent conservators and institutions alike have published guidelines related to collecting, storing, conserving, and exhibiting works on paper. See Elizabeth Edwards and Christopher Morton, "Between Art and Information: Towards a Collecting History of Photographs," in *Photographs, Museums, Collections: Between Art and Information*, ed. Elizabeth Edwards and Christopher Morton (Bloomsbury Academic, 2015), 3–23; Margaret Holben Ellis, *The Care of Prints and Drawings*, 2nd ed. (Rowman & Littlefield, 2017); "Light Duration Guidelines for Exhibited Works of Art," National Museum of Asian Art, Smithsonian Institution, 2025, https://asia.si.edu/research/conservation-scientific-research/exhibitions-conservation/light-duration-guidelines/; National Park Service, "Appendix J: Curatorial Care of Paper Objects," in *The Museum Handbook*, pt. 1, *Museum Collections* (National Park Service, Museum Management Program, 2003), https://www.nps.gov/museum/publications/mhi/appendix%20j.pdf; Northeast Document Conservation Center (NEDCC), *Preservation Leaflet: The Environment, 2.5 Protecting Paper and Book Collections During Exhibition* (NEDCC, 2020), https://www.nedcc.org/free-resources/preservation-leaflets/2.-the-environment/2.5-protecting-paper-and-book-collections-during-exhibition; and "Light Exposure for Artifacts on Exhibition," Conservation Center for Art & Historic Artifacts, 2021, https://ccaha.org/resources/light-exposure-artifacts-exhibition.

Part I

Framing the Question and Creating the Space

"Yearning" is the word that best describes
a common psychological state shared by many of us,
cutting across boundaries of race, class,
gender, and sexual practice.
Specifically, in relation to the post-modernist
deconstruction of "master" narratives,
the yearning that wells in the hearts and minds
of those whom such narratives have silenced
is the longing for critical voice.

—bell hooks,
1990

1

Teaching to Transgress

AMBER N. WILEY

IT WAS A BOLD PROPOSITION. In the spring of 2020, when contemplating the courses I would teach that fall, I chose to prepare a new class that relied on sources that were out of my immediate control and to which I had little to no access. We were in the midst of a global pandemic. All teaching had gone virtual. No one really knew what they were doing. We were learning innovative technologies, trying novel approaches to teaching, brainstorming ways to keep our students engaged—from afar. But I was determined. For some time I had wanted to explore Rutgers University's resources related to Black American art. I was entering my third year of institutional affiliation with no better understanding than I had when I first started. I opted to go bold, because I was *yearning* for something more. So were my students.

When I recommended an exhibition seminar focused on Black women artists in the Zimmerli Art Museum's (ZAM) collection, I was operating from a desire to address student needs and to fulfill my obligations as a professor, a scholar, a community member, and a Black woman. While I did not know what I would find, I knew that the result would provide the answer to my own "longing for critical voice," as described by bell hooks. What I discovered is that by designing an exhibition around Black women artists, I was also creating space for my students to find their respective critical voices.

Within the confines of core curriculum and graduation requirements, one can create assignments, classes, and public-facing work that is groundbreaking and vitally relevant. To demonstrate that, I discuss herein two courses that I offered at Rutgers—the undergraduate survey African American Art and the graduate-level Exhibition Seminar. I provide a how-to section using these courses and the resultant *Collective Yearning* exhibition as case studies. Moreover, in addition to satisfying humanities and diversity requirements, the students received a greater gift—that of rigorous instruction, a more complete pedagogy, and new methods for assessing value and creating knowledge. Most institutional rhetoric on topics such as humanities-based inquiry and diversity (the latter term falling out of fashion for more contemporary frameworks of justice and belonging, equity and inclusion) treat them as boxes to tick off to signal a moral high ground. This book aims to show that this work is more than necessary ornamentation—it is central to the intellectual work of the university. We are all better—more enlightened, more empathetic, and more engaged—because of it.

MY PHILOSOPHY

My path to becoming a professor began with my dissatisfaction with my own learning process in an esteemed Ivy League institution. In the classroom I was confronted by the silenced histories that shaped my world view as an adolescent. The personal narratives and trials and tribulations of my forebears, my great-grandparents and their progeny—Black Oklahomans, Arkansans, Washingtonians (DC), North Carolinians, Marylanders—were left out of my curriculum. I was shocked at the disparities between what I understood to be true, what my professors taught, and what my classmates learned (and, through omission, did not learn). Whether intentional or not, those omissions were carefully crafted and particularly revealing. As the author Toni Morrison argues: "Just as the formation of the nation necessitated coded language and purposeful restriction to deal with the racial disingenuousness and moral frailty at its heart, so too did the literature, whose founding characteristics extend into the twentieth century, reproduce the necessity for codes and restriction. Through significant and underscored omissions, startling contradictions, heavily nuanced conflicts, through the way writers peopled their work with the signs and bodies of this presence—one can see that a real or fabricated Africanist presence was crucial to their sense of Americanness."[1] In other words, the pedagogical hegemony that attempts to sidestep race, especially Blackness, as a social construct that has material consequences in the real world, betrays through its silence a willful ignorance that gives itself over to carefully crafted master narratives.

I went into academia to teach, but I realized along the way that academia was not primarily about teaching. This was a major disappointment, as someone who lived for the classroom as a student and wanted to inspire student curiosity in the classroom. Indeed, as hooks asserts, "The classroom remains the most radical space of possibility in the academy."[2] But I am not convinced the academy agrees. Part of my academic journey has been to figure out how to navigate the responsibilities of research, teaching, and service, the three main components of a professorial occupation. Each part of this triad can complement the others in ways that are fruitful for my students' learning process. Academia does not make it easy, since it is constructed of silos that represent disciplinary expertise. The breaking down of those silos, for some, would symbolize the breakdown of their own academic selves. I counter that the breaking down of the silos activates the teaching and learning processes, rather than invalidating them.

I have been teaching on the university level for two decades. As a doctoral student, I instructed students taking American studies courses. I held successive positions in a school of architecture, a small liberal arts college, a large research 1 state school in the Northeast, an Ivy League design school, returning back to a large research 1 state school in the South. Over various summers, I taught at summer camps—one for privileged, majority white high schoolers in Connecticut; another serving economically disadvantaged K–6 graders in northeast Washington, DC; and yet another for racially and economically diverse K–12 students in rural North Carolina. Through these experiences, I have gained multifaceted perspectives in pedagogical methods and concerns. I see the process of posing questions, exploring, and coming to new conclusions as the basis of my work as a teacher, whether instructing kindergartners or future professors.

These experiences have been my substitute for formal training in instruction along the doctoral journey. Doctoral candidates, with little preparation, are often thrown into the classroom as graduate teaching assistants, learning to imitate their professors by observation or consulting with one another to teach themselves how to teach. Useful training, unfortunately, usually only happens after freshly minted doctorates secure a job.

My primary experience crafting a teaching philosophy came when I was a fellow in the Center for Engaged Learning and Teaching (CELT) at Tulane University, a fairly new initiative at the time that "empowered faculty to reflect on pedagogy specific to their disciplines and provided resources to create an atmosphere of engagement both in and out of the classroom."[3] It was there that I learned to think of the classroom as a dialogic space, instead of a captive space where expertise is dispensed. I crafted learning goals for student inquiry, skill development and practice. At the time I was teaching required history of architecture courses in a professional degree-granting program. I reformatted architectural survey courses that had long outlived their utility, a process central to addressing obstacles that the architecture school faced ahead of accreditation by the National Architectural Accrediting Board (NAAB).[4] My methods for evaluating pedagogical efficacy began with my training at the CELT, and assessing the achievement of learning goals in my architectural survey courses in support of the accreditation process.

The Intergroup Relations (IGR) program and the Center for Leadership, Teaching, and Learning at Skidmore College grew my confidence to get creative within the classroom space and to support students through challenging conversations. The IGR program's goal was "to support student learning and competencies around inter- and intragroup relations, conflict and social justice across a range of social identities, including race, gender, sexuality, social class, religion and nationality."[5] Under the tutelage of my colleague Jennifer Mueller, who was then the director of the IGR program, I began to understand the vulnerability, discomfort, humility, and, ultimately, rewarding experience of dialogue-based learning.

IGR was offered as a minor and focused on student learning and facilitation, however my growth as a professor expanded tremendously through offering American studies courses as electives in relation to the minor—specifically Diversity in the United States and African American Experience. Those electives attracted students who desired credit for the IGR minor and had training in group facilitation. As such, they came to the classroom with a demonstrated capacity, as Mueller argues, "to build understanding and suspend assumptions, actively listen to how other people understand their reality, and create a greater understanding of the whole."[6] The IGR process forced students and teachers alike "to descend into the chaos of knowledge," a necessary step in the learning process, as the poet Audre Lorde describes, in order to "return with true visions of our future, along with the concomitant power to effect those changes which can bring that future into being."[7] These journeys are not easy. They require a commitment to self-actualization, and to improving communications in environments outside the classroom. IGR training is structured to support applied learning in the real world.

As junior faculty on the tenure track at Rutgers, I participated in two initiatives—the Office of Academic Affairs' Program for Early Career Excellence (PECE) and the Office of Undergraduate Education, Teaching and Learning's Flexible Pedagogy Summer Seminar. While a member of PECE Cohort 3, I attended research and pedagogy workshops, refining the goals for my academic career and interrogating approaches to the classroom environment. The Flexible Pedagogy seminar, led in part by my Department of Art History colleague Jenevieve DeLosSantos, introduced me to the concept of backward design for online course planning and the principles of universal design for learning to develop accessible and equitable assignments in a virtual world. Both planning frameworks were particularly important given the dual crises of COVID-19 and racial unrest in 2020.

Combining these varied proficiencies, I developed several pedagogical approaches that have been consistent across my career. The first is my adherence to interdisciplinarity. The second is my commitment to offer opportunities in applied learning and public history.[8] Finally, is my dedication to the serious issues of accessibility and opportunity. It is the obligation of cultural and educational institutions to actively engage the communities in which they reside and to increase their accessibility through innovative programming. While universities pay lip service to these very ideals, they are not structured to reward them.[9] Grounded in my desire to broaden the dimensions of knowledge production, the work of interdisciplinarity, applied learning, and increased accessibility has often been relegated to the realms of "practice," or "service," inferior substitutes for research and theorizing. Indeed, as the sociologist Patricia Hill Collins asserts, "Resistant knowledge projects also have a presence within academia, but their inquiry and praxis are rarely confined to academia. For this reason, they may not be seen as sufficiently critical to merit the term *theory*, yet they are essential for intersectionality."[10]

What I have grown to understand, especially as I couple my teaching experience with Black feminist theory, is that my *yearning* in the classroom, the narratives of my forebears, and my hodgepodge background in architecture, history, urbanism, and African American cultural studies, has informed my personal Black feminist approach to the academy. While I readily accept the label *Black*, I have been less excited to think of myself as a *feminist* because of its historical associations with racialized white feminisms. I generally have gravitated toward the term *womanist*, coined by the writer Alice Walker. Yet the philosopher Lindsey Stewart tells us, "Black feminist scholarship comprises many eras, theoretical traditions, forms of activism, and disciplinary commitments."[11] With a capacious definition of Black feminist scholarship and theory, I can elevate the triad of research, teaching, and service as equal parts of a critical activist-scholar praxis.

AFRICAN AMERICAN ART SURVEY

In September 2018, I offered the undergraduate survey African American Art for the first time in years at Rutgers University. Surveys necessitate superficial depth—their main purpose is to advance a breadth of knowledge. Students acquire basic tenets on a topic, from specialized terms and familiarity with historical movements to key examples of foundational events related to the evolution of the topic. Yet, in refashioning the course, I hoped to incorporate touchpoints and moments of pause within the semester where we could go deeper, and students could develop and apply approaches to description, analysis, and synthesis that would lead them to new insights.

The first step toward this process was reckoning with the canon. By that, I mean the global art historical canon, its subdivisions and dependencies—the American art canon and the Black American art canon. In each of these categories sat an ever-present but silent antagonist. The art historian Linda Nochlin, in her groundbreaking essay "Why Have There Been No Great Women Artists?," puts it plainly: "In the field of art history, the white Western male viewpoint, unconsciously accepted as *the* viewpoint of the art historian, may—and does—prove to be inadequate not merely on moral and ethical grounds, or because it is elitist, but on purely intellectual ones. In revealing the failure of much academic art history, and a great deal of history in general, to take account of the unacknowledged value system, the very *presence* of an intruding subject in historical investigation, the feminist critique at the same time lays bare its conceptual smugness, its meta-historical naïveté."[12] My job was to battle these time-honored biases within the field to inspire in my students intellectually rigorous methods with which to understand the production of Black American art over the course of four centuries.[13] How to do that, when, as the art historian Gwendolyn DuBois Shaw instructs us, "the historian of African American art writes about what was, effectively remembering the disremembered from the materials that have been purposefully undervalued and disregarded by white supremacist historians of American art"?[14] How do you excavate that which is purposefully hidden? How do you create new value frameworks to understand that which is purposefully misunderstood? How do you introduce these ideas to young people who may be learning about the topic for the first time? You must present the truth, in its multiple, messy, contradictory, and real forms. What the historian John Hope Franklin called, in an aptly art historical metaphor, "the unvarnished truth."[15]

The survey course covered the work of African American artists, from the colonial era to the present. We used artwork as a means of understanding the lived experiences of Black Americans—that is, Americans of African descent, whose origins are from across the diaspora. Lectures covered a range of material culture, including the built environment, ephemera, film, installations, painting, photography, and sculpture. The course paid particular attention to themes of Black American life, including migration, notions of home, citizenship, social segregation, expatriation, gender norms, colorism, music, sport, and family. It also stressed rural, urban, and international African American experiences. Finally, the course considered the role of the African American artist within the Du Boisian concept of double consciousness—of looking at the world through one's eyes and the eyes of the outside world.[16]

The survey was interdisciplinary in nature: our investigation into African American art included methods and theory from African diaspora studies, anthropology, critical race art history, environmental studies, ethnomusicology, geography, history, literary studies, Marxist and materialist theory, and postcolonial/anti-colonial theory.[17] We used both primary and secondary sources to gain an understanding of the African American experience as depicted through various art forms; the course readings were coupled with artist interviews, exhibition overviews, film, music, and poetry.

I required students to purchase a Black American art survey text (the specific text varied across the years) and hooks's *Art on My Mind: Visual Politics*.[18] *Art on My Mind* is hooks's manifesto on the importance, nay, the imperative, of developing a critical Black discourse in the art world. It was published in 1995, and many of her main arguments still hold up today. hooks believed Black people must engage in and write cultural criticism and art theory, "acts of critical resistance that actively introduce change within existing visual politics." She argued, "As we critically imagine new ways to think and write about visual art, as we make spaces for dialogue across boundaries, we engage a process of cultural transformation that will ultimately create a revolution in vision."[19] Here hooks is channeling the cultural critic Michele Wallace, who openly proclaimed the "potential for a revolution in vision" three years prior.[20] By introducing these notions to my students, I intended to inspire them, from the outset, with a revolution in vision.

The survey assignments included two papers and three exams. Couching the assignments within the educational scholar L. Dee Fink's taxonomy of significant learning, the exams were meant to develop foundational knowledge as well as application. Students demonstrated agility in art-term definitions and artwork identification. They also utilized critical thinking by applying correct terms to artworks and comparing aesthetic, social, historical, and political aspects of art production.[21]

The two paper assignments were scaffolded to move from object-based reflections to larger contextual observations of the power of art and art institutions. The first paper was an art analysis, which was new to most of my students. Its aim was to aid in the development of visual literacy. The second paper was an exhibition analysis, which would empower students to develop a vocabulary for exhibition layout, critically assess the interpretive work done in museums, and engage in discourse on museum outreach. For the latter assignment, I secured a charter bus to New York City to take students to Firelei Báez's 2018 *Joy Out of Fire* exhibition in the Latimer/Edison Gallery at the Schomburg Center for Research in Black Culture. The show was presented in partnership with the Studio Museum of Harlem, which was under renovation. In 2019, we bused to the Barnes Museum to see the Philadelphia version of *30 Americans* curated by Shaw. There, students responded to the prompt: "What are the most pertinent challenges facing Black artists in the twenty-first century?" Students taking African American Art in 2020 during the height of the pandemic did not have the luxury of visiting an exhibition in person, so we had to settle on virtual access to exhibitions instead.

ART ANALYSIS ASSIGNMENT

One of the most exciting components of teaching at Rutgers was the presence of an art museum on campus. Prior to my time at Rutgers, I actively incorporated artwork from the Frances Young Tang Teaching Museum and Art Gallery into my classes at Skidmore College, where I lectured in American studies.[22] My approaches to the African American Art course at Rutgers built on that earlier experience. The Art Analysis assignment fulfilled the undergraduate core requirement learning goals for the Arts and Humanities proficiency, which required students to successfully analyze art in itself and in relation to specific histories, values, languages, cultures, and technologies. I expanded those goals to include students' ability to develop a method for analyzing visual resources through a critical race art history lens.

This assignment had multiple components. The first part was a worksheet that listed art by Black artists on display at the ZAM, identified by artist name, artwork title, and date of production (if known). Students visited the museum and, after viewing all the choices in person, selected the artwork they would write about. After selecting the piece, they then answered a series of questions based on their personal reactions to the piece. Their instructions were as follows:

1. Summarize your initial thoughts and reactions to the piece:
   a. Why were you drawn to it?
   b. What aspects of the piece stood out to you?
   c. Your impressions can help you reach your thesis.

2. Work through the Art Analysis Worksheet to analyze the artwork that you chose for this project. You should not consult any other primary or secondary source material at this time to complete these answers. No artist biography, no art reviews, nothing. It is only you and the artwork. You do not have to answer in full sentences; you can do bullet points.

I tried to limit any pre-emptive student research. When they conducted research ahead of time, the students often relied more on historians' views of the artworks than on their own insights. I wanted to push my students to find their own voices in the arena of art critics, and to trust their instincts. We had practiced visual analysis and interpretation from the first day in class, so the idea of discussing art pieces that were new to them was not foreign.

The worksheet questions followed a straightforward formula. Building on resources for primary source analysis available through the Library of Congress, the National Archives, and art textbooks outlining analytical method, I had students contemplate the art piece's title, formal characteristics, and content; the creator's intent; and the assumed audience for the piece.[23] They had to answer these questions while in the museum, standing or sitting in front of the artwork.

The second part of the scaffolded assignment was a continuation of the exercise that forced students to spend time with an art object, contemplate it on its own accord, then move forward with research to create an analytical argument about the piece. Therefore, the Art Analysis paper would do three things—discuss the artwork on its own merit; discuss it within the social, cultural, political milieu in which it was produced; and discuss its impact on the student.

Only after they turned in their worksheets and received feedback from me were they allowed to conduct primary and secondary source research on their artworks. They would then return to their worksheet and try to answer any lingering questions through that research. Sample investigative prompts included the following questions: What does the title mean? Are there other artworks with the same title? Does the artwork depict a common art subject? Is the title a play on words? How was the piece made—what materials were involved in the production process? What kind of technical knowledge did the artist need to possess to create the piece? Who is the artist—what is his/her/their life story? art training? significant life events? How does the art world characterize the artist? What was life like for African Americans during the time that the art was produced? When students finished their research, they revisited their worksheet to remind them of their first impressions. Then they answered the final two questions: How has the research impacted your understanding of the piece? Do you appreciate or regard it in a different way?

The different steps and reflective nature of the final product were intended to accomplish a number of goals. The first was to have students immersed in the art experience, which included the spatial aspects of finding the museum, figuring out what was allowed inside (bookbags, pencils or pens, etc.), perhaps speaking to a museum employee, orienting themselves to the American art gallery, and maybe even getting lost. The second was seeing the artwork in person, understanding its dimensions, its relationship to other pieces on display, and to the broader museum. The third was following their own instincts—allowing the option to decide which piece they would write about, understanding what caused excitement in themselves, what they found interesting or novel about the piece—in effect, developing their singular voices. Only after those experiences did the assignment prompt them to see what "experts" had to say. And from the more traditional method of research, they would then come to a resolution about their initial feelings and observations.

The process I described is part of what Fink calls "learning how to learn."[24] Not only does it offer autonomous and embodied experiences—how often do students have the opportunity to visit another part of campus for an assignment?—but it also requires reflection on what they learned in the process of research. They are actively engaged in the construction of knowledge, and they are acutely aware of what has changed in their understanding of an artwork from the time they first experienced it to the day they write the concluding sentence in their analysis paper. More often than not, students expressed excitement about new revelations, rather than disappointment if their initial perceptions were not "right."[25]

EXHIBITION SEMINAR

It was the Art Analysis paper that was a major impetus for the creation of the Exhibition Seminar focusing on Black women artists in the Zimmerli collection. Over the course of the three years that the assignment was offered, students often voiced disappointment with the small number of Black artists on display at the university museum relative to its other holdings. I had wanted to explore Black artist representation in the permanent collection to create novel ways to engage students in the classroom. One way to do that was by offering an upper-level graduate seminar that took stock of the collection's artwork by Black artists and developed an exhibition around it. The Curatorial Studies program in the Department of Art History at Rutgers requires students to take a seminar in which a faculty member develops an exhibition in tandem with students over the course of a semester. The seminar is not beholden to the Zimmerli; in fact, it can focus on a private collection, a topic or theme, or any other inspiration that a professor proposes. Thus, my Exhibition Seminar: Black Women Artists in the Zimmerli Collection was born, with the specific aim to fulfill a need in my survey class.

The upper-level graduate seminar was a collaboration between the Department of Art History, the ZAM, and the Center for Women in the Arts and Humanities (CWAH, now the Center for Women in the Arts at Douglass). Using the collection of the Zimmerli as a resource, the course built on the range of Black women artists represented in the museum's permanent collection to develop an object-driven exhibition. The partnership with the CWAH came through the advocacy of my colleague

Tatiana Flores. Despite my attempts to hold the entire exhibition at the Zimmerli, I was informed that the museum's exhibition schedule was full for several years. When discussing my options for alternate locations in New Brunswick, Flores suggested that I investigate the gallery space run by the CWAH on the campus of Douglass College. Upon my discovery that the gallery had availability for 2022, the focus on Black women artists was solidified. And it made sense. In the years that I taught the African American Art survey course, Black women were sorely underrepresented in the Zimmerli. Focusing on a subset of Black artists in this way would also help my students and me work with a manageable number of resources over one semester.

During my time at Rutgers, the ZAM had rarely showcased Black American women artists in its galleries. This is particularly true of its American gallery. While we had a celebrated visiting exhibition on Angela Davis in the 2021–2022 academic year, that was based on pieces on loan from a collection outside Rutgers.[26] I wanted to investigate what artworks we had in our permanent collection to make sure I knew what was consistently available for students and the greater public that the Zimmerli serves.

Outside Rutgers and the Zimmerli, there is still a paucity of research and celebration of the work of Black women artists. Survey books, including those concerned with Black American art, are primarily filled with work by Black men, even when Black women are the writers, researchers, and curators. As hooks has asserted, "Race does not mediate patriarchal politics in the realm of visual arts."[27] In this and myriad other ways, the African American Art survey replicates the larger American art survey based on the Western canon. This disparity highlights how women art makers (quilt makers, seamstresses, yard workers) have had their artistic production discredited and stymied because of a lack of access to education, as well as child-rearing and homemaking responsibilities that restrict time for studio work.

With these concerns in mind, the Exhibition Seminar came to be. My students and I would comb through the Zimmerli permanent collection and display the artwork at Douglass College in the main library. The exhibition space, the Mary H. Dana Women Artists Series (DWAS) in the Douglass Library, is the oldest continuously running exhibition space in the United States dedicated to making visible the work of emerging and established contemporary women artists.[28] Douglass College, in fact, had been founded as the New Jersey College for Women and was later renamed for its first dean, Mabel Smith Douglass. The institution merged with Rutgers University in 2007. The Exhibition Seminar built on the long history of women's education and empowerment at Douglass, and the history of women artist activists who founded the DWAS.

The renowned artist and Douglass College alum Joan Snyder was the first curator of the DWAS. As Snyder later reminisced, "At first, I wanted to show women [artists] that the students would love to see, who would be important for them to see. Then I wanted to show women who needed a break, who were wonderful artists, but hadn't been showing their work."[29] What I did not realize when I first proposed the Exhibition Seminar was that I was building on a longer tradition of women activists who yearned for critical voice and representation in the curriculum offered to students and who created the space to do so. That connection was magical.

Almost six hundred women exhibited in the DWAS between 1971 and 2021. Of that number, I identified thirteen Black women artists.[30] If I counted the Black women artists who exhibited multiple times during the first fifty years of the series, they would represent no more than 3 percent of all artists in the DWAS. Even in an art series dedicated specifically to representing women artists, Black women were shockingly underrepresented. The Exhibition Seminar would rectify Black women's erasure on a number of levels within the art spaces at Rutgers University.

With an exhibition space and access to the ZAM holdings secured, I sought out students for the specialized course. I drew up an illustrated one-page course description to advertise the class to students across a number of fields. I sent it to faculty and administrators in the Departments of Africana Studies, American Studies, Art History, Design, English, History, Visual Arts, and Women's, Gender, and Sexuality Studies. While the course was designed for graduate students, I also welcomed upper-level undergraduates with instructors' permission. I handpicked a few undergraduate students who had taken the African American Art survey based on their abilities and experience in completing the Art Analysis and Exhibition Analysis papers. From prior experience I knew they were capable of the upper-level independent and collaborative work.

The students in the Exhibition Seminar came from a variety of racial, ethnic, socioeconomic, sexuality, and gender-based backgrounds. They consisted of fourth-year undergraduates and first- and second-year master's students. They were in the Mason Gross School of the Arts, the Department of Art History's Cultural Heritage and Preservation Studies and Art History programs, and the Department of Women's, Gender, and Sexuality Studies. They were from Michigan, Missouri, New Jersey, and North Carolina. They came to the class from different positionalities. Granted, this was a self-selected group. They chose to take part in an upper-level graduate seminar on Black women artists whose work was held by our university museum. And they poured into their work, one another, and the exhibition. Our process really was discursive. We had to arrive at a common point, even if we didn't start there. That is the very essence of the learning process—being open to novel experiences, information, and perspectives.

Our investigation into the Zimmerli collection and approach to exhibition design included methods and theory from art history, critical race theory, Black feminist theory, and new museology. We used both primary and secondary sources to gain an understanding of the holdings of the Zimmerli and the extent to which Black women artists were represented. One goal for student learning was that, by the end of the semester, they display a general understanding of mid- to late twentieth-century Black women artists and the social conditions in which they worked. Students would also develop a critical analysis of museum collection holdings and engage in discourse about the museum curatorship and representation.[31] This they would do by exploring elements of museum exhibition planning, problem solving, interpretation, and design.[32]

Our project-based learning process reflected what DeLosSantos proclaims in *Poetries—Politics*, that "rest[ing] on a central driving question, and the contemporary relevance of the driving question or 'problem' [was] a key student motivator."[33] Indeed, the problem was the lack of Black women artists displayed at the Zimmerli. Students were motivated to find out why this disparity existed and to work together to create a proper solution. I had already determined one vehicle to address the problem—an exhibition. The staff at the ZAM helped me gather the resources—a list of Black women artists, thumbnails of some of the artworks, and as much information as they had on the artists and the works' provenance. The class was structured to allow student creativity but also scaffolded to go from big ideas to more specific, actionable deliverables, all the while requiring collaboration across assignments.[34]

As idealistic as this setup was, we faced gargantuan obstacles. The Zimmerli had just unexpectedly lost its director, the late Thomas Sokolowski, in spring 2020, and museum leadership was in transition. The challenges of the pandemic were numerous. Operating in a limited virtual environment, we had no physical access to the museum or the art library. I had no idea nor indication of whether students would be able to visit the gallery spaces or collection storage to see artwork. But that was the reality of our present. The challenges remained in the face of an uncertain future, but we moved forward anyway. This meant that I had to develop a significantly more flexible syllabus than normal.

To combat these issues, I leaned heavily on outside expertise in the classroom. Zimmerli staff members Nicole Simpson, assistant curator of prints and drawings, and Donna Gustafson, interim director, curator of modern and contemporary art, and Mellon Director of Academic Programs, gave virtual guest lectures early in the semester, discussing the history and holdings of the ZAM and the preponderance of Black women artists in the print collection. Rutgers art history alum and arts advocate Stephanie Johnson-Cunningham, founder of Museum Hue, discussed problems affecting artists of color and museums that support them. Rutgers Mason Gross faculty member and visual artist Heather Hart, co-founder of the Black Lunch Table, highlighted the importance of the archive and led my students through a Wikipedia edit-a-thon focused on the Black women artists they were researching in the class. All of these class visits were virtual and took advantage of technology as a tool for student engagement in the Zoom classroom. Student participation in the virtual classroom was of utmost importance; thus, it constituted 20 percent of their final grade. Working on the exhibition was both exciting and exceedingly difficult. Since we were fully remote, we had to pull on a lot of disparate resources, lean heavily on one another, and use our collective imaginations.

EXHIBITION PROPOSAL ASSIGNMENT

The first assignment for the class gave students the opportunity to develop an object-based exhibition proposal. Students familiarized themselves with the missions and recent exhibitions of both the ZAM and the DWAS.[35] Students had access, via a folder on Canvas, to a list of artworks by Black women artists developed for our purposes by Simpson. To support their proposal thesis, they were encouraged to use texts that we had already discussed in class, as well as any outside scholarly sources they deemed relevant.

For students, the goals of the exhibition proposal were as follows:

- Illustrate their primary survey and analysis of Black women artists in the Zimmerli collection.

- Discuss the history and mission of the Zimmerli and the DWAS and how their proposed exhibition related to these institutions and venues.

- Articulate the main concept and framework for an exhibition based on the Zimmerli's collection of Black women artists.

- Develop public-facing programs that connected to the artistic themes of the exhibition.

To successfully complete these tasks, students were given a proposal checklist. They had to discuss their exhibition concept, the "big idea" that would frame their exhibition. They would connect the exhibition's relevancy and benefits to the ZAM and DWAS. The budding student curators then listed the artwork to be displayed, stating whether the works were newly commissioned, existing works, or a mix of both. The assignment required that a fraction of the pieces had to come from the ZAM permanent collection. Students also outlined the target audience and the programming around the show. Programs could include artist talks, panel discussions, roundtables, or hands-on workshops geared toward engaging the general public.[36]

Students presented their proposals to the class and gave one another feedback. Afterward, we used a Google Jamboard—a digital whiteboard—to highlight commonalities across all the proposals.[37] From these sessions, the thematic focus of the exhibition began to appear: "Self-Making and Identity," "The Brodsky Center and the Rutgers Print Collaborative," "Process and Materiality," "The Art of Storytelling," and "Alchemy and Spirituality." But we still needed to discuss the central message, as well as the ways students could bring these themes to life. That would require further research into the artworks themselves, with an eye on our emergent themes.

DEVELOPING DIDACTIC MATERIAL

After students presented their exhibition proposals and found common themes, they moved on to their next assignment—artist biographies and catalog entries. The student curators listed their top three preferences for the artists they wanted to research, and I matched them as best I could. Since there were nine students in the class, and each student researched three artists, we had to exclude other Black women artists in the collection out of necessity. We also discovered that two artists in the collection were incorrectly identified as Black.[38] We were restricted from incorporating Black women artists who had been recently shown, like Renée Green, whose prints were acquired for the Angela Davis exhibition. We did not have access to artworks by Black women artists included in an upcoming exhibition, *American Stories*, which highlighted a major gift from the Jersey City Museum. That particular gift, a result of the unfortunate closing of the museum, was a major boon to the ZAM, since it significantly increased contemporary artist representation across diverse races and ethnicities.

Students created two-page bibliographies on their selected artists as a foundation to the development of didactic materials for the exhibition. Several issues came to the fore in this process. The ZAM had a range of less prominent Black artists who did not even have published biographies. Some were living, others had passed on. For those living, students reached out via e-mail, LinkedIn, Facebook, and galleries, to speak with the artists, if possible. For others, students relied on obituaries or information they gleaned through art auction catalogs.

The parameters of the biographies and later, catalog entries, were developed from professional standards published by the Association of Art Museum Curators, among others.[39] With concise yet accessible language, students interpreted the items in the exhibition to speak to an informed art public. They were instructed in the art of peer review, and we workshopped artist bios and catalog entries together. They also corrected misinformation in the Zimmerli catalog, such as artist names and artwork titles.

Our next step toward interpreting the pieces for the exhibition was the development of wall texts. The section texts would highlight the major themes in the exhibition, while the focus texts and object labels would draw specific connections between the artworks and speak to a diverse, non-expert audience. The student curators created interpretive materials following professional standards in the museum field, using guidelines produced by the Minneapolis Institute of Arts and the Getty Museum.[40]

Given that we were virtual, it was particularly difficult to figure out object placement in the galleries. Over the course of the semester, we learned that, in addition to the two galleries at the DWAS, we would be able to display artwork at the Zimmerli in its Focus Gallery, a small room on its ground floor that was once the museum store. Two separate Jamboard sessions helped us contemplate pieces we would like to see in conversation with each other. The first session focused on the exhibition themes. Students dropped JPEG files of the artworks onto a Jamboard slide, then rearranged them on subsequent slides that stood for each of the five exhibition themes: "Self-Making and Identity," "The Brodsky Center and the Rutgers Print Collaborative," "Process and Materiality," "The Art of Storytelling," and "Alchemy and Spirituality." These categorizations were necessarily fluid, as many of the pieces could fit into multiple themes.

Next, we attempted to replicate that process, moving from the two-dimensional space of the Jamboard slide to the three-dimensional spaces of our three galleries. I procured floor plans, sections, and installation images of previous exhibitions for both DWAS galleries and the Focus Gallery. We struggled to correctly match our representative JPEGs to the scale of the mock-ups. In the second Jamboard session, we placed artworks in different areas on floor plans and in room sections, failing at times to get the proportions right. We discussed where the section and focus texts would go and how to balance content and aesthetics. We were concerned with sight lines—what would be the first pieces a visitor would see when approaching each gallery, and from various entry points? When did we consider a wall too crowded? While we wanted the pieces to be arranged thematically, we did not prescribe a static route that people would follow. How would we arrange the works to handle a loosely defined traffic flow, and account for COVID-19 6 feet distancing protocol?

Given that we did this work all online, in some ways the design workshops felt like excercises in futility. Yet I returned to these very exercises a year later when it was time to install. The results of the conversations with my students were the guiding principles by which I made placement decisions in both the DWAS and the Zimmerli galleries.

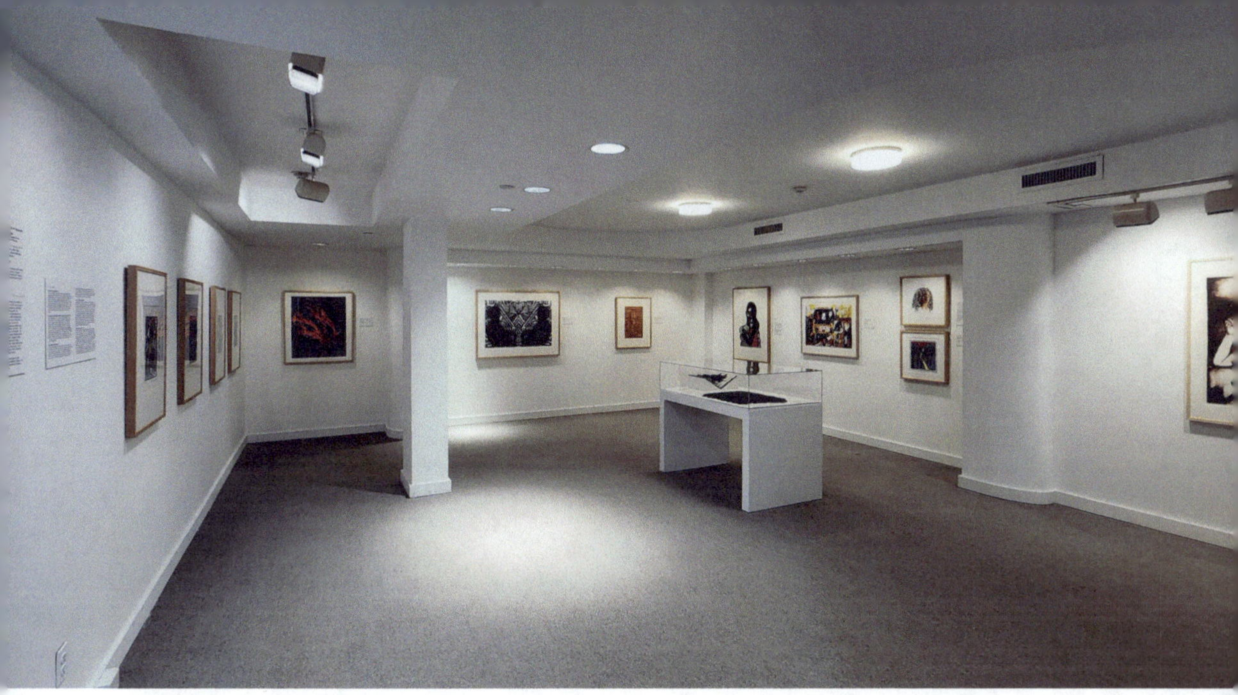

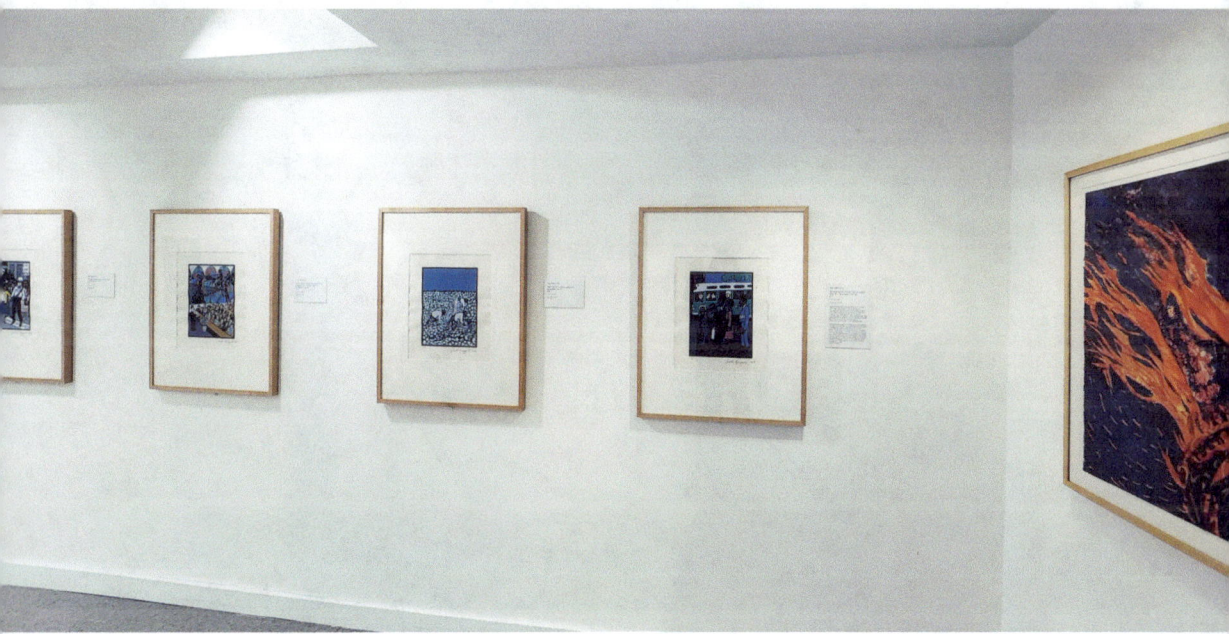

Fig. 1.1. General installation view of the Focus Gallery at the ZAM. While I collaborated with Nicole Ianuzelli, then senior program coordinator at the Center for Women in the Arts and Humanities, in the installation process, the principles developed by students in the Exhibition Seminar directed my decisions. Introductory text and student curator-produced section texts, focus texts, and object labels accompany the art. 2022. Nicole Ianuzelli, photographer.

Fig. 1.2. Installation in the Focus Gallery at the ZAM. Four prints from Faith Ringgold's *Letter from Birmingham City Jail* portfolio in conversation with Betye Saar's *Blow Top Blues: The Fire Next Time.* 2022. Nicole Ianuzelli, photographer.

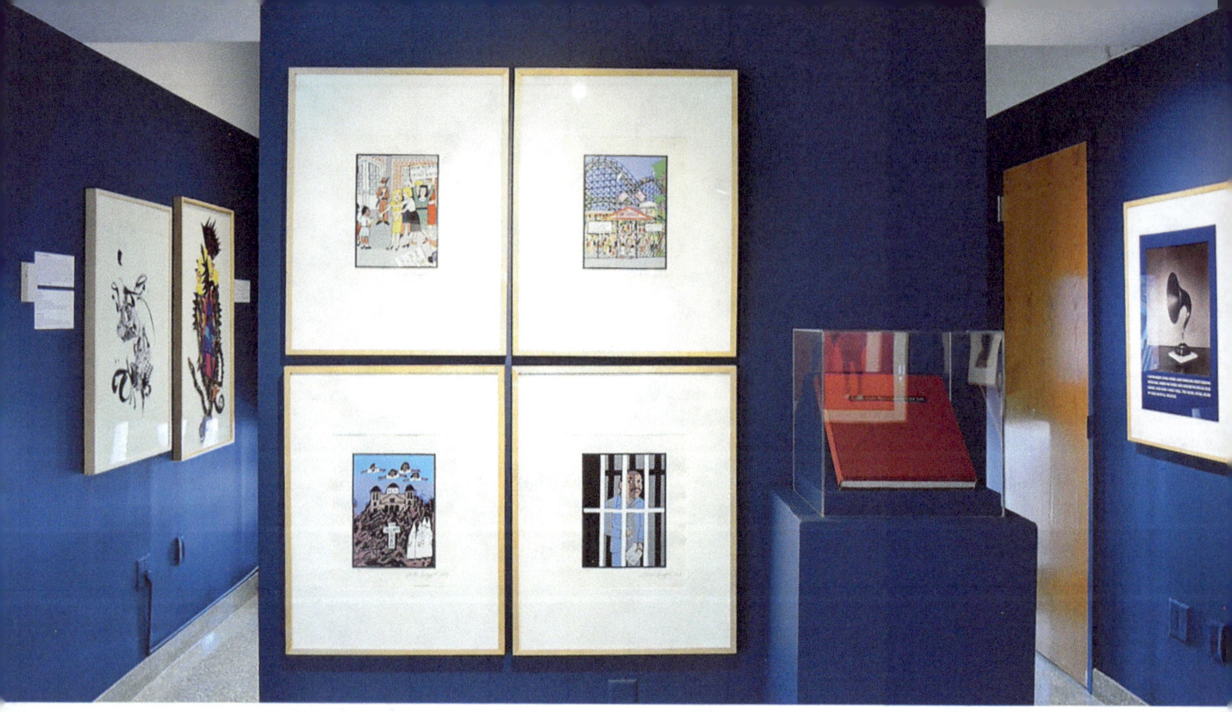

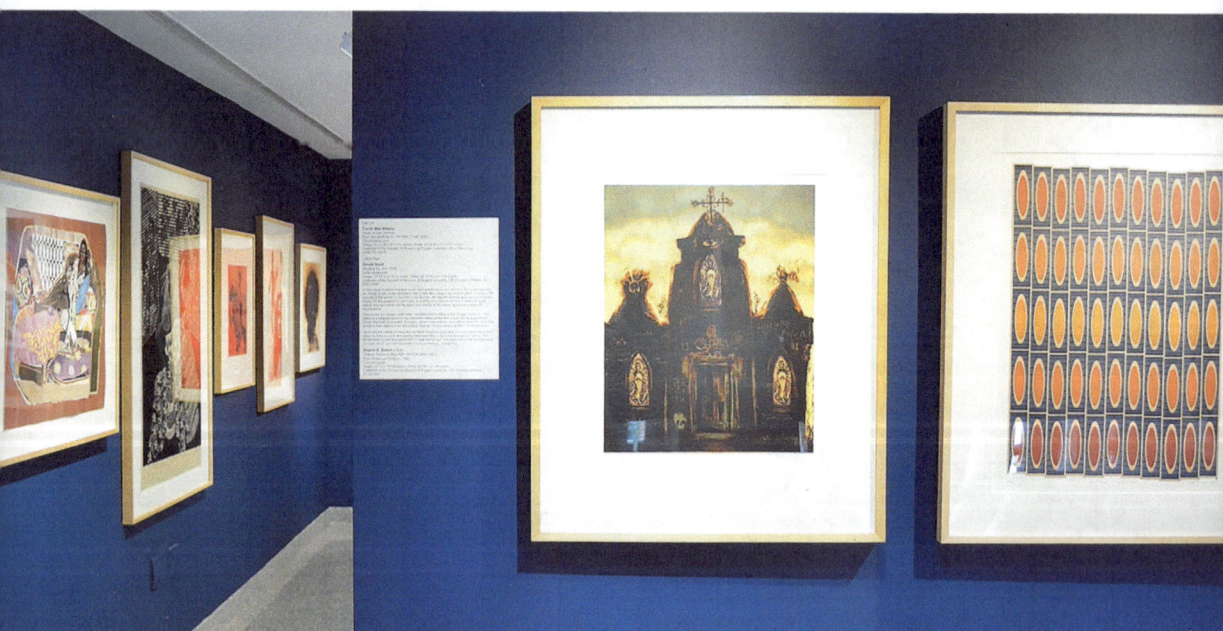

Fig. 1.3. The remaining four prints from Faith Ringgold's *Letter from Birmingham City Jail* portfolio with the book edition of the serigraphs in the pedestal case to the right, installed in Gallery104A at the DWAS. Splitting the Ringgold series between the ZAM and the DWAS created balance between the galleries. 2022. Nicole Ianuzelli, photographer.

Fig. 1.4. Renée Stout's *Waiting for Jimi* and Sharon E. Sutton's *Streets Paved in Moonlight and Candlelit Cafes* in the foreground. Note the complementary aesthetics of the two pieces. Student curators' focus text and object labels visible on the left. The Stout piece represented "Alchemy and Spirituality", while the Sutton piece is discussed in relation to "Process and Materiality." Gallery 104A of the DWAS. 2022. Nicole Ianuzelli, photographer.

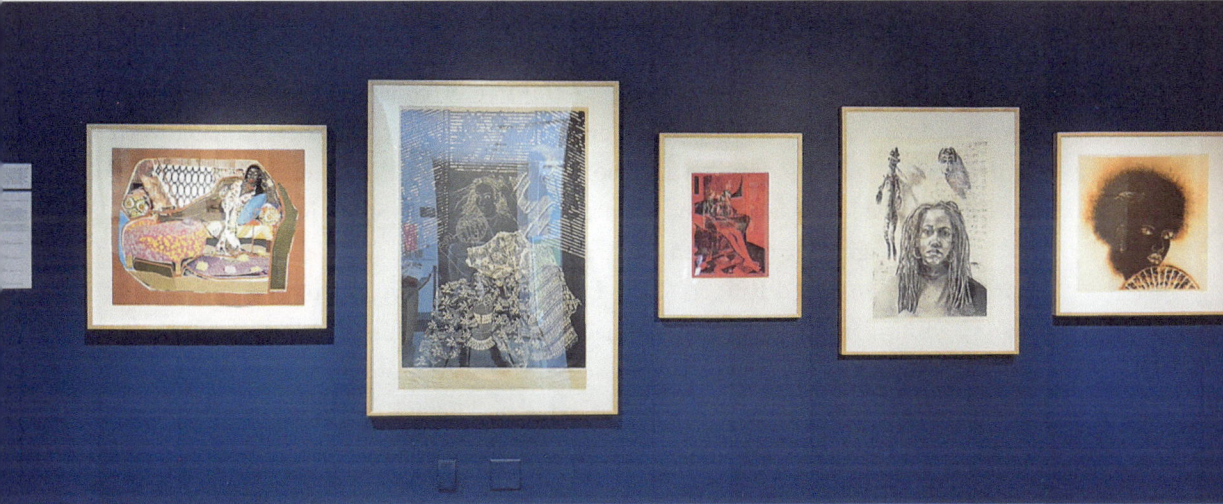

Fig. 1.5. Prints highlighting "Self-Making and Identity." Gallery 104A of the DWAS. 2022. Nicole Ianuzelli, photographer.

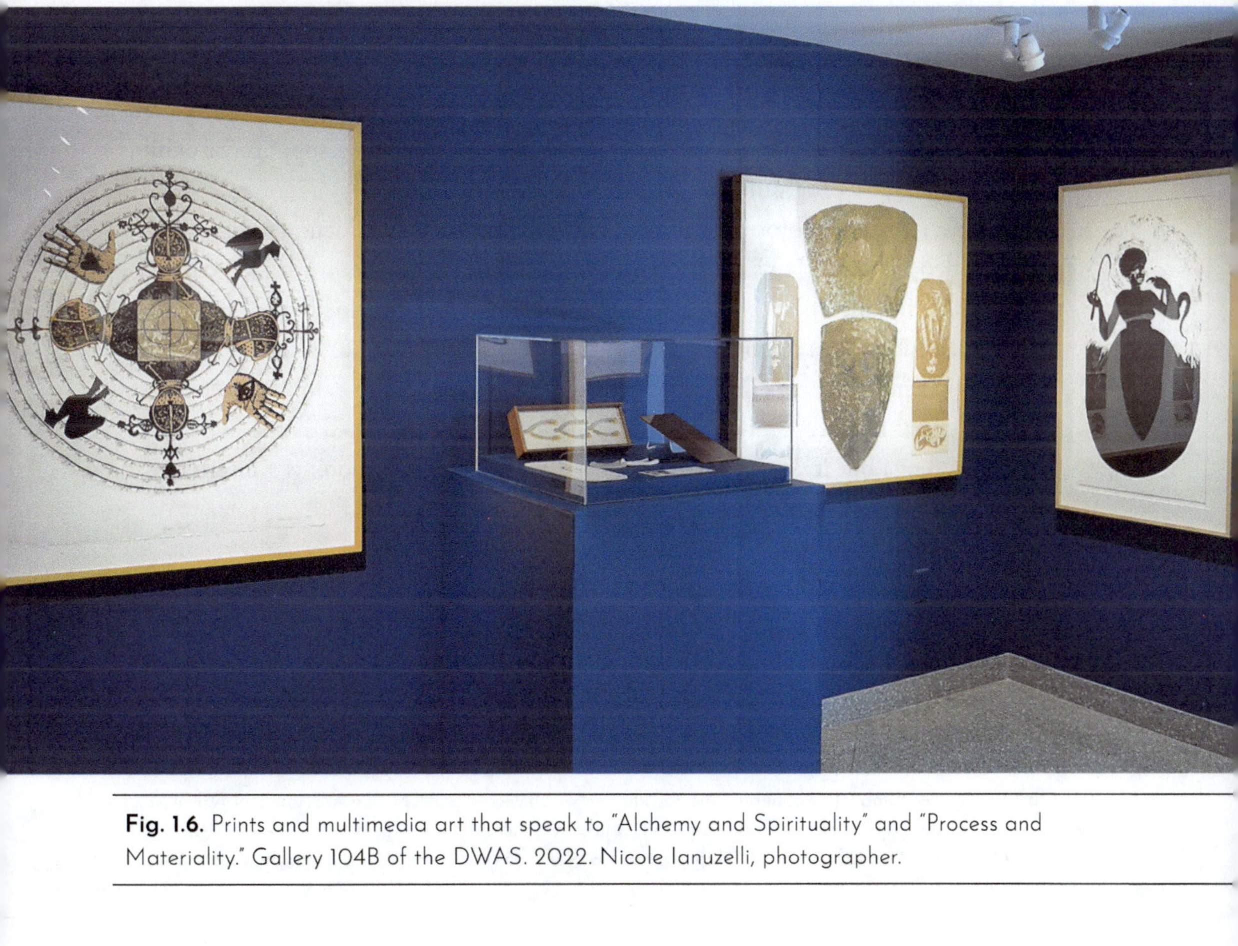

Fig. 1.6. Prints and multimedia art that speak to "Alchemy and Spirituality" and "Process and Materiality." Gallery 104B of the DWAS. 2022. Nicole Ianuzelli, photographer.

TRANSFER OF KNOWLEDGE

The last deliverable for the course was a transfer of collective documents to the DWAS and the ZAM, and a virtual Zoom presentation to stakeholders affiliated with the university. I asked students with whom they would like to share their findings. I also revisited the list of faculty and departments with intersecting interests that I had created at the beginning of the semester. The range of invited audience members was impressive. We included Rutgers–New Brunswick, Rutgers Library, Zimmerli, and CWAH administrators and staff. We had faculty from Mason Gross School of the Arts and members of the faculty from across the School of Arts and Sciences. The student curators were not shy—they asked that I invite the university president, Jonathan Holloway. He was unavailable, but the senior vice-president for equity and inclusion was on the Zoom because of a student's request.

The final presentation was a chance not only to highlight important revelations about the Black women artists and artworks in the Zimmerli collection, but also to suggest areas of expansion for future collecting in view of the collection's strengths and weaknesses. Over the course of two hours, the student curators shared their findings and engendered excited responses from their engaged audience of Rutgers faculty, staff, administrators, and classmates. Audience members expressed their enthusiasm for the upcoming exhibition and their appreciation for all the new knowledge created. Some of the same people on the call would end up offering support for exhibition financing and programming that following year.

The last requirement for the course was a collaborative final document, into which students deposited their twice-revised artist biographies, catalog entries, and wall texts, as well as their collective bibliographies. Each student curator added to the exhibition checklist, which was a tallying up of all the artworks to be included in the show. At every step over the course of the semester, students developed an exhibition according to professional industry standards—and delivered. I may be listed as the main curator of the show, but it was not really mine. It was theirs. This book is a testament to their work. Please enjoy.

Notes

1. Toni Morrison, "Playing in the Dark: Whiteness and the Literary Imagination" (1992), in *Racism in America: A Reader* (Harvard University Press, 2020), 2.

2. bell hooks, *Teaching to Transgress: Education as the Practice of Freedom* (Routledge, 1994), 12.

3. "About CELT," Center for Engaged Learning and Teaching, Tulane University, accessed November 14, 2025, https://celt.tulane.edu/about-celt.

4. For detailed information about my approach to the NAAB accreditation process, see Amber N. Wiley, "Pedagogy," paper presented at the Black in Design conference, Harvard Graduate School of Design, Cambridge, MA, October 9, 2015, https://youtu.be/P46hVD6YmkQ?si=WG1NUdgQuzD9gTxg&t=1109;

"Pedagogy and Diversity: Amber Wiley and Jessica Varner," *Constructs: Yale Architecture*, Spring 2016, 12, https://www.architecture.yale.edu/publications/42-constructs-spring-2016; and Aaron Smithson, "Black Students Demand Action on Institutionalized Racism at Harvard's Graduate School of Design," *Architect's Newspaper*, June 17, 2020, https://www.archpaper.com/2020/06/black-students-demand-action-on-institutionalized-racism-harvards-graduate-school-of-design/.

5. "Intergroup Relations," Skidmore College, 2025, https://www.skidmore.edu/igr/index.php.

6. Jennifer Mueller, quoted in Emilka Jansen, "Understanding Skidmore's Intergroup Relations Department," *Skidmore News*, October 14, 2020, https://skidmorenews.com/new-blog/2020/10/14/understanding-skidmores-intergroup-relations-department.

7. Audre Lorde, "The Master's Tools Will Never Dismantle the Master's House," in *Sister Outsider: Essays and Speeches* (Crossing Press, 2007), 111–112.

8. For examples from Tulane University, see Amber N. Wiley, "Integrating Architecture into Digital and Public Humanities: Sites and Sounds + MediaNOLA," *Journal of Digital Humanities* 2, no. 2 (Spring 2013), https://journalofdigitalhumanities.org/2-2/integrating-architecture-into-digital-and-public-humanities-by-amber-wiley/; Brentin Mock, "A History of New Orleans Public Housing, Through No Limit and Ca$h Money Music Videos," CityLab, August 28, 2015, https://www.bloomberg.com/news/articles/2015-08-28/no-limit-and-cash-money-music-videos-provide-a-visual-history-of-pre-katrina-public-housing-projects; and Jan Ramsey, "Sites and Sounds: Preserving New Orleans Historic Musical Landmarks," *Offbeat Magazine*, September 21, 2013, https://www.offbeat.com/news/sites-sounds-preserving-new-orleans-historical-music-landmarks/. At Rutgers, I took preservation students to East Jersey Old Town Village. They authored papers on the efficacy of the site's interpretation. That led to my later engagement with Monument Lab's Revolution NJ project, a collaboration with the New Jersey Historical Commission and the New Jersey State Council on the Arts. See Amber N. Wiley, "East Jersey Old Town Village, Piscataway, NJ," in *Revolution Research: Revolution NJ Artistic Research Residency* (Monument Lab, Summer 2021), 29–32, https://data.monumentlab.com/uploads/monument-lab/originals/2462f74e-5c0f-475b-a79f-5529cffc0553.pdf.

9. For this reason, several committees and task forces of professional organizations have striven to articulate the value of interdisciplinary, nontraditional work for faculty on the tenure track. I have consulted these resources and shared them with other tenure-track colleagues throughout my career. See College Art Association and the Society of Architectural Historians, "Guidelines for the Evaluation of Digital Scholarship in Art and Architectural History," Task Force to Develop Guidelines for Evaluating Digital Art and Architectural History for Promotion and Tenure, January 2016, https://www.collegeart.org/pdf/evaluating-digital-scholarship-in-art-and-architectural-history.pdf; Big Ten Arts Administrators, "Guidance for Rewarding and Recognizing Community-Engaged Scholarship in the Arts," September 2020, https://www.a2ru.org/wp-content/uploads/2020/09/Big-Ten_Evaluating-Community-Engagement.pdf; Committee on Promotion and Tenure of the National Council for Preservation Education, "Toward Promotion and Tenure: Guidelines for Assessing the Achievement of a Preservation Educator," October 27, 1984, rev. 2013, https://www.ncpe.us/wp-content/uploads/2015/12/PresEdGuidelines2013update.pdf; Association of Collegiate Schools of Architecture, "Research and Scholarship for Promotion, Tenure, and Reappointments in Schools of Architecture," 2017, https://www.acsa-arch.org/wp-content/uploads/acsa_tenurepromotion_17.pdf; and American Historical Association, Organization of American Historians, and National Council on Public History, "Tenure, Promotion, and the Publicly Engaged Academic Historian," 2010, rev. 2017, https://www.historians.org/resource/tenure-promotion-and-the-publicly-engaged-academic-historian/.

10. Patricia Hill Collins, *Intersectionality as Critical Social Theory* (Duke University Press, 2019), 145.

11. Lindsey Stewart, "Black Feminist Figures: Interventions and Inheritances," *Southern Journal of Philosophy* 59, no. 1 (March 2021): 10. Alice Walker used the term *womanist* to specifically tackle the notion of what it means to be Black, or a woman of color, *and* a feminist, since the larger feminist movement was born out of white women's needs, desires, and priorities, such that the unspoken modifier for feminist was *white*. Walker famously argued, "Womanist is to feminist as purple to lavender." Alice Walker, *In Search of Our Mothers' Gardens: Womanist Prose* (Amistad Press, 2023), ix.

12. Linda Nochlin, "From 1971: Why Have There Been No Great Women Artists?," *ARTnews*, January 1971, reposted May 30, 2015, https://www.artnews.com/art-news/retrospective/why-have-there-been-no-great -women-artists-4201/. Kymberly N. Pinder also highlights these discrepancies in "Black Representation and Western Survey Textbooks," *Art Bulletin* 81, no. 3 (September 1999): 533–538.

13. Rhea Swain, "Art History Professor Highlights Iconic Black Artists," *Daily Targum*, February 19, 2020, https://dailytargum.com/article/2020/02/honoring-black-artists-zimmerli.

14. Gwendolyn DuBois Shaw, *The Art of Remembering: Essays on African American Art and History* (Duke University Press, 2024), 3.

15. Franklin's quote is emblazoned on an introductory panel in the Smithsonian National Museum of African American History and Culture's permanent exhibition *Slavery and Freedom, 1400-1877*. Franklin served as the chair of the museum's Scholarly Advisory Committee.

16. W.E.B. Du Bois, *The Souls of Black Folk: Essays and Sketches* (University of Massachusetts Press, 2018), 3.

17. This approach builds on the work of Camara Dia Holloway, "Critical Race Art History," *Art Journal* 75, no. 1 (2016): 89–92; and Anne D'Alleva, *Methods & Theories of Art History*, 2nd ed. (Laurence King Publishing, 2012).

18. I tested two different survey books for the course: Lisa E. Farrington, *African-American Art: A Visual and Cultural History* (Oxford University Press, 2016); and Sharon F. Patton, *African-American Art* (Oxford University Press, 1998). bell hooks, *Art on My Mind: Visual Politics* (New Press, 1995) was required reading every year.

19. hooks, *Art on My Mind*, xvi.

20. Michele Wallace, "Why Are There No Great Black Artists? The Problem of Visuality in African American Culture" (1992), in *Dark Designs and Visual Culture* (Duke University Press, 2004), 191.

21. L. Dee Fink, *Creating Significant Learning Experiences: An Integrated Approach to Designing College Courses* (Wiley, 2013), 34–36.

22. Much of the work I completed at the Tang was a part of various initiatives and grants secured by my colleagues at the museum and in different departments. I served as a faculty collaborator for the following grants: the Teagle Foundation, Teaching and Learning with Museum Exhibitions: An Inter-Institutional Approach (2017), and the Mellon Foundation, Accelerate: Access and Inclusion at the Tang Teaching Museum (2017). I wrote two essays through the latter collaboration: "Amber N. Wiley on Teaching with the Tang Collection," 8–9, and Amber N. Wiley, "Carrie Mae Weems, *When and Where I Enter the British Museum*," 10–13, in *Accelerate: Access and Inclusion at the Tang Teaching Museum*, ed. Ian Berry and Rebecca McNamara (Frances Young Tang Teaching Museum and Art Gallery, Skidmore College, 2017), vol. 1. Two of my students' essays were also included in the *Accelerate* publication.

23. For the full worksheet, see the appendix. The worksheet combined methods, questions, and resources from Lisa E. Farrington, "The Art of Perception: How Art Communicates," in *African-American Art: A Visual and Cultural History*, 3–13; Anne D'Alleva, *How to Write Art History*, 2nd ed. (Laurence King Publishing, 2010); National Archives and Records Administration, Education Resources, "Document Analysis," accessed January 25, 2025, https://www.archives.gov/education/lessons/worksheets; and Library of Congress, "Primary Source Analysis Tool for Students," Teacher's Guides and Analysis Tool, accessed January 25, 2025, https://www.loc.gov/programs/teachers/getting-started-with-primary-sources/guides/.

24. Fink, *Creating Significant Learning Experiences*, 56–61.

25. By putting *right* in quotation marks, I am highlighting the misconception that students often carry, that their observations after sufficient research need fall in line with what experts—credentialed historians, cultural critics, and the like—have already said.

26. Gerry Beegan and Donna Gustafson, eds., *Angela Davis: Seize the Time* (Hirmer Publishers, 2020).

27. hooks, *Art on My Mind*, xiv.

28. Mary H. Dana was a New York Public Library historian and Douglass College alum. In 1987, her friend and Douglass professor emerita Nellie Smither endowed the art series in Dana's honor. Beryl K. Smith,

"The Mary H. Dana Women Artists Series: From Idea to Institution," *Journal of the Rutgers University Libraries* 54, no. 1 (1992): 11.

29. Joan M. Marter, *Women Artists on the Leading Edge: Visual Arts at Douglass College* (Rutgers University Press, 2019), 134.

30. The thirteen artists were Howardena Pindell (the first Black woman shown in the series, in the 1972–1973 academic year), Beverly Buchanan, Jane Taylor Pickett, Betye Saar, Faith Ringgold, Loïs Mailou Jones (from her estate), Vivian E. Browne, Emma Amos, Kara Walker (listed by her married name, Kara Walker-Bürgel), Clarissa Sligh, Renee Cox, Adrienne Wheeler, and Maria Magdalena Campos-Pons. Some artists exhibited more than once over the years. Pindell, Saar, and Ringgold all exhibited twice. Browne and Amos exhibited three times. For transparency, I did not screen every woman artist listed in the DWAS but instead looked for names I identified as Black women. I may have overlooked some less prominent Black women artists. Nevertheless, the numbers speak for themselves. The list of artists who exhibited in the DWAS can be found online: Center for Women in the Arts at Douglass, "Mary H. Dana Women Artists Series: List of Exhibiting Artists by Academic Year from Spring 2024–Fall 1971," 2025, https://douglass .rutgers.edu/sites/default/files/2024-08/Mary%20H.%20Dana%20Women%20Artists%20Series _Artist%20List_spring%202024-fall%201971.pdf.

31. Required reading included, but was not limited to, Diana Greenwald, "What Data Can Teach Us About Museum Collections," *Alliance Blog*, American Alliance of Museums, April 27, 2020, https://www.aam-us .org/2020/04/27/what-can-data-teach-us-about-museum-collections/; Nicholas Miller, "The History of the Group Exhibition from the Harmon Foundation to *Black Male*," in *The Routledge Companion to African American Art History*, ed. Eddie Chambers (Routledge, 2020), 301–310; Caroline V. Wallace, "Exhibiting Authenticity: The Black Emergency Cultural Coalition's Protests of the Whitney Museum of American Art, 1968–71," *Art Journal* 74, no. 2 (2015): 5–23; Valerie Smith, "Abundant Evidence: Black Women Artists of the 1960s and 1970s," in *Entering the Picture: Judy Chicago, the Fresno Feminist Art Program, and the Collective Visions of Women Artists*, ed. Jill Fields (Routledge, 2012), 119–131.

32. Students were oriented to standards in museum interpretation through the J. Paul Getty Museum, *Complete Guide to Adult Audience Interpretive Materials: Gallery Texts and Graphics* (J. Paul Getty Trust, 2011), 1–21. They also read reviews of recent exhibitions that focused on Black women artists, including Shannan L. Hayes, "Wanting More," *differences* 31, no. 1 (2020): 64–97; Renée Ater, Review of *Creating Their Own Image: A History of African-American Women Artists* and *African Queen, African Arts* 38, no. 2 (Summer 2005): 82–83; and Jennie Hirsh, Review of *Material Girls: Contemporary Black Women Artists, Art in America* 99, no. 10 (2011): 177.

33. Jenevieve DeLosSantos, "The Pedagogy of *Poetries—Politics*: How to Craft Your Own Project-Based Learning Course," in *Poetries—Politics: A Celebration of Language, Art, and Learning*, ed. Jenevieve DeLosSantos (Rutgers University Press, 2023), 72.

34. DeLosSantos, "The Pedagogy of *Poetries—Politics*," 72–75.

35. They could refer to the ZAM website, https://zimmerli.rutgers.edu, and to the Mary H. Dana Women Artists Series Records, New Brunswick Special Collections, Rutgers University Libraries, https://archives .libraries.rutgers.edu/repositories/11/resources/852.

36. The checklist was condensed from Art Museum of the Americas, "Instructions on How to Present Exhibit Proposals to AMA," 2013, http://museum.oas.org/img/forms/exhibition-proposal-english.doc; Phillips Museum of Art, "Exhibition Proposal & Planning Guidelines," 2025, https://studylib.net/doc/6736162 /object-labels; and Museums Victoria (Australia), "Exhibition and Display Basics," 2025, https:// museumsvictoria.com.au/learning/small-object-big-story/5-exhibition-basics/.

37. Google discontinued the Jamboard application in 2024.

38. Those artists excluded from our research were Laylah Ali, Vivian E. Browne, Nanette Carolyn Carter, Barbara Chase-Riboud, Collaborative: Girls of Baltimore, Shamia Gaither, Gladys Barker Grauer, Jennie C. Jones, Samella (Sanders) Lewis, and Norma Gloria Morgan. One artist, Joan Eda Byrd, was researched for the class but not included in the exhibition. The two artists incorrectly identified as Black were Irene Clark and Davira Fisher. There are two Irene Clarks who are artists, one white and one Black. The artwork in the Zimmerli collection is by the former. Fisher was misidentified as Black in several sources outside the Zimmerli; my student's research bore out that she was not, in fact, a Black woman.

39. Association of Art Museum Curators (AAMC), *Professional Practices for Art Museum Curators* (AAMC, 2007), https://www.collegeart.org/pdf/AAMC_Professional_Practices.pdf; Sylvan Barnet, "How to Write an Exhibition Catalog," in *A Short Guide to Writing About Art*, 9th ed. (Pearson, 2008), 151–158; "Writing a Museum Catalog," Purdue Online Writing Lab, Purdue University College of Liberal Arts, accessed January 25, 2025, https://owl.purdue.edu/owl/subject_specific_writing/writing_in_art_history/museum _catalog.html.

40. Minneapolis Institute of Arts, Interdivisional Committee on Interpretation, *Interpretation at the Minneapolis Institute of Arts: Policy and Practice* (Minneapolis Institute of Arts, 1993); The J. Paul Getty Museum, *Complete Guide to Adult Audience Interpretive Materials: Gallery Texts and Graphics* (J. Paul Getty Trust, 2011), 12–21, https://www.getty.edu/education/museum_educators/downloads/aaim _completeguide.pdf.

2

Echoes
Speaking from the Threshold

HEATHER HART

I AM ONLY A HISTORIAN in that I remember. I am only an archivist in that I collect. I am only a scientist in that I pay attention. My practice is art. My father, a carpenter, taught me to build. But I am neither a carpenter nor an architect, and it's often difficult to call my artwork sculpture. I want to amplify human resonance in built space. My work begins with engaging the everyday person in a new translation of our sociopolitical and racial climates through spaces, through structures, through architectures. It is about asking people to reclaim power, a territory, a space, a relationship that they may not have recognized.

> Storytelling teaches us how to navigate the world. Architecture influences our navigation of space and thus our perception of the world.

This work is about captivating the viewers in their rich and fraught histories (the gravity) through a playful and disarming disruption of physical engagement (the levity), creating an experience that echoes further than a pass-through, a walk-by, or a pause to sit. I want participants to take an active role in considering the built environment, in the collective, mining their relationship to power in and of a space. I want to share with you a few strategies I use to process the world. This is an invitation to participate.

STORYTELLING

I sat nestled under my dad's arm, examining the blurred blue tinge that his navy tattoo gave his skin, following the shape of his arm to where it shifted under his silver watch clasp into his heavy hand. He was telling me about his grandfather (Harry Sr.), who migrated north as a teenager at the turn of the twentieth century. Harry Sr. traveled north by caring for racehorses in a train car, leaving his family behind. He became a chef and a musician. Dad told me about how Harry Sr. won a Carnegie Medal for saving an electrician and how he later saved a little white girl from drowning in the river behind his house. He told me about the times Sr. would tour upstate New York and western Massachusetts playing music with Harry Jr. and his band, the Virginians. One day they would open for Cab Calloway, and the next day Sr. would create a banquet for the frat house he worked for as a cook. As I grew older these stories became lessons in carving out space, in power and survival.

> We live among echoes from our past. Everything is a passing moment. And although we move on, and things change, as they should, the moment continues to ricochet into the future even if we can't always hear it.[1]

> There are documents, thoughts, and memories, and stains. When a building is felled, there are scars in the concrete that remain. All these echoes affect our foundation and direct where we build in the future.

Most Black Americans came from people who had no space of their own after landing on this continent. They no longer owned land, no longer had a home, and even their bodies were a space that didn't belong to them. Stolen, beaten, and tightly packed into ships as cargo, enslaved people could never own physical space. That which remained was a psychological, spiritual, historical space kept alive through oral traditions when physical space was forbidden. This remainder is a trace, the enduring residue of history in our midst.[2]

Communities continue to look to storytellers, like oracles, for guidance and truth, to help navigate the world. This has been the artist's role in society since the beginning. I'm thinking of stories I learned from an elder on my block in Brooklyn, Grandmaster Kham, about intentionality and centering among chaos. I am thinking about James Baldwin. I am thinking about watching Maya Angelou on television during Bill Clinton's presidential inauguration. I am thinking about bell hooks, Zora Neale Hurston. I am thinking about first hearing Monie Love and Queen Latifah. I'm thinking about Kaitlyn Greenidge, Ladee Hubbard, Killer Mike, and W. Kamau Bell. I am thinking of Sista Souljah in the 1990s, who catalyzed systematic change at Rutgers and helped us feel like we might be able to make an impact in our world after all.

A good storyteller lends empathy.[3]

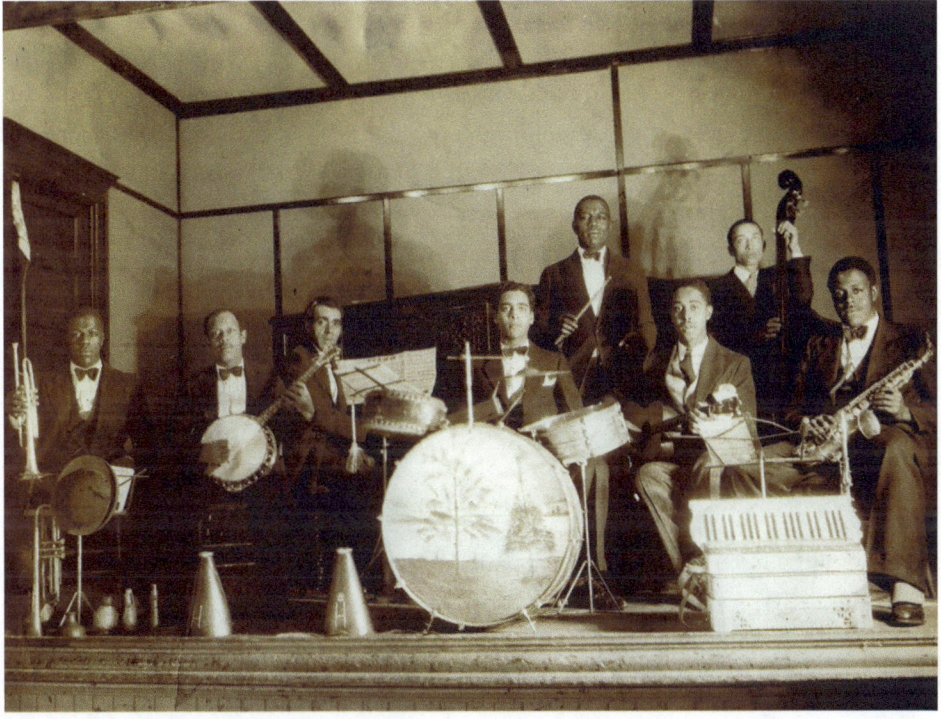

Fig. 2.1. *Harry Hart and His Virginians*, ca. 1935. Harry Herbert Hart Jr. sits far left holding trumpet, Harry Herbert Hart Sr. stands fifth from left holding baton, in Williamstown, MA. Hart family personal collection.

When people see themselves in a story, they not only hear why something is important but they feel it and relate to it. They picture themselves as part of the narrative. A lesson without empathy, without involving the collective is rote memorization. What use is memorization if we don't understand how to use it, how it fits into our lives?

> An artist/storyteller can bridge those who think and
> theorize with those who do the thing.

In this world of violence, delusion, denial, I want to nurture the ability to catalyze "feels." Intentional work in empathy is crucial.[4] I don't believe this needs to be sappy, or that artwork doesn't need a critical eye, or that someone should get lazy about their tastes and judgments; but rather that they should become self-aware and fully understand their positionality within the world. I believe the most universal way toward building empathy is multisensory storytelling, which includes physical experience. People learn from discovery—so prove it. As hooks proclaims, "Our capacity to generate excitement is deeply affected by our interest in one another, in hearing one another's voices, in recognizing one another's presence."[5]

SOMATIC RESONANCE

There is the moment you hear about something, and you imagine what it could be. There is the moment you see something and judge whether you are its audience, if you have space for it in your memory, and if it has space for you in its concept. There is then a somatic moment where every part of your body is involved in making decisions and perceiving your environment. This may be linked to safety (fight or flight), it could be linked to the fact that we are social animals. This somatic experience could also relate to us literally absorbing our environment.[6] But making the decision, putting your body into a situation—to smell, feel, hear, see—how to navigate a space leaves residue in you, not just intellectual experience/memory but physical memory (i.e., you never forget how to ride a bike).

Lorraine O'Grady talks about the somatic experience in her *Inheritance* series and her collaborative and performative work. Howardena Pindell, Shinique Smith, Steffani Jemison, Daonne Huff, generations of Black women artist-storytellers work through somatic space. This is why I do the work I do. Our experiences are in our bodies.

Scientists traditionally assumed that fear (as well as certain memories, anxiety, and addiction) is built up over a lifetime and must be a lived experience or passed on through direct teaching. The pediatric neuroscientist Brian Dias and his team of researchers published a study showing that information like trauma can be inherited through RNA.[7] This proved, in the Western scientific sense of the word, the concept of collective memory and the reason it is taking generations to shake the systemic violence that has been bequeathed to us. This corporeal fear is a very real PTSD (post-traumatic stress disorder) for Black Americans.

NAMING SPACE

I'm interested in how we inhabit the world. I'm interested in how we take up space, and in the notion of audacity. How we feel entitled to space. How it affects us, affects our navigation, the way we move through our lives, and how it influences our identity, our sense of self, our interactions with others, and visions of our shared future. Who is the author of these spaces, might the author change? What is my territory? What is yours? Do they overlap? What parts of a space hold its power? If space was fragmented, would its power be fractured? Would its power reduce or would it multiply? Would the same spatial aura come through? If space were to be recontextualized, would it be legible?

I began searching for notable spaces in my own narrative and those of other Black folx. Spaces that could act as a threshold to shift energy, an interstitial space. Between the field and the big house, lies the porch. So, I built porches, stoops, and rooftops.

Lately I've been researching more specifically Black space through storytelling that I iterate into sculpture. Originally, I intended a series of sculptures that centered on unpacking and replicating overlooked elements and thresholds in architecture that held Black narratives—essentially architectural quotes.

I wondered, what happens to the legibility and meaning of a space if only the railing from the Lorraine Motel was installed in a gallery? As a visitor climbs to the balcony, will tracing the structure with their hand make them remember? Will there be clues through somatic experience? Would the smell of the wood that I cut to make the sculpture disrupt the line a visitor follows to the recognition of this space? Would this white cube holding the sculpture become a Black space?

I was reminded early on, as I researched these spaces, of the Western archive's relationship to Black trauma. It was challenging to see my understanding of Black space in the records I was finding; the archive flattened what I knew, through my own family stories, to be Black. I decided that although I wouldn't edit out the pain, I needed to broaden my approach to sourcing what "notable narratives of Black space" meant.

I complicated my methodological framework a bit and took time for a more comprehensive approach to find spaces that felt connected to my research, or my own narrative. I traveled to the South, headed to the West, North, and back East. Through this research and experimentation, I discovered, first, that what I was looking for was not necessarily formal architecture and, second, that some of these spaces of trauma could be read as spaces of resistance and optimism. I'm thinking of the abolitionist Henry Brown's wooden crate, the Edmund Pettus Bridge, or the platform from Tommie Smith and John Carlos's 1968 Olympic medal ceremony.

Sometimes the spaces I noted were an arrangement of rocks, like the Great Barrington site of W.E.B. Du Bois's childhood home, and sometimes they were cartographic, like the Green Book guides. Other times there was empty space with the tangible form only described in words and left to the imagination, like Octavia Butler's Acorn. My frame of reference just needed a shift. So, I began looking at oral history, fantasy and broadening my definition of *architecture* to "structure" or "built environment." What if I included Nyota Uhura's workstation or Nola Darling's bed, Carrie Mae Weems's kitchen, Oprah Winfrey's couch, or the place where my neighbors fell in love?

I am investigating powerful forms of claiming space, drawing space digitally, printing space in three dimensions as stereolithographic sketches, so I can identify relationships and find how claims to space support each other or how they live alone. I can iterate, and fragment, to abstract a space enough to talk about its aura, but not so much that the space loses meaning.[8] At least its meaning for someone who investigates enough or brings the space with them in their memory to the next place or the next space. So, this work is about the future.

HEALING THROUGH SPACE

If a strong trauma can carry into the next generation, could a powerful joy? Dias, the neuroscientist, answered this question in 2020 by stating, "Just as our biology can accrue marks associated with negative experiences, so also our biologies must accrue marks associated with positive experiences."[9]

I began thinking about repair—how, through the stories my father had told me, he inevitably left things out, emphasized certain things, even fantasized something. This was a demonstration of reclaiming a space of trauma. There is power in how he navigates the world. I want to learn from that. How can we propose alternative spatial readings as acts of power, to accrue new, positive marks through experience, art making/storytelling? How can transforming/reading/claiming space as a Black space be reparative for everyone? How can an artwork open a radical space of restoration and repair? Can this work exist without readers? My artwork might have included objects, but the art was more about the interaction between my audience and the situation I placed the audience in.

And the forms, if there were any, mimed these thresholds: a roof, a porch, a staircase, a stoop, a space of transition. In this between-space was where the heart was, the aura, the essence, the lesson, and the growth. I believe in the power and possibility of a threshold space. Liminality holds a prompt for the future that can offer transformation and reclamation of a space that plays with mystery, or affect, that can be reparative or claimed. These are the margins that hooks talked about. The in-between, the hold.[10]

As an artist, I've been trained to see, to pay attention. This is how you learn to draw in your first class in art school. To slow down, to not make assumptions, to really look and understand form to ultimately have command of a medium, command of reality as a tool to dream.

> The goal was to become fluent in reality to have the choice
> of when to control it and when to let go.

I have been motivated to understand why I still initially miss seeing certain things, and what it is that I'm not actually seeing at all. In Charles Burnett's 1978 film *Killer of Sheep*, I know that an engine was carried to the back of a vehicle by two men . . . three men? But I don't remember what kind of car or truck was used. I went back to watch this film for what feels like the twentieth time and noticed a scene where the children climb out of a hole in the wall of a house. I also do not remember this image at all from my previous viewings, yet that space they emerged from spoke so clearly to the work I have been doing for over a decade. What connects one bit of what I notice of my experience to another? To find the answer, I investigated cognition research in attention—perception; what is most relevant for a visitor; how folks decide what they witness, whether we are really talking about space or actually about objects in space.

The cognitive neuroscientist Marlene Behrmann has argued that "space is the medium through which the visual system operates," and "space-based processing yields much faster processing than object-based attention."[11] Which led me to think more about context and installation in my artistic practice. People understand an object or form because of their relation to it, their frame of reference, the semiology of space, the context of their body and that object in space. There is a constant negotiation between space and object, a collaboration, that we all witness, where the object and the space that surrounds it vie for attention. When I want a visitor to access a story in my artwork, I need to compose the work in a way that speaks dynamically, intersectionally, through an arrangement of objects in a space so they can be read deeply and more intuitively.

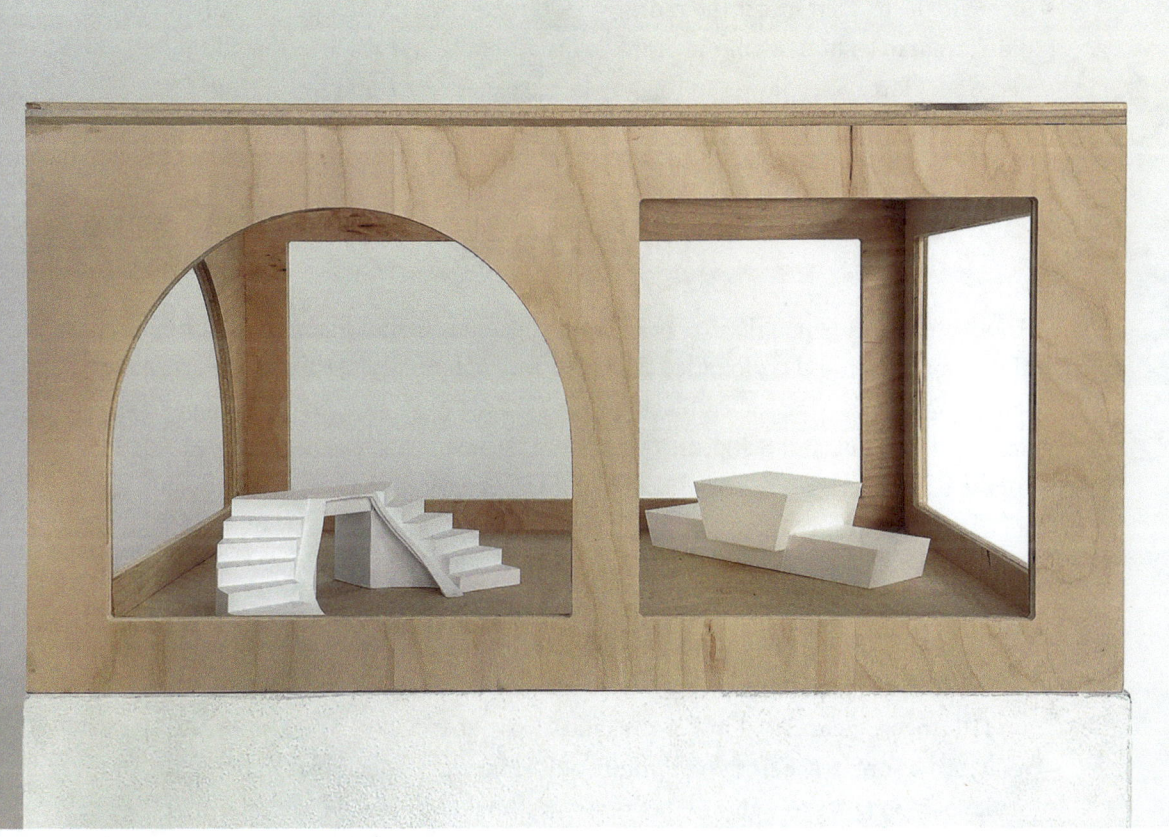

Fig. 2.2. Heather Hart, *"It's Not a Code," She Repeated. "It's a Language."* (Delany), 2022. Wood, polylactic acid. 12 1/2 × 24 × 17 3/4 in. (31.75 × 45.1 cm). Photograph courtesy of the artist.

Lately I am working with sculptural fragments (the "sketches"/3-D prints). By themselves they *are* objects, but in association with each other, in a collective, we find space. The resulting sculptures prompt a continual shift of framing, a grouping of prints that live together inside a container. These individual 3-D prints may be read as words in the sentence within a container. An individual print might appear again, paired with a different print or two in a different container, and embody an entirely new meaning. For example, a print of Oprah's yellow couch paired with a print of Uhura's workstation inside a container reads one way; pairing Oprah's couch with Nola Darling's bed completely transforms the meaning of the prints. The work that I am doing is really focused on that liminality, the gap, the lacuna, the space.

My focus on space is about healing, and also as healing pertains to inheritance. I admire my father's unflinching cognition of space, which is an inspiration in my life and work. I once went with my father back to Williamstown, Massachusetts, and parked in the driveway of the place where he had grown up. He wanted to know if a memento he had left under the stairs was still there. But it was a police station now. I didn't want to let him out of the car to go inside, but he has a charm about him, inherited from Harry Sr., a power in the way he navigates space, and he was fine.

"Liberation is a spatial practice."[12]

TOGETHER

Another part of my practice has been more collaborative and focused on storytelling and historical gaps—I co-founded an oral history nonprofit project with the artist and professor jina valentine, called Black Lunch Table. We met in 2005 at the Skowhegan School of Painting and Sculpture in Madison, Maine, where we began the project as tricksters, wondering what would happen if we segregated the lunchroom by race, in the way we had experienced outside the residency at work and at school. We thought about perception and (self-)identification. We thought about who would be left out of our Black Lunch Table because of our personal perception of race and who might be incorrectly included. We all squeezed into one picnic table—Whitfield Lovell, Steve Locke, Hank Willis Thomas, Loul Samater, Yashua Klos, Jamal Cyrus, Ernest Bryant III, Angela Hennessy, Linda Earle, and Shervone Neckles. By claiming this space we reified our presence in the community and exposed implicit bias in the space. We made space to talk through whether or not we would exhibit our work during February for Black History Month and if we felt a civic responsibility with our practices. There was no real agenda at that time, just convening together. We didn't need to solve a problem or exit with a plan of action. The conversation meandered; together we explored the space we created. It felt like the beginning of something even then.

We knew this activation resonated and we thought about the incredible artists that participated; artists neither valentine nor I were introduced to in our art history courses. Our textbooks covered only the Harlem Renaissance and, perhaps, Jean-Michel Basquiat. We didn't see ourselves in the class content. The inception for this ongoing project was the surging desire to make sure the future generations had access to the vast world of contemporary Black artists in a way that valentine and I did not.

The Black Lunch Table grew from a performative activation into a nonprofit that now has employees and has received prestigious grants. We realized it was a legacy far beyond what we were capable of on our own. There are still Artist Roundtables that host Black visual artists in small conversations all over the world. But in 2014, in the wake of the murder of Michael Brown, as the movement for Black Lives was also beginning, we used the form of our roundtable conversations to create the People's Table, an integrated and local space for cross-demographic conversation. That same year, we also hosted our first Wikipedia workshop to convene and teach volunteers to edit Wikipedia in the hope of filling the gaps in the art historical record. These forms of work persist, and the organization has grown, adding partnerships, residencies, and a photo initiative. The idea, beyond recognizing and documenting these spaces, is also to focus on self-authorship—a reclamation of space.

Anything worth having is going to take energy, intention, and collaboration, and if I choose not to do that work, that's on me. I am not obligated to be responsible. It is my privilege to be *possessed* as an artist, as Baldwin has so eloquently characterized this state of being.[13] This energy and intention is not always comfortable, it is sometimes heavy and feels hopeless, but it does teach me to be adaptable and flexible. And if I do want something, I must face toward it, and sometimes I must fight for it, and I need collaborators to help me keep my head up. I need to speak up when I can and accept the process with love while I keep an eye on the goal. I do this work to create spaces that can begin to rectify purposeful erasures.

ARCHIVES, AUTHORSHIP, IMAGINATION

I began my search for space, really, with my own story, or rather
I began with the story of my father's father's father's mother, Minnie.

I was following my father's line, searching for Minnie Wells in "the archives," as my dad calls them, before the advent of Ancestry.com. My father took us to the National Archives regularly, and we were able to trace most of his family to 1860, when slavery robbed our forebears of identities. But we hadn't been able to find my great-grandfather's mother, Minnie Wells, further than the 1880 census, not a huge surprise since she was born a slave in North Carolina. So, in 2011, I took a research trip with my sister that led me from my home in Brooklyn to the very small Maney's Neck, North Carolina, the place where Minnie was last "seen."

After listening to a mixtape of my mother's vast record collection, following paper maps, far out of range of my mobile service, we found a local library in the nearest town. In its catalog was a microfiche for an 1877 marriage license of my great-grandfather's father. It was a marriage between a Julius Hart and Winnie Wells. But I knew her name was Minnie.

With a one-letter error in transcription, Minnie had disappeared for over a century. The census taker's transcription lost her. Our "factual" records are full of errors like these; a census taker's handwriting, perception, or translation changes a name, a race, or a date. And that changes our history, in turn our truth, and our reality. Yet there is a faith we have in written records, valuing them more than oral histories. I'm captivated by this slippage, this liminal space between truth and fiction, between what I say and what you hear, and what we all value.

There is power in this threshold of interpretation.

The literary critic Frank Kermode wrote that authors' and readers' forgetfulness helps interpretation. The world is constantly providing us with infinite bits of information, and we cannot possibly process and remember it all; an author presents their story, a simplification of reality, and a reader perceives a bit of that story, and remembers even less. As readers, we read ourselves into the story, we come to it with our personal frames of reference and understand it based on our place in the world. We must collaborate as we author and as we read. Because of the human brain, there is space for creativity and space to claim and to gift power in these stories, these histories.[14]

My dad, Harry Herbert Hart III, grew up down the block from Williams College. Most of his formative years were spent living in an apartment above a frat house. His father grew up near there too, since my great-grandfather moved there ten years before the start of the Great Migration. So, the next step in my genealogical and artistic research was to make my way there, wandering past my family landmarks— the Green River, the house my great-grandfather built, the apartment where my dad grew up—to the Williamstown Historical Museum, where I unexpectedly encountered a photo of my grandfather, Harry Jr., on its entry wall. After I shared that surprise with the archivist, she was excited to bring me boxes of Hart ephemera, an archive, where I found an essay that was based on an interview of my great-grandfather, Harry Sr., written by a student at Williams.

I knew my great-grandfather Harry Sr. had been a chef at the college for almost fifty years, a position that was eventually bequeathed to his son, my grandfather. And I knew Harry Sr., the son of a slave, had moved north from Virginia at seventeen years old, alone, sending for his family years later. But the essay included information that was new to me. It mentioned the tribe in Africa from which my great-grandfather was descended. This is the dream of so many Black Americans and I was emotionally overwhelmed, so I called my father, who sounded . . . unimpressed. After prodding him to tell me why he wasn't as moved as I was, he told me that this detail about our family line was likely fabricated, saying of Harry Sr., "He was the town character." Yet, I don't think my great-grandfather had constructed a persona just to forge his fantastic life. He didn't do it for attention, or for honor, but instead, for his time, it created a space for a small amount of power, and it was crucial for survival.

My dad once compared me to Harry Sr., likely meaning that I may be a bit of a character in his eyes too (I think it may have passed through Dad, though). I may have some trickster tendencies. I mean, I am an artist, so I fabulate and fabricate spaces, and systems and ritual (what else might I have inherited from Harry Sr. or Junior, or III?). My job is to fantasize and to be audacious.

Saidiya Hartman described a similar approach to her writing as "critical fabulation." The intention here is not anything as miraculous as recovering the lives of the enslaved or redeeming the dead but rather laboring to paint as full a picture of the lives of the captives as possible. This double gesture can be described as straining against the limits of the archive to write a cultural history of the captive and, at the same time, enacting the impossibility of representing the lives of the captives precisely through the process of narration.[15]

I value fantasy as a tool for building and reclaiming space for marginalized stories; fantasy incepted by artists/storytellers/educators/curators, mingled indistinguishably with fantasy in a real-world conversation; fantasy as mutable reading of space. It is from this world that we can picture the breadth of possibility.

And what *are* these spaces, these forms that are inherited? What are we doing to reclaim and redirect what we bequeath? What is between the lines; what is left unsaid; what and why is the fantastic for Black Americans? And let's talk about the importance and power in authorship!

I'd like you to pause for a moment and visualize along with me.

First, find a space with nothing but this book in your peripheral vision, a blank wall, or go under a blanket, and close your eyes between each instruction or find an empty space in your mind . . . take a deep breath in . . . and out. . . .

. . . Take another, breathe in all the positive vibes . . . and a slow breath out . . . any kind of tension, nerves, negativity. . . .

. . . OK, while you slow your breathing, please think of a favorite project you've completed, one that you are most proud of; if you are not an artist, feel free to think about projects in your field or at home too . . . we are all creative. . . .

> . . . So, you have that project in your mind now. . . . Now imagine that
> you had the opportunity to re-create that project . . . with no limits . . .
> no space, location, or budget limitations—unlimited resources.
> What would that look like? Picture that for a moment.
>
> And breathe. . . .
>
> Beside you in this vision there is someone else, maybe more than one person . . .
> others, they are coming into focus . . . colors . . . settings. . . . Who is beside you in
> this project, who is making this happen with you?
>
> Inhale. . . . Exhale. . . .

Take that revised vision of your project and make it even more ambitious than you imagined. Write all the impossibilities down so you will always have a log of ideas that you can make into possibilities and then into realities. Because this world needs more imagination; we need visionaries. We need more women artists and more subaltern artists and more Black artists, more artists speaking from the threshold. I will leave you with this mantra that Octavia Butler wrote in her journal and used. I invite you to post it to your wall, as I have: "I will find the way to do this. So be it! See to it!"[16]

Notes

1. *32 Sounds*, directed by Sam Green (ArKtype, Department of Motion Pictures, Impact Partners, Wavelength Productions, and Free History Project, 2022).

2. Édouard Glissant, "Dispossession," in *Caribbean Discourse*, trans. J. Michael Dash (University Press of Virginia, 1989), 13–32.

3. See Fred Moten and Stefano Harney, "Debt and Study," *e-flux Journal*, no. 14 (March 2010): 1–5, https://www.e-flux.com/journal/14/61305/debt-and-study.

4. adrienne maree brown, *Emergent Strategy: Shaping Change, Changing Worlds* (AK Press, 2017).

5. bell hooks, *Teaching to Transgress: Education as the Practice of Freedom* (Routledge, 1994), 8.

6. Prerna Bhat, "Think like an Animal: Understanding Animal Decision Making for Conservation," *Yale Environment Review*, September 28, 2018, https://environment-review.yale.edu/think-animal -understanding-animal-decision-making-conservation; Louise Barrett, *Beyond the Brain: How Body and Environment Shape Animal and Human Minds* (Princeton University Press, 2015); Sabrina Strang, Christina Hoeber, Olaf Uhl, and Soyoung Q. Park, "Impact of Nutrition on Social Decision Making," *Proceedings of the National Academy of Sciences* 114, no. 25 (2017): 6510–6514, https://doi.org/10.1073/pnas.1620245114.

7. See Ewen Callaway, "Fearful Memories Haunt Mouse Descendants," *Nature*, December 1, 2013, https://www.nature.com/articles/nature.2013.14272.

8. Walter Benjamin, "The Work of Art in the Age of Mechanical Reproduction," in *Illuminations*, ed. Hannah Arendt, trans. Harry Zohn (Fontana Press, 1968), 214–218.

9. Brian Dias, "Halting Legacies of Trauma," lecture presented at TEDxEmory 2020, Atlanta, GA, February 15, 2020, YouTube, https://www.youtube.com/watch?v=OhrW08fqiP0.

10. bell hooks, *Feminist Theory: From Margin to Center* (South End Press, 2000); Stefano Harney and Fred Moten, "Fantasy in the Hold," in *The Undercommons: Fugitive Planning and Black Study* (Minor Compositions, 2013), 84.

11. "Marlene Behrmann—Spatial vs. Object Based Attention," interview by Cynthia Peng, GoCognitive, September 25, 2011, YouTube, https://www.youtube.com/watch?v=CUhOo1ftQmo; Marlene Behrmann and Craig Haimson, "The Cognitive Neuroscience of Visual Attention," *Current Opinion in Neurobiology* 9, no. 2 (1999): 158–163.

12. Mario Gooden, *Dark Space: Architecture, Representation, Black Identity* (Columbia Books on Architecture and the City, 2016), 21.

13. James Baldwin, "The Moral Responsibility of the Artist," lecture presented at the University of Chicago, May 21, 1963, YouTube, https://www.youtube.com/watch?v=PlnDbqLNv-M.

14. Frank Kermode, *The Genesis of Secrecy: On the Interpretation of Narrative* (Harvard University Press, 1996), 14.

15. Saidiya Hartman, "Venus in Two Acts," *Small Axe* 12, no. 2 (June 2008): 1–14.

16. "So Be It, See to It: From the Archives of Octavia Butler," *The Paris Review*, March 23, 2018, https://www.theparisreview.org/blog/2018/03/23/so-be-it-see-to-it-from-the-archives-of-octavia-butler/.

3

"Pass the Mic"
A Conversation with Student Curators

AMBER N. WILEY, KYLE B. CO.,
AND DESIREE MORALES

THIS INTERVIEW OCCURRED VIA ZOOM in June 2023. Kyle b. co. and Desiree Morales were both student curators who developed content for the *Collective Yearning* exhibition. Additionally, they are practicing artists who received their master of fine arts degrees from the Mason Gross School of the Arts at Rutgers University–New Brunswick and have also taught at Mason Gross. This conversation reflects their experiences across those four positionalities—as students, curators, artists, and teachers. The text has been lightly edited for clarity but retains the general feel and flow of the conversation.

AMBER N. WILEY: Could you tell me what inspired you to take the Exhibition Seminar in the spring of 2021, and where were you at that point in your respective academic and artistic journeys?

DESIREE MORALES: What inspired me? Honestly, I wasn't even aware of this class. I think Bomi [Kim] was still the grad coordinator and she sent out that there was a new course thing offered in the art history department, and it was going to be creating an exhibition of Black women artists. And I was like, "OK, you know, that sounds good, like something I'd be interested in taking," and that was also influenced by me wanting [to take] other classes outside of my department. I will say, when I did take the class, I was like, "Oh yeah, this is a grad class." And then I was like, "Do I want to do this?," and then I was like, "All right, yeah, I'm doing this. I'm here. I signed up for grad school. Let's do grad school." Because, you know, our art [department] seminars are nothing like that. There's a lot of reading, depending on who your instructor is, but it's not structured in the same way. Everything is very free-flowing, self-directed. This was the first formal graduate class that I took while I was at Rutgers. And probably the only one, honestly. Yeah, I think it is.

KYLE B. CO.: In the same breath as Desiree, we wanted to take something outside of the department, and part of that push was to take a class that has a more informed discussion, practice, or something like that. A practice where people actually read the work and then they are talking about the work, not bringing [up] some random anecdote, and also for us, it was to possibly [be] in a space where we're explicitly talking about race, as part of the discourse and not necessarily being the initiator of that conversation, or the subject of that conversation. So there was an aspect that I guess is somewhat similar to the founding of the [Mary H.] Dana Women Artists Series, where there were no women artists, and where . . . there were Black artists [at Mason Gross], a lot of them were on sabbatical, and there was a lack of conversation or discourse around race and art for us. So, the opportunity to take the Black women exhibition course, it was exciting for us. But we also had the same hesitation as Desiree, like, "I don't know if I could do this writing!" And that shifted halfway through, just like, "I don't think I have enough space because I want to write so much!"

And it really kind of prompted us to think about the particulars of an exhibition in a way that felt very practical, because we had taken a class previously with Park McArthur that was talking about contracts in the art world, being part of exhibitions, not necessarily making the exhibition or being in the curatorial space. So it felt like a full circle moment for our experience where we're able to experience both on the curatorial side, but also in our other classes, you know, what is the proper way to be a part of an exhibition, like with release contracts and artist fees and whatnot. Yeah, that was our initial kind of push to take the class, was just to address something that we felt was lacking in our graduate experience.

WILEY: Second part of this question, where were you at that point in your respective academic and artistic journey? Spring 2021 is when we had the class, and then fall 2022 is when we had the exhibition.

B. CO.: OK, that was our third year.

MORALES: Let's say that was my second year. That was y'all's third year.

B. CO.: Yeah, this is my third year. Because we were also the pandemic class of Mason Gross, we had an additional year to our program, so that was technically my third year. It was my final semester that I was able to take classes, and then the spring semester we had kind of a residency, where we were allowed studio space but not necessarily funding to take classes. It was our last set of classes at Rutgers. There was an aspect of . . . just doing stuff to finish the coursework that we need to do for our degree, but also, because we had already taken everything we needed, it was a chance to do something that brought us joy or excitement. Yeah, I was on my way out. I guess you could say that, a senior in a certain sense.

MORALES: Yeah, I also had a third year because I came in as the COVID class. The seminar was my second year. I would say the academic and artistic journey definitely overlapped. For starters, a big reason that I came to Rutgers was that I wanted to work with Black faculty. That was something I had not [done] in my undergrad experience. So, you know, just off top, that was already a goal of mine. And then again, because of my [academic] background, there were holes in my knowledge of Black art history. Most of what I've obviously learned is from the white canon, right? Because that's who's teaching it to me. Outside of any kind of information that I find on my own, this was my first Black art history class essentially. Because, for the first half of the class, that's what it was, right? With all the readings and things to contextualize the work, to be able to create an exhibition. There was a catch-up that I think collectively everyone had to do. That was something that I think was a big part of my experience and where I was during the time.

WILEY: I have to say, this is rather alarming. But I hear you.

B. CO.: The Black faculty on staff at Vassar was Didier William, in the art department. But I mean, I was taking classes with other Black professors, because my undergrad [degree] is in anthropology, so I took classes with professors of color in the English and anthropology departments.

MORALES: See, I went to art school. So, who we had was who we had. It wasn't a university.

WILEY: Another question, how does your knowledge of printmaking inform the direction you took in the course? For instance, the artists that you researched and the interpretive texts that you created for the exhibition.

B. CO.: At first, I thought [the first assignment for an exhibition proposal] was a joke. I thought it was a trick question. [And] we were like, "Oh yeah, figure out an exhibition from this work [of Black women artists in the Zimmerli collection]," because when we got the PDF of all the work, I'm just like, "Oh! It's a print show!," because most of the work was print work. I know after taking that course and learning more about the Zimmerli, partially due to their limited budget for acquisitions and/or their reliance on donations, for us it felt very obvious, and maybe it was obvious to us, because we come from a printmaking background as well.

My initial thought around the exhibition was always focused on being Black in the printshop, which for us has a lot of historical ground. This historical presence for us, just due to how, well, you could say more broadly the printing press allowed for the dissemination of information, but then specifically thinking about Black newspapers, and I even think about the proliferation of Jacob Lawrence's Great Migration images, and I grew up with some of those images in various families' houses, where it was a way for Black art to be disseminated. Printmaking is a medium of access. A print is not super expensive in relationship to a painting or a sculpture. But that is to say that printmaking is something that immediately relates to a community, both in terms of community access [and that] its production is dictated by community.

Like the infrastructure of the printshop, . . . [there are] the people who are the master printers and the associated folks who are there to execute especially large editions. I know for a fact their relationships to these prints probably also represented a more sustainable income stream, or in terms of how people can access their work, or even how maybe in some f-cked up way, how people [primarily connoisseurs] value—or the value they're willing to [put] on—a Black artist's work. They may not buy a painting, but they will buy a print. And whether that be from resource availability, like that's what they can afford, or a larger value judgment.

That's highlighted by the fact that the majority of the Black art in the collection was prints. There's the question, "How do you reconcile that in some ways? What is the institution prioritizing?" In [our] original . . . conception of the exhibition there was a component of looking into the demographics of the collection more explicitly, as part of the work of the exhibition, because it felt as if [Black women artists] had not been celebrated up until this point. And I mean, it just so happened to align tragically with the murder of George Floyd. But this is something [I am] trying to address in my work now, trying to create conversations around race that are not dictated by trauma. But in some ways [Black women artists'] absence at the time felt like a trauma. . . . The fact that none of what was in the collection was on display or framed or even accessible, there was a question of "What are y'all doing with this work?"

So, in coming [back] to the exhibition [proposal,] that [we] thought it was a joke or a trick or something, because it felt very obvious to us, "Oh, it's a print exhibition of Black women," and [it was] talking about the relationship to space. . . . The space of the printshop in which they're given a voice and allowed to express their voice in a way that the institution was supporting—the Brodsky Center and the Rutgers Print Collaborative.

But then there's also this simultaneous other conversation, I guess the privilege of entering a museum collection, but what happens once you're in that collection? Are you valued as part of that collection? Are you addressed in a way that acknowledges that they see you or that they care that you're there. And that part of the exhibition for us brought up some conflict because it felt like we shouldn't have been the first ones to be like, "Oh, let's do a print exhibition of all the Black women." Or even the Black artists in the collection. Because it felt like [that was] the most cohesive thing they had in relationship to Black women. But that made me think maybe [the Zimmerli] just had never addressed them as a demographic that needed to be celebrated or put on display or seen as part of the collection, where it seems like most of the labor or work has been in maintaining the Soviet-era kitsch majority of their collection.

WILEY: It's funny that you say that, because you sit down and you look at what's in front of you [in this case, Black women artists in the Zimmerli collection] and you go, "Well, the obvious path forward is XYZ." And you don't understand why no one's taken that path forward before, until you realize that no one has sat down and looked, and that is part of the issue.

Desiree, I want to hear your thoughts on, you know, bringing your knowledge of print-making and such, because you did the Rutgers Print Collaborative too, didn't you?

MORALES: I took the last one after the class, but I had zero printmaking experience. I didn't come into this [exhibition seminar] assuming that it was just going to be printmaking. So, I was like, "OK, I'm not familiar with printmaking. I know that Kyle's obviously, like, very familiar with printmaking." I feel [that] based on their experience with printmaking in the department, I got information from them that I wouldn't have known, obviously just because, you know, when you have certain information you're privileged to. That was a big thing. I guess I would say that I approached this more just from the perspective of being an artist and a person who makes [things]. There's this way when you make art, even when stepping into a curatorial role, it's treated very differently.

I heard this artist speak, and she said that a big issue with curators today is not enough of them are artists, a lot of them are admin[istrators]. And that really sat with me because, I mean, it's true, right? Even that became apparent to us going through the class. I think that me and Kyle would bring different things to the conversation that weren't necessarily considered, and you see things differently because you make things. You experience work in a different way, or there's a certain way that you interpret works. I feel like my catalog writing was just me looking at the work and being like, "OK, how can I interpret this work? What does this look like? What references do I feel like they're making? What do I feel like the work is saying?," versus me trying to find research about the work. I just think that's how I took my experience into account with preparing.

WILEY: It's funny because my [art history] students want to know what other people have said and written about artwork before they form their own opinions. They didn't trust their own knowledge of the art-making process, because they didn't have the same intimate knowledge of the art-making process that y'all had.

MORALES: There is this interesting takeaway that I got [as an] undergrad. A lot of my learning in grade school and up was me learning information and being able to regurgitate information. And when I was an undergrad in art school, my experience completely shifted, and it was more about "How are you interpreting this?" [and] thinking more critically about things. I felt like now I'm being taught how to think about things versus how to relay information that had been found previously that I know how to say. That's just a structural issue with higher education, but it is a little disappointing in a situation where, say, you are an art history major or something like that. When you leave Rutgers, and you want to do this kind of work, they're looking at what you think, not just all this information that's already been passed down. Or even, you know, we have enough Picasso books. We have enough of that. What kind of artists can you bring up and what kind of critical thought can you contribute to the conversation?

WILEY: Do you want to talk about the challenges of having the class in a virtual space?

B. CO.: Yeah, it was hard learning in a virtual space. I think part of it was just kind of gauging other folks' commitment to the conversation without necessarily being able to read body language or [tell] whether their screens were on or off. There were a couple of students who didn't have their screens on, which is fine, but sometimes I felt like I was talking too much, or it was hard to gauge whether people were with me in an understanding or how involved folks were. But that was also my experience in other courses that I was teaching, and during that time people were dealing with the pandemic in different ways, so that was different for us.

MORALES: I feel like . . . it's not even necessarily a limitation of a virtual space. But it was because [Black women artists were] something that [the Zimmerli] clearly hadn't even considered exploring. What does this work look like, right? You don't know. We don't know. Nobody knows. OK, well, I guess we can Google what [the artists] usually make and put together some ideas of what it could be like. That was wild to me. How are there pieces in your collection that you don't know exist? Why has Barbara Madsen been donating her grad portfolios, and you've never opened them? All these questions that I just have that I'm like, "You know, I could go in there and walk out with these. You don't even know they're there." This is a disservice to the small portion of this collection that really makes it expansive, because otherwise it's a very limited art history resource in terms of looking at art collectively. That was a big thing for me, "Why don't I know what this [art] looks like?"

B. CO.: It seems like [the Zimmerli] only photographs things [from] shows that they deem worthy [of] a catalog or have been in a catalog previously. So yeah, there is a question of access. That was a big thing for us too, because [the class] was online we really felt the lack of access to the museum's collection.

WILEY: You both work as instructors at Rutgers. Can you describe your teaching responsibilities? And then, were you able to apply things that you learned in class to your teaching or the content of the exhibition to your teaching?

B. CO.: We teach in the drawing department and the printmaking department. We've taught screen printing, relief, and sometimes cover some intaglio classes. And then in drawing, we currently teach the collage course. And then we recently started teaching with Rutgers Art Online. During the spring of 2022, we taught a student docent class where we looked at the work of the *Collective Yearning* exhibition and were able to be in person—the class and the exhibition. It was intensive, over spring break and then sometime in the fall. And then in the fall [the student docents] essentially led tours of the exhibition. And they were paid very well. They were asking me, you know, "Are you doing this next semester?"

MORALES: Yeah, Kyle made sure their students got paid. I was like, "Can I take y'all's class?"

B. CO.: It was nice to get people paid. In that regard, it felt like you were also addressing [the fact that] there were a lot of students of color, some Black women who were learning about Black art in a way where they're also becoming confident and talking about it. It was nice to have these conversations with femme-identified folks[, who] are all trying to come to terms with the fact that they are going to be the mouthpiece for this work and trying to reconcile what they feel comfortable talking about, whether or not they're relating back to their experience, how they're talking about Black women's experience. And I mean, there's a lot with us teaching it where we have to check our authority because we were raised by Black women, but we are not Black women. But those conversations we found very helpful and very fruitful.

I realized during that time that I prefer teaching situations where the students are also getting paid. Or we've been in youth programs where the youth are getting paid to be there. They're also learning. Because I think there's a level of motivation, but it feels like a more even exchange in some sense, where learning new things shouldn't necessarily be to the detriment of your survival, [that] we're going to take up your time when you could be doing a nine-to-five or something that helps you sustain in this world. There's an aspect of that dynamic that we wish we could bring to more of our other classes, but there's not always a budget. You know, I would love for lunch to be provided every time I teach, and it can't necessarily be the case. There was something about that that felt utopian in some sense.

WILEY: That funding in the position was because you were the faculty fellow at Douglass College?

B. CO.: Yeah, Douglass fellow, but it was due to the dean that was in the class.

WILEY: Jacquelyn Litt. You know, based on the work that y'all did and the ability to provide that fellow position, it was worth it.

Desiree, can you describe your teaching responsibilities and in what ways you apply either what you learned in class or the context of the exhibition to your teaching?

MORALES: The semester that I took this class was actually my first semester teaching. I was teaching an introductory digital photography class. The way I approached that was teaching basics—a little photo history, a little photo theory. But I always push [the idea that] you have to learn the rules first, and then if you want to break them, you can do that. And you know, it's a different generation, right? This is the iPhone / cell phone with the camera generation. So, their experience with digital cameras, physical output of prints, and all these things, it's completely different. It's like, "All right, let's talk about it."

But yeah, I'm always like, "OK. No, don't say you don't focus on technique. That's a cop-out. You just started. You do focus on technique and then, you know, do whatever you want after you learn the technique." I'm always like, "Once we can get past the hang-ups of technical things and worries about your tools, we can really get into talking about what the work is doing. How is it functioning? What are you saying?" All these things start to come together in a significantly more expansive way, when we're not just hung up on tools and equipment. That's something I heavy hit every time I teach Intro Photo.

Then, the context of the [*Collective Yearning*] class being carried over. Which is a little different than what you're asking, but [that] was really important for me. So again, this was my first time teaching. I was really anxious about teaching that semester because I had never done it before. I wanted to do a good job and [thought about] what kind of teacher am I going to be and things like that. I had your class the day before I was supposed to teach my class. There was something about having a Black woman professor right before I was about to be a Black woman professor, [that] was something that really struck me, especially because you still have a personality, right? You're so you. It's not like, you know, super uptight wound-up academic, because that's not who I am, you know, and that's not how I portray myself in my class. I know people tend to code-switch. I try to do that as little as possible, and just like all aspects of life, I prefer

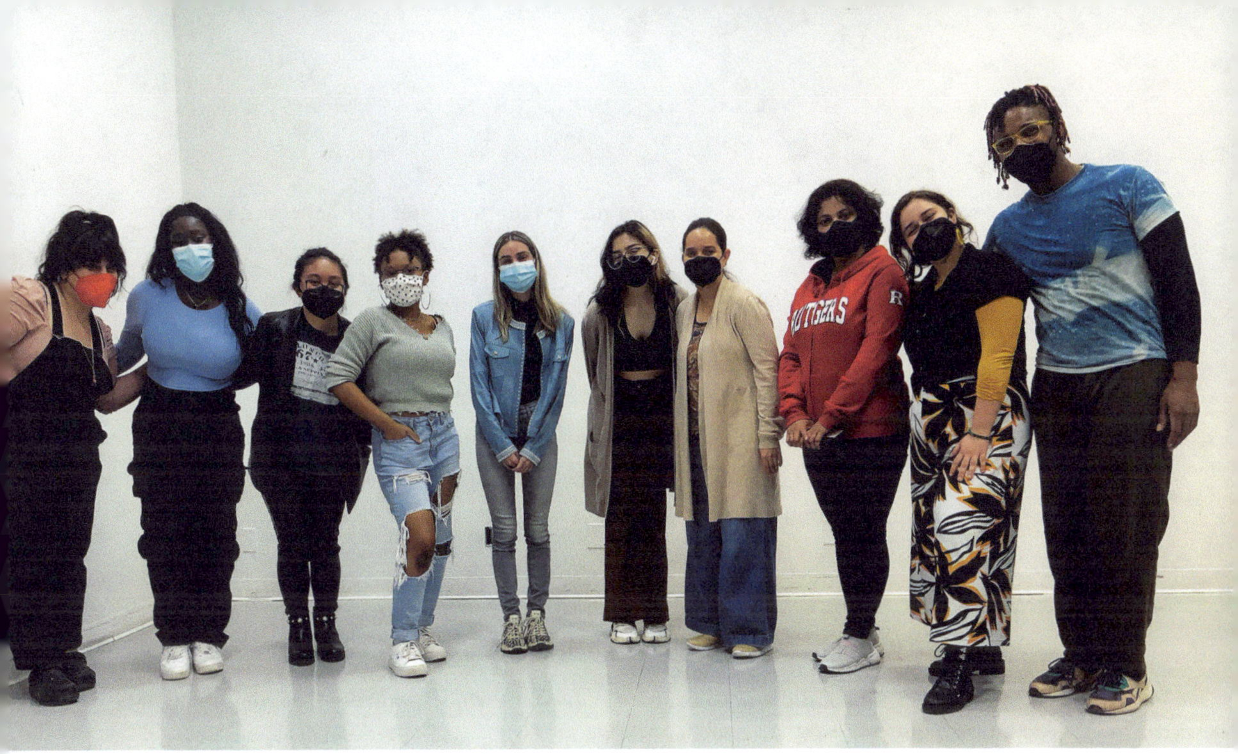

Fig. 3.1. Student curator and instructor Kyle b. co. with their students from the Douglass Faculty Fellows Program. 2022. Courtesy of Kyle b. co.

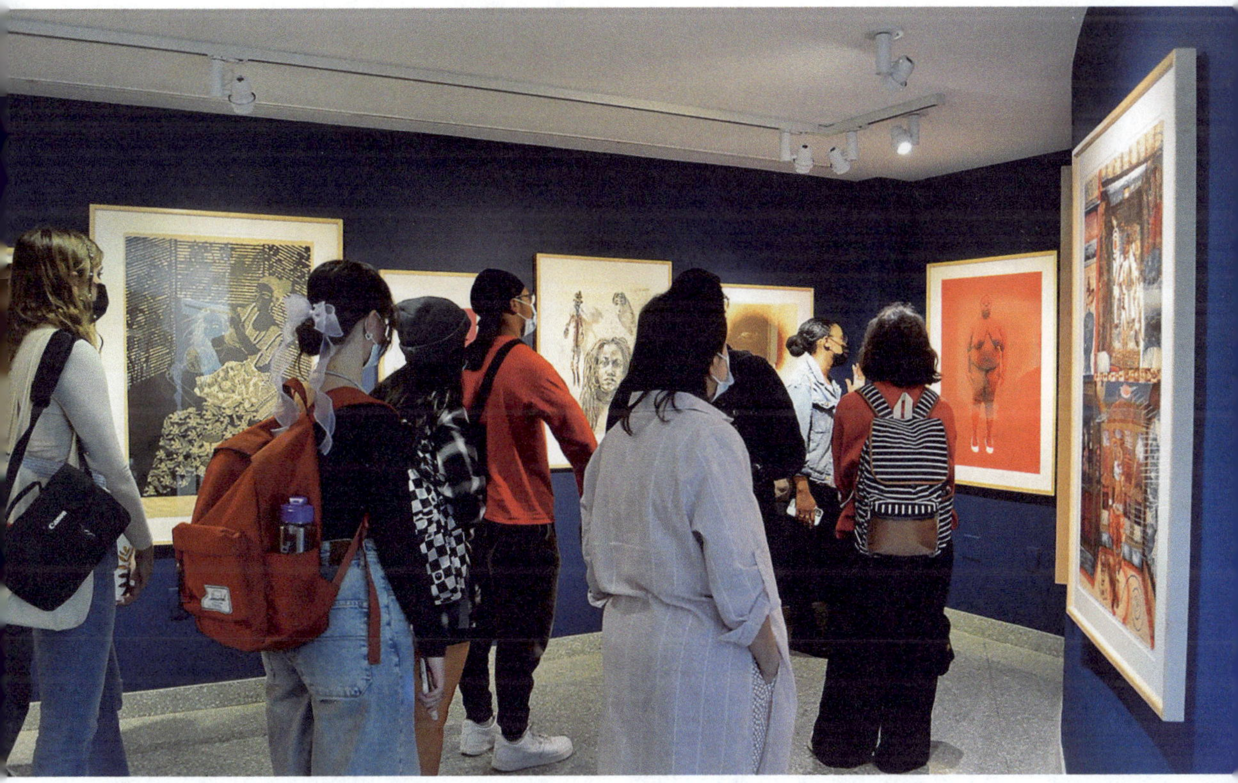

Fig. 3.2. Student curator and instructor Desiree Morales discussing Nona Faustine's *Scarlet and Black* with her students. 2022. Nicole Ianuzelli, photographer.

to be very fluid. That was a big thing for me. I want to say you may have been my first Black woman professor.

WILEY: I never ever had one. I'll just say that I never had one.

MORALES: Yeah, you know, and I came to Rutgers. But all the Black instructors were on sabbatical. And so, honestly, I was like, "Damn, I was trying to avoid this." But yeah, it ended up really influencing me, and definitely I want to say kind of put me at ease, like, "OK, I can still be myself and do this and not have to have these expectations of what I should be like or what this looks like." So I think it kind of all circles back to representation is important, always.

WILEY: I appreciate your willingness to sit down with me. If you have any last thoughts you want to share, I'd be happy to hear them.

MORALES: OK, I did write a couple of notes on the questionnaire that you sent for the interview. And so, for the next [question], "What would you consider your own curatorial or pedagogical priorities?," I just wrote, "Pass the mic." Because that's a big thing for me. Regardless of who you are, becoming a curator means it's not about you. So, center who it's about. And then [the question], "What are some things you hope to impart to your students and public about the artistic process?" "Follow the work" is something that I've started to integrate into my practice. So, it may not play out how you think. You know, bodies of work, they expand, they contract, they shift, right? I came in exclusively as a photographer and now I really don't photograph. And probably the last thing I showed is technically a painting. You can't dictate the process, you just have to let it reveal itself.

WILEY: That's some sage advice.

B. CO.: Yeah, I agree with that sentiment and thinking about pedagogy as passing the mic. I really appreciate the opportunity of this class and the experience doing the docent program because it really situated an understanding of art that is involved in a community and that comes back to our initial understanding of the exhibition and recognizing that art is not made in a vacuum and it requires a community in its production and its support. Whether that be childcare for Black mothers or—in thinking specifically about the institution of a printshop—who they're inviting in and who they're supporting.

It comes back to opportunity. For us, this class showed us we need to be involved and seek ways to provide opportunities for the people that we want to see in the arts. For people of color, Black women, queer and non-gender-conforming folks to be seen. And part of that is creating the spaces in which we can have the conversations, where we can invite folks in. Sometimes that's a literal thing. Sometimes that's institutionally allotting or fighting for space. It was nice to come into a class where we were both addressing a history of institutional unrest, [joined by] the organizing of Faith Ringgold and other folks, [and] trying to shape up the institutions that we're actively operating in and not acting in a passive way and allowing folks to continue to go unnoticed, unaddressed or to be invisible. Yeah, so I'm both thankful for the opportunity and for the opportunity to provide opportunities.

MORALES: Yeah. Reciprocity.

B. CO.: Reciprocity. There we go.

Part II

Collective Yearning and Curatorial Action

Nothing I accept about myself
can be used against me
to diminish me.

—AUDRE LORDE,
1984

4

Self-Making and Identity

JASMINE DARIA CANNON, GRACE LYNNE HAYNES,
EMILY HU, AND MICHAEL RANDALL

WOMANIST YEARNING, COINED BY KARA WALKER, unites the host of Black women artists held in the Zimmerli collection. In line with bell hooks's offering of the singular term *yearning*, in "Self-Making and Identity" the artists across the collection share a common desire to voice themselves after being silenced and excluded from the art history canon for so long.[1] These artists all have a critical eye and praxis dedicated to sharing their artistries as Black women, demonstrating their care for issues that affect Black women, and exploring the long history of what it means to be a Black woman. They enter and leave the studio, exhibition, and classroom as such.

Black women's artistic identity is unbounded by traditional time. For Black women artists, the past is present is future, simultaneously. In this collection, Black women's art is both critical theorizing and social practice. Whether artists are critiquing an institution's tenuous history with slavery, like Nona Faustine, or painting their likeness on historical figures, like Renée Stout, or creating something beautiful like they have never seen before, like Mickalene Thomas, their art transcends, expands, and makes anew the traditional boundaries of the canon.

–JASMINE DARIA CANNON

EMMA AMOS (1937-2020)

Identity from the Femfolio portfolio, 2006

Femfolio is a publication from the Brodsky Center that brought together works of twenty women who were influential figures of the Feminist Art movement of the 1970s. *Identity* is an exploration of the various components that create the "self" through a lens of gender, race, and cultural heritage. A chimeric woman, likely the artist herself, gazes at the audience with a face split down the center by a line that creates an optical illusion, presenting a brown face in profile and a tan face as a three-quarter portrait. Her wavy hair consists of multicolored strands and seemingly random shapes. The woman embodies multiple features—and therefore multiple identities—simultaneously.

One side of the woman's face features brown skin and a brown eye. The other half features tan skin and a blue eye. A series of diagonal and horizontal lines accentuate both sides of her face. The direct implication of a multiracial identity is there, but the more engaging question is how exactly race or racial phenotype shapes personal identity. The woman's face is split down the center, and the two halves are identical aside from the skin and eye colors. In other words, melanin is the only thing that separates the two halves. This is an image of unity.

The woman's hair is a vibrant combination of colors and symbols that answers the question posed by her face. Fingers, lips, eyeballs, vines, twigs, planets, a clef sign, a braid, and other items signal the external factors that we experience that shape us. Her hair even features the glove of Michael Jackson, a musician who shaped generations of people's perceptions of themselves and their identities. It is the combination of physical features, the material world, and the cultural identities within that world that shapes the "self."

–MICHAEL RANDALL

LITERATURE: Brodsky Center at PAFA

Fig. 4.1. Emma Amos, *Identity* from the *Femfolio* portfolio, 2006. Color digital print with hand lithography on Hahnemühle German Etching paper. 12×12 in. (30.5×30.5 cm). Collection Zimmerli Art Museum at Rutgers University. Gift of the Brodsky Center at Rutgers, The State University of New Jersey. 2010.006.001.01. © 2026 Emma Amos / Licensed by VAGA at Artists Rights Society (ARS), New York.

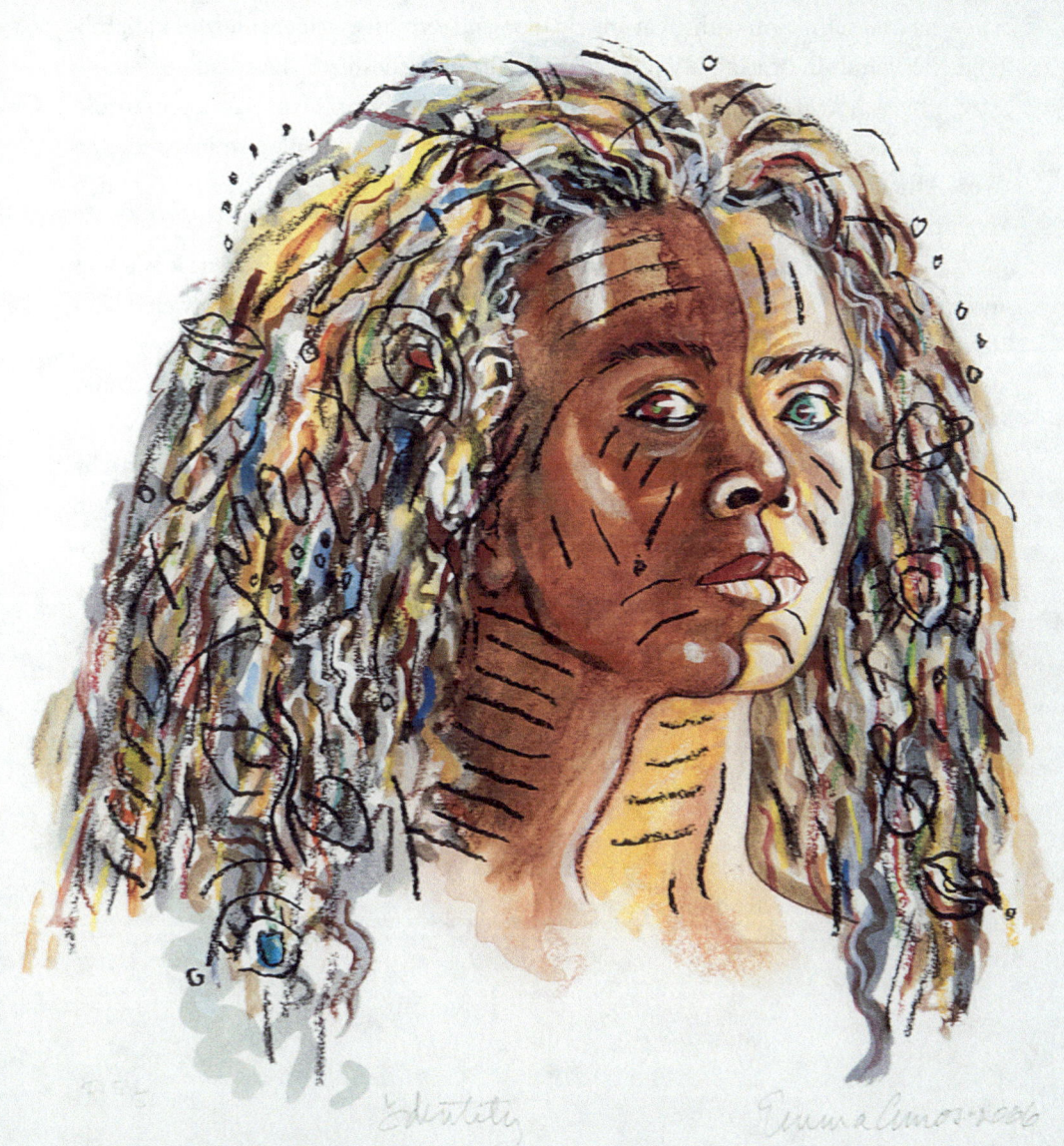

Identity   Emma Amos · 2006

ELIZABETH CATLETT (1915-2012)

Gossip, 2005

Gossip gives us a glimpse into an absorbing conversation between two women. One woman leans inward, head resting on her hand. She is present and available to receive a new bit of information with great anticipation and seriousness. Her companion lightly holds her hand, indicating a sense of familiarity and comfort. The friends solemnly gaze into each other's eyes. One woman's floral shirt contrasts with the angular fold creases on her arms. In the background there is a simple stripe pattern inspired by a West African textile that Catlett admired. It grounds the image, but the two women remain the focal point.

Catlett's work celebrates womanhood and all aspects that derive from it, such as motherhood, female friendships, and strength. Her women are regal, empowered, and dignified. She argued, "I have always wanted my art to service my people—to reflect us, to relate to us, to stimulate us, to make us aware of our potential. We have to create an art for liberation and for life."[2] She shows us who Black women are outside of the public sphere and the intimacy that exists within female friendships. Patriarchy can often attack female relationships, encouraging competition and slander. However, Catlett combats these notions, emphasizing the important bond that these two Black women share.

–GRACE LYNNE HAYNES

LITERATURE: Rosenberg

Fig. 4.2. Elizabeth Catlett, *Gossip*, 2005. Color digital and photo lithograph. 227/16 × 243/16 in. (57 × 61.4 cm). Collection Zimmerli Art Museum at Rutgers University. Gift of the Brodsky Center at Rutgers, The State University of New Jersey. 2007.0033. © 2026 Mora-Catlett Family / Licensed by VAGA at Artists Rights Society (ARS), New York.

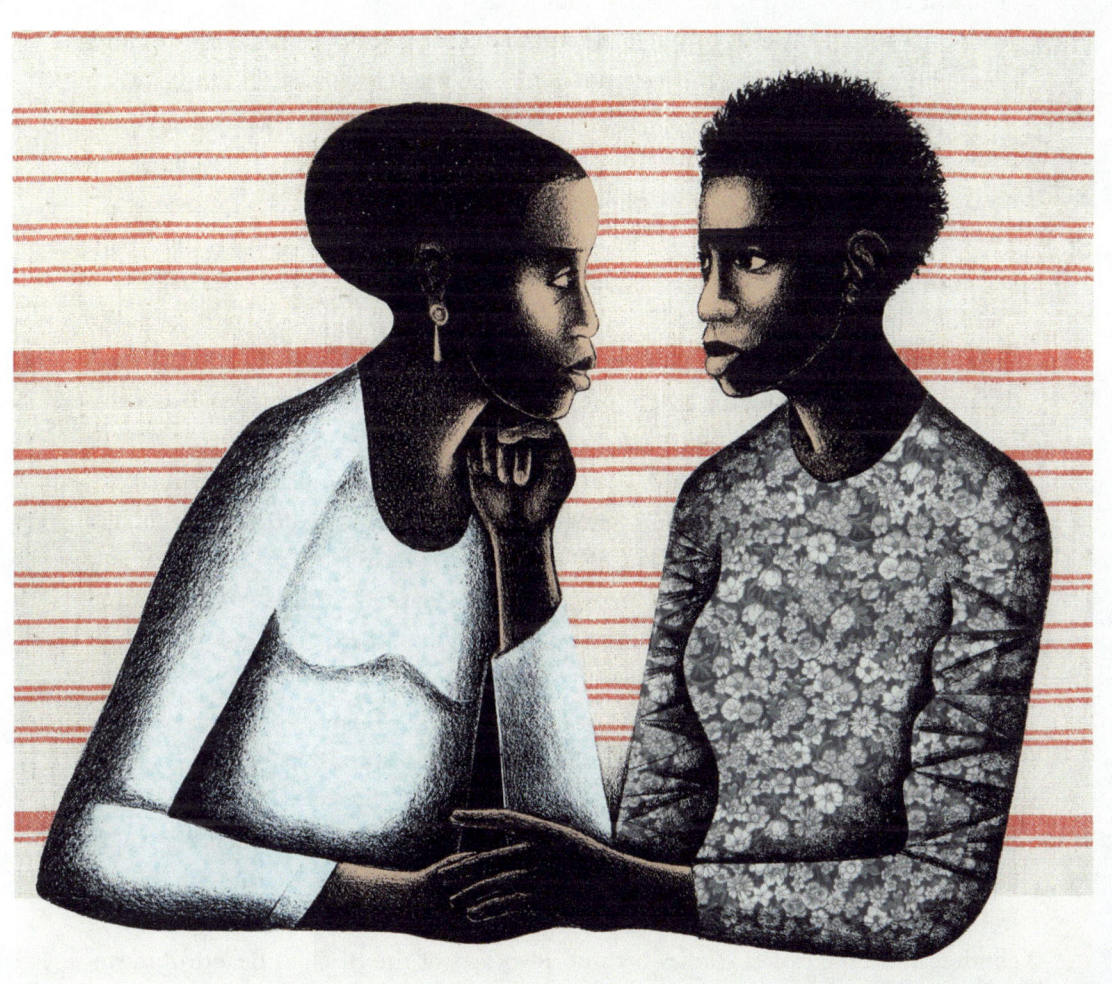

AP 17/50   Gossips   E Catlett 2005

NEFERTITI GOODMAN (1949-)

Getting Fixed to Look Pretty, 1978

A young woman fans herself leisurely as another woman stands behind her, a fistful of hair to braid in her left hand, and the right hand holding the comb to gather the hair. Both women are lavishly dressed. The lively geometric patterning of the braider's dress captures the viewer's attention, and the organic leaf and feather-like motifs of the sitter flow down to the fish swimming across her skirt. Their florid clothing echoes the flora that peeks through the window shades, but contrasts with the quiet tranquility within the private space. The woman braiding closes her eyes, relaxed while she performs her task. She leans close to the seated woman, who stares ahead in a meditative trance, head held high regally. The calm dignity of the woman braiding is not unlike that of the stately sitter to whom she is attending.

The print bears formal similarities to Japanese ukiyo-e prints featuring courtesans and their attendants. In the relief style of printing, the artist carves the image into a sheet of linoleum and then presses the raised ink-covered surface onto a piece of paper. This technique can yield the application of an expanse of opaque, solid color, like the dark, empty floor behind the two women. The ornate patterns of their gowns are also reminiscent of the robes of the women in ukiyo-e prints.

Black women in particular have a culturally, historically, and socially informed collective consciousness about the subject of hair. Black mothers and female role models have taught Black girls from a young age not only how to style and care for their hair but also the significance of hair as an expression of identity, heritage, femininity, and creativity. This experience is an intimate one, a way for mothers, daughters, and sisters to bond and for young women to care for and empower themselves.

Goodman made this print toward the end of the Black Power movement, which brought ideas about political and social rights alongside cultural expression and beauty to public discourse. The famous "doll tests" in the 1940s by the social psychologists Kenneth and Mamie Clark opened the public's eyes to how segregation negatively affected Black children's sense of self-worth. By the 1960s and 1970s, through the collective power of the Civil Rights and Black Power movements, the same generation of children from the earlier studies became advocates of the Black Is Beautiful movement, which celebrated Afrocentric beauty. It proved that the act of caring for one's own appearance or "getting fixed to look pretty" as the central figure is doing in this print is enormously powerful.

—EMILY HU

LITERATURE: Banks, Bell, Camp, Rowe, Suzuki

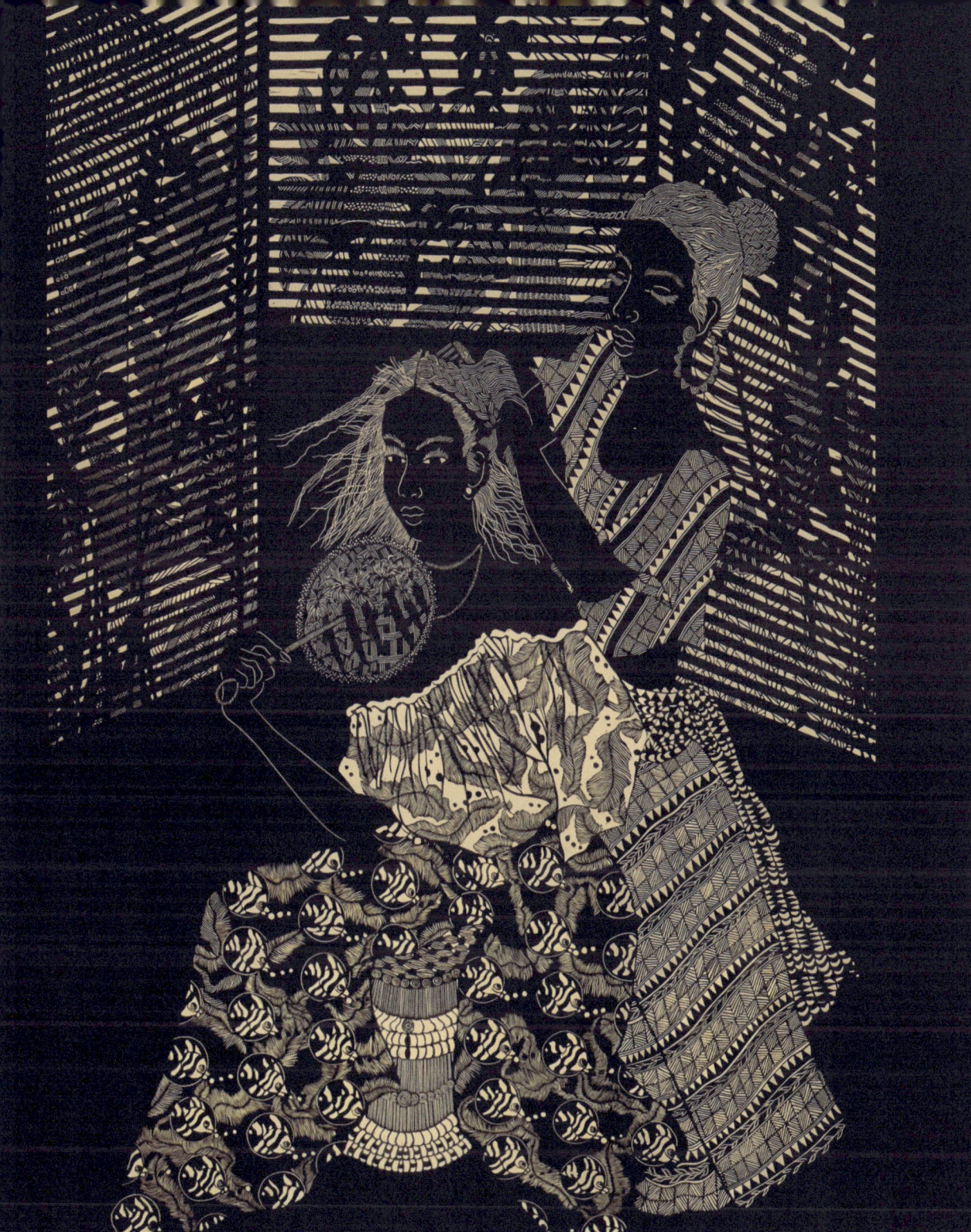

Fig. 4.3. Nefertiti Goodman, *Getting Fixed to Look Pretty*, 1978. Linocut. 43 13/16 × 29 7/8 in. (111.3 × 75.9 cm). Collection Zimmerli Art Museum at Rutgers University, Promised Gift of Barbara Sunderman Hoerner. TR9927.012. © Nefertiti Goodman.

MARGO HUMPHREY (1942-)

The History of Her Life Written Across Her Face, 1991

Identity plays a central role in Humphrey's work. *The History of Her Life Written Across Her Face* is a self-portrait of the artist. Humphrey depicts herself with myriad bright and colorful autobiographical words and images on her face, neck, and shoulders. Her skin is black, while her hair is a light brown accentuated with strokes of red. Her golden-brown eyes stare out mysteriously, and her distinctly shiny red lips are puckered. The yellow sun glows on her forehead as a "third eye," indicating wisdom and enlightenment. Below the sun is the word *BALANCE* and a scale featuring the words *MOM* and *DAD*, respectively.

What becomes increasingly clear is that travel and adventure played a significant role in the story Humphrey chooses to tell. Just above the eye on the left, or what she describes as her "carnal eye," she illustrates Michigan Avenue in Chicago. This image plays into a storytelling sequence: "She met a man in Michigan Ave Chicago," with "man" reading as a picture of a gentleman with a white hat, coat, and cane. Bold red surrounds the eye to the right, what she calls her "spirit eye." A woman in an orange dress climbs a ladder toward a question mark and away from a storm cloud, a lightning strike, and a flame. The full narrative on the left side of the print describes her journey to New York in 1979; her encounters with art; the people, protections, and challenges she came across; and the birth of her twins, among other details.

Humphrey places crosses on both shoulders, a bright one on the left and a dark one on the right. The two crosses (and the third on her face, next to a representation of the Devil) stand as symbols of her unwavering faith during the darkest and most challenging moments of her life, in alignment with biblical themes and stories. This piece is a story of courage and perseverance. Humphrey takes her experiences and presents them with a raw, passionate, and proud honesty that engages and inspires.

–MICHAEL RANDALL

LITERATURE: Childs, Powell

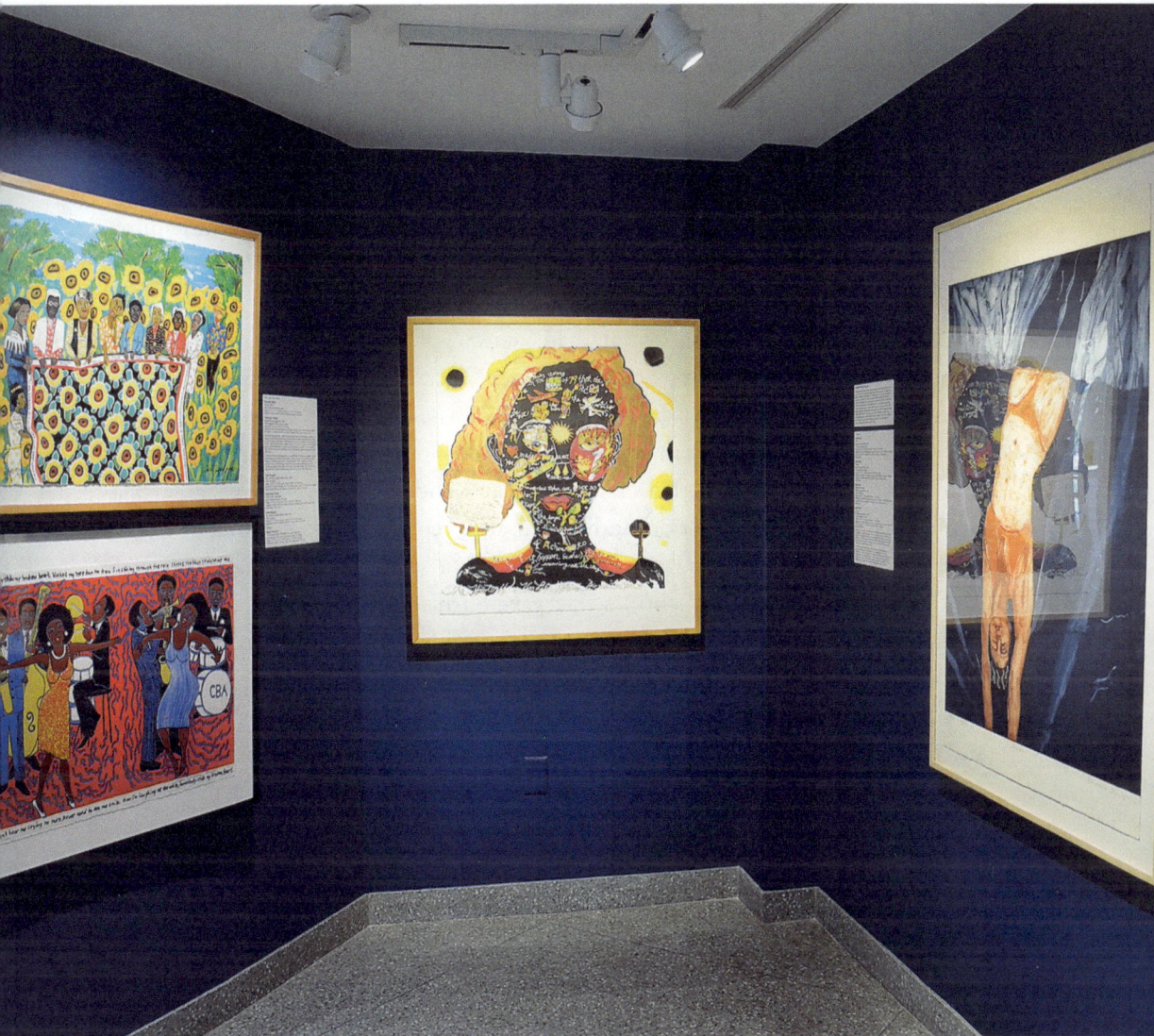

Fig. 4.4. Installation view of Margo Humphrey, *The History of Her Life Written Across Her Face*, 1991. Color lithograph with metallic leaf, bronze powder, and collage. 325/16×293/4 in. (82×75.5 cm). Collection Zimmerli Art Museum at Rutgers University. Gift of the Brodsky Center at Rutgers, The State University of New Jersey. 1991.0083. The Humphrey print is flanked by prints by Faith Ringgold on the left and Emma Amos to the right. Gallery 104B of the DWAS. 2022. Nicole Ianuzelli, photographer.

BETYE SAAR (1926-)

Blow Top Blues: The Fire Next Time, 1998

Blow Top Blues: The Fire Next Time is illustrative of Saar's unique ability to generate intense messages and imagery through the reappropriation, dissection, and fusion of images from popular culture, the occult, and more. Explosive sparks and flames charge a dark and ominous blue and purple sky. The fire rises from the scarf of Aunt Jemima, who menacingly grins from the bottom right corner of the image. *LIBERATION* is imprinted on the scarf.

Aunt Jemima is a recurring character in Saar's work. An example of the "mammy" stereotype, Aunt Jemima represented and defined Black women as large, motherly, submissive, and one-dimensional beings. Saar's 1972 assemblage *The Liberation of Aunt Jemima* turned the caricature into a radical symbol of resistance, keeping her mammy features while arming her with a shotgun and a grenade. *Blow Top Blues* is an escalation of that famous composition. In her refusal to "correct" Aunt Jemima's exaggerated features and presenting the character with a sense of rage, Saar is directly confronting the systems and entities that gave birth to the stereotypical imagery of Aunt Jemima and the relentless oppression of the Black women the mammy figure was meant to visually represent.

The phrase, *Blow Top Blues,* references a 1944 song performed by Lionel Hampton and Dinah Washington that describes a woman's descent into madness, and *The Fire Next Time* recalls James Baldwin's 1963 book of the same title. While one might label this print as a depiction of madness, considering Aunt Jemima's empty stare and wide grin, we can take it a step further. In the face of endless injustice, what does it mean to reduce the justified rage and anger of the oppressed and call it insanity? What does it mean to plant seeds of doubt in an individual or group in opposition to their lived experiences? It is gaslighting. In a gas lamp, a stream of gas fuels a combusted flame. What the world does to Black people and Black women especially, is what fuels the violent flames rising from Aunt Jemima's head.

—MICHAEL RANDALL

LITERATURE: Baldwin, McCabe, Tani, Wolfskill 2017

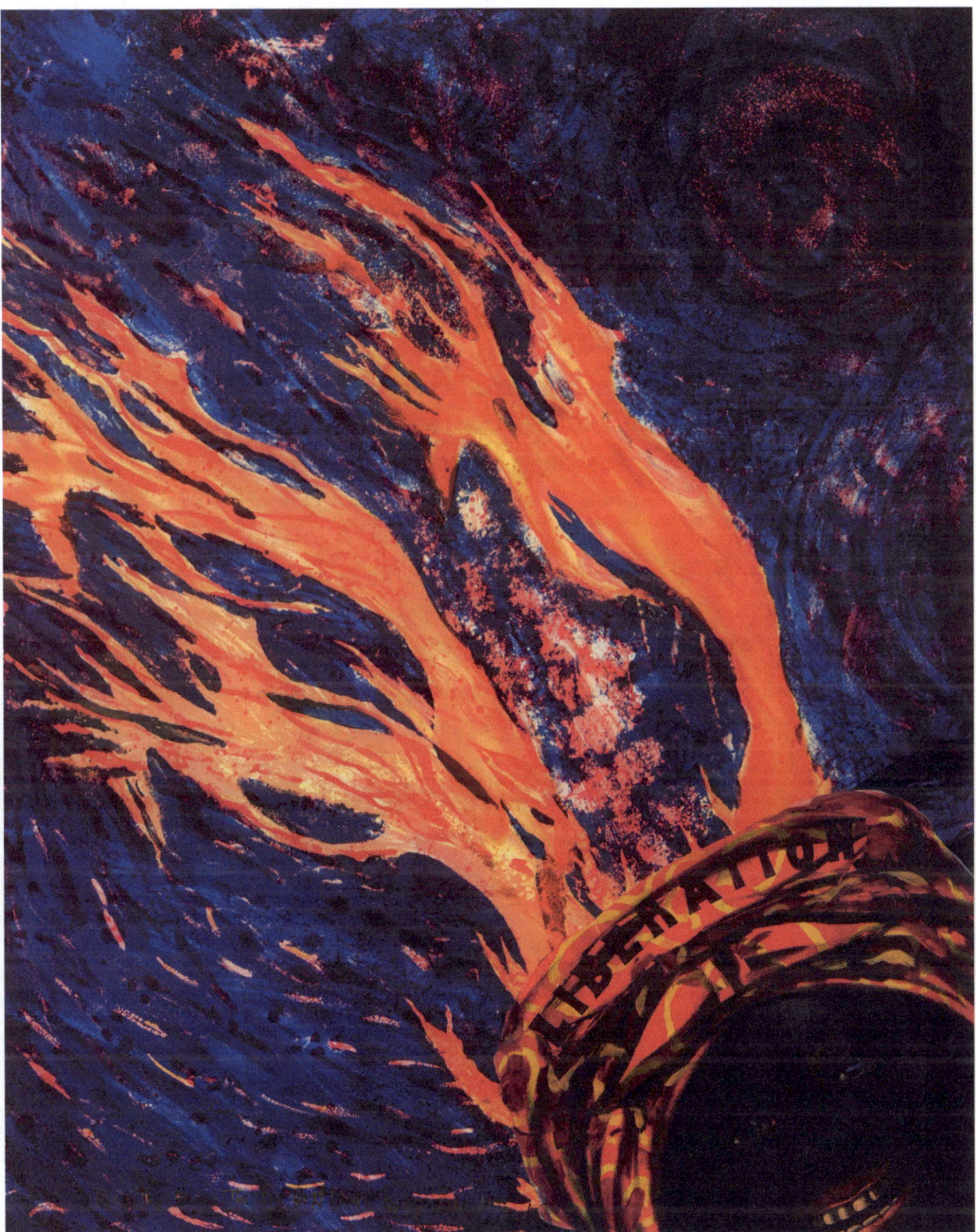

Fig. 4.5. Betye Saar, *Blow Top Blues: The Fire Next Time*, 1998. Color lithograph and photoelectric transfer with chine collé on Rives BFK white paper. 271/16 × 227/16 in. (68.8 × 56.9 cm). Collection Zimmerli Art Museum at Rutgers University. Gift of Judith Solodkin, SOLO Impression. 1998.0979. Courtesy of the artist and the Roberts Projects, Los Angeles, California.

CARMEN CARTINESS JOHNSON (1954-)

The Get Together, 2005

Seated around a rectangular coffee table, a group of close friends and family engage in lively conversation. They are relaxed, facing one another, and leaning into each other's company. A cooking show plays on the television in the background.

Johnson is a painter and a storyteller. Her works tell stories about ordinary people, family gatherings, and individuals. She imbues her subjects with individuality through the variety in their fashion, hair, skin tone, and body shapes, from the older pear-shaped woman with a curly ponytail in a black and white polka-dot shirt on the couch to the short-haired goateed man pouring out a drink and reclined on a rug on the right. Despite the vivid personalities shown by their clothes and features, the party members are also faceless and anonymous. Johnson's figures are both specific and generalized—they are characters of her imagination and could be anybody in the world.

Johnson began teaching herself how to paint after her grandmother died. Her earliest works look back on her memories of summers with her grandparents in Arkansas. Warmth, affection, community, and belonging have since become central to the stories she crafts. She counts among her inspirations Diego Rivera's use of color, political content, and composition; the simplicity of Jacob Lawrence's shapes; and the complexity of Romare Bearden's collages.

Her interest in composition and shape are evident in this piece that looks down at the living room scene from the vantage point of the ceiling. The four walls of this room contain the vibrancy and richness of everyday life, with good company and the beauty of a well-lit home full of plush rugs, furniture, and plants. The bright scarlet red pops against the soft yellow and brilliant azure blue. In the right corner, two people bring another chair to the table to close in the cheerfully raucous circle.

—EMILY HU

LITERATURE: Cole, Johnson, San Antonio Art League and Museum

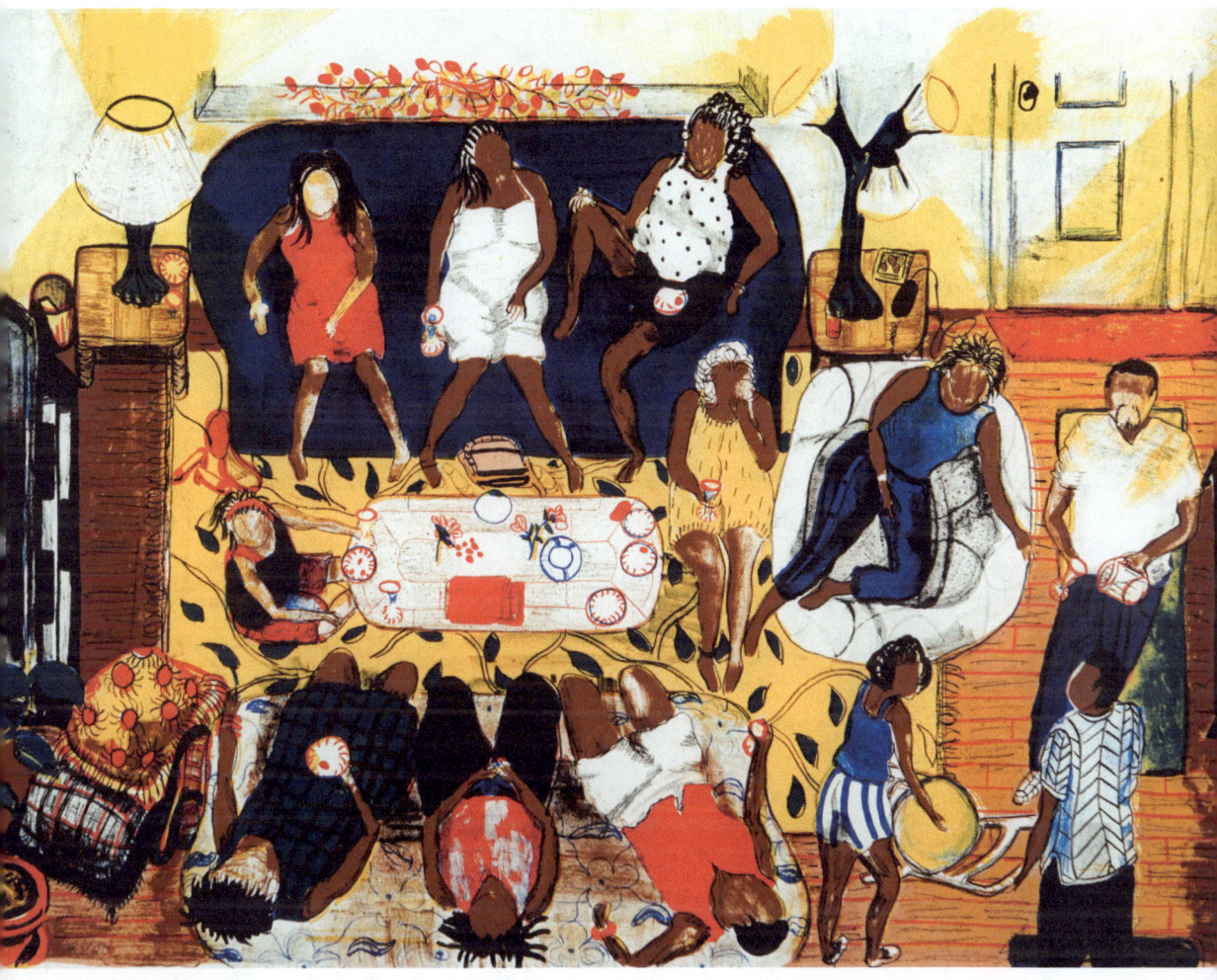

Fig. 4.6. Carmen Cartiness Johnson, *The Get Together*, 2005. Color lithograph on Somerset paper. 19 3/16 × 27 in. (48.8 × 68.6 cm). Collection Zimmerli Art Museum at Rutgers University. Gift of the Brodsky Center at Rutgers, The State University of New Jersey. 2007.0065. Courtesy of the artist.

RENÉE STOUT (1958-)

Marie Laveau, 2009

In *Marie Laveau*, Renée Stout creates a portrait of the famous nineteenth-century Voodoo priestess. She models Laveau in her own likeness, thus crafting an imagined self-portrait. Laveau's intense beauty and mystical powers captivated New Orleans in the 1800s. Although Laveau was a Creole woman with a light complexion, Stout took artistic liberty to depict her in a darker, nearly black skin tone, emphasizing her African heritage. The soft edges of her afro span outward, creating a sense of unruliness and pride.

A snake's head peeks out from the afro as its tongue slithers and red eyes beam with curiosity. In biblical histories and mythologies snakes often symbolize evil, like in the story of the mystical and powerful Medusa. These reptiles covered Medusa's head; she possessed such a striking beauty that it cursed anyone who glanced upon her. Stout intentionally hides her snake, buried deep in her hair. It appears as a trick up her sleeve. Her face is partially obscured by a fan, creating a sense of mystery. She turns her head to look directly at the viewer, simultaneously revealing her strength and femininity.

Stout's imaginative portrayal gives the piece a powerful presence and otherworldliness. Through this portrait she brings awareness to New Orleans Voodoo and honors the practitioners who have sustained the religion.

–GRACE LYNNE HAYNES

LITERATURE: Flint Institute of Arts

Fig. 4.7. Renée Stout, *Marie Laveau*, 2009. Color lithograph. 221/2 × 231/4 in. (57.1 × 59 cm). Collection Zimmerli Art Museum at Rutgers University. Gift of Maurice Sánchez, Derrière L'Étoile Studios. 2011.015.019. © Renée Stout.

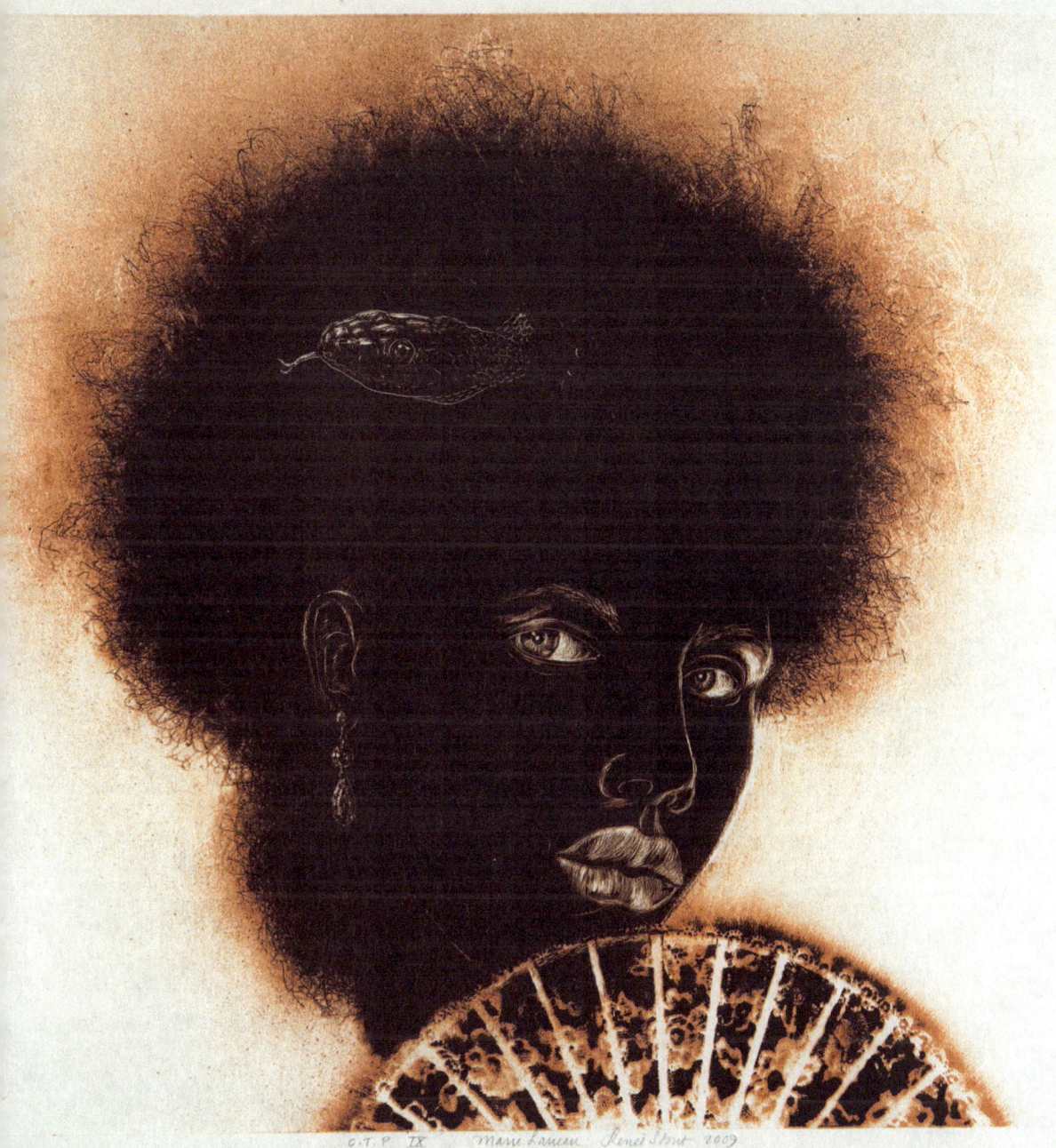

C.T.P. IX   Marie Laveau   Renee Stout   2009

MICKALENE THOMAS (1971-)

You're Gonna Give Me the Love That I Need, 2010

This collaged print is reminiscent of a 1970s Blaxploitation set, featuring a wood-panel background and an eclectic mix of colorful and textured furniture. Thomas gives character to every object within the frame, using techniques such as digital print and silk-screened pulp paper, but the busyness of this piece never detracts from the model's control of the viewer's gaze. Her reclined pose and face anticipate the arrival of a lover or a future self, who has taken on the responsibility of loving her. The pillows, loveseat, ottoman, and rug all have different designs, patterns, and colors—none more vibrant than the rest, and all making the subject of the work, with her brown skin and red lips, stand out even more.

Thomas's work is frequently generalized and simplified as just an interest in bringing Black female subjects into art history; however, her work is even more deeply personal and political than that. Using Jacques Lacan's psychoanalytic theory of the mirror stage, her paintings reproduce self/ego and are intended to offer validation for Black women seeing reflections of themselves. She undermines dominant social norms by giving the gaze (and the power associated with it) to women. Additionally, her work follows an avant-garde genealogy from Édouard Manet, Henri Matisse, and Romare Bearden that explores the role of the Black model in art history, yet Thomas departs from that tradition with her specific eye for amplifying Black women's beauty.

—JASMINE DARIA CANNON

LITERATURE: Kino, Landers, Loos, Murrell, S. Smith, M. Thomas, Walker 2009

Notes

1. Kara Walker is specifically describing how Mickalene Thomas's depictions of Black women offer "the promise of womanist agency," borrowing the term *womanist* from Alice Walker, who saw a need to distinguish Black women's freedom struggles from those of the more mainstream (and white) feminist movement. Kara Walker, "Mickalene Thomas," Artists on Artists, *BOMB*, no. 107 (Spring 2009), https://bombmagazine.org/articles/2009/04/01/mickalene-thomas/; bell hooks, "Postmodern Blackness," *Postmodern Culture* 1, no. 1 (September 1990), https://dx.doi.org/10.1353/pmc.1990.0004.

2. Samella S. Lewis, *African American Art and Artists* (University of California Press, 2003), 134.

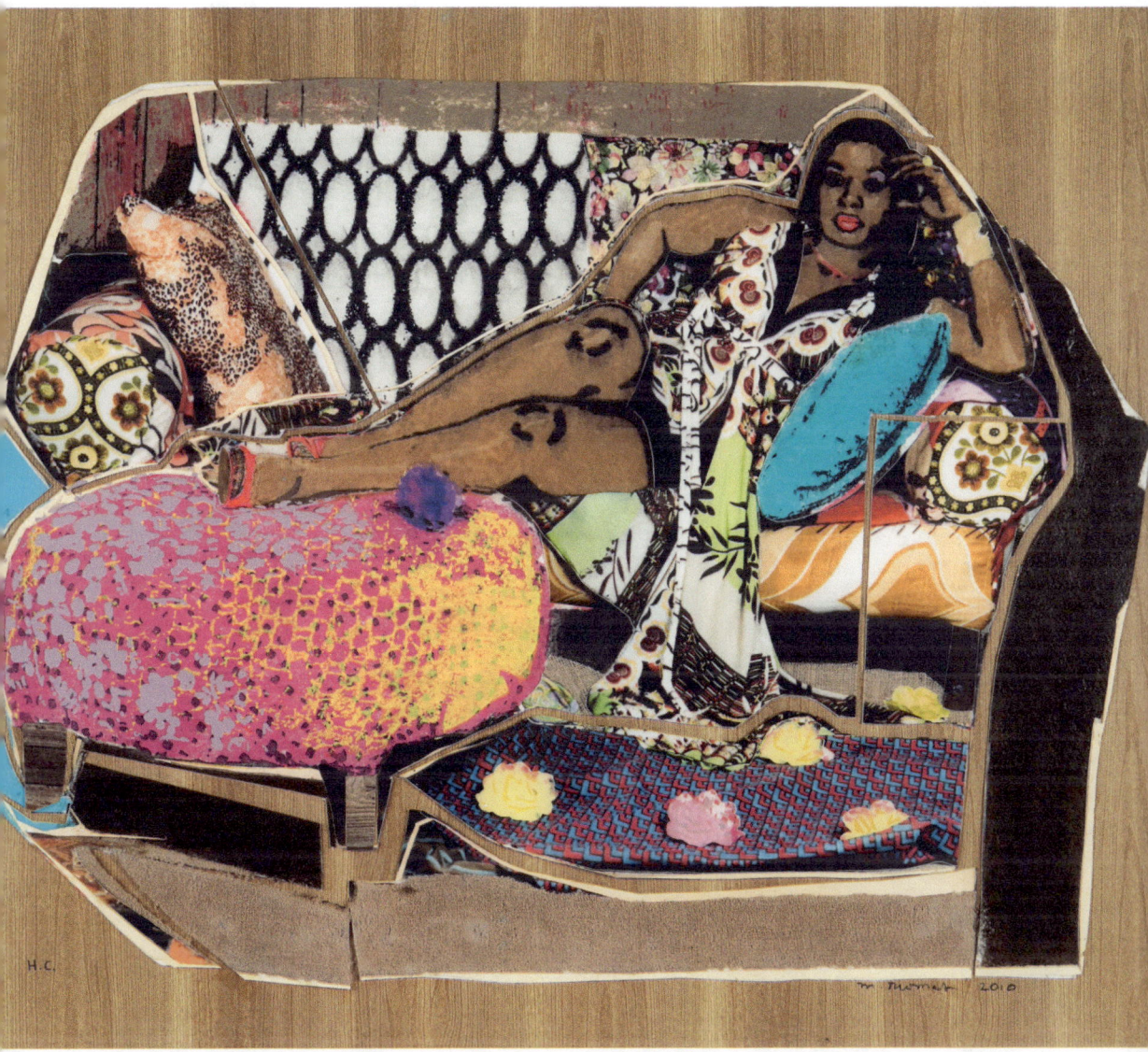

Fig. 4.8. Mickalene Thomas, *You're Gonna Give Me the Love That I Need*, 2010. Collaged handmade paper with silk-screened pigmented paper pulp, pochoir, digital print, and appliqué of cloth and glitter. 24×291/4 in. (60.9×74.3 cm). Collection Zimmerli Art Museum at Rutgers University. Gift of the Brodsky Center at Rutgers, The State University of New Jersey. 2018.034.003. © 2026 Mickalene Thomas / Artists Rights Society (ARS), New York.

It's always been my contention
that, for me,
a Black woman artist,
to walk into the studio
is a political act.

— EMMA AMOS

5

The Brodsky Center and the Rutgers Print Collaborative

KYLE B. CO., GRACE LYNNE HAYNES, EMILY HU, AND DESIREE MORALES

THE ARTIST AND PRINTMAKER JUDITH K. BRODSKY founded the Rutgers Center for Innovative Print and Paper in 1986 as a forum for the exchange of new ideas in print, papermaking processes, and education. In 2006, Rutgers renamed the center in her honor. Originally located at the Mason Gross School of the Arts, the Brodsky Center relocated to the Pennsylvania Academy of the Fine Arts in 2018. The primary mission of the Brodsky Center is to enable artists, both established and emerging, to create new work in paper and print. Since the conception of the Brodsky Center, diversity has been central to its mission. The center has consistently supported women and artists of color. Presently, the Brodsky Center is responsible for one-third of the Zimmerli Art Museum's collection of works by Black women artists.

In 2013, Barbara Madsen founded the Rutgers Print Collaborative as part of her graduate print portfolio class. The annual portfolio invites artists to collaborate with a collective of graduate students on an edition of unique prints. The Brodsky Center also reflected this mode of communal print production. The Brodsky Center and the Rutgers Print Collaborative are representative models of a practiced intersectional feminism. These institutions have invited Black women in to take up space, give lectures on their work, and, ultimately, exist. The *Collective Yearning* exhibition gathered these stories for the first time.

—KYLE B. CO. AND DESIREE MORALES

BLACK AT THE PRINTSHOP

Historically, the printshop has served as a crucial tool for Black communities in the imagining of a collective identity following the institution of slavery. The printing press allowed for the mass dissemination of information, and African American access to the printshop and the eventual network of Black printshops are responsible for producing a new paradigm of thought through imagery and language that uplifted the race and produced more accurate depictions of Black life. As derogatory racialized imagery like pickaninnies, Sambos, and minstrels circulated in popular media, Black voices in print served as counternarratives, a new polarity to displace the negative.

With the rise in popularity of fine art print editions after the Great Depression, due in part to organizations such as Associated American Artists and the Works Progress Administration (WPA), it became more common for artists to work directly with a printshop that could house and maintain the otherwise cumbersome resources and techniques the printmaking process required. In 1947, for instance, Black American artist Robert Blackburn, who had attended WPA-operated classes at the Harlem Arts Community Center, founded what would become the oldest and longest-running community printshop in the United States. The Robert Blackburn Printmaking Workshop and the Brodsky Center are two examples of printshops oriented toward artists of color.

–KYLE B. CO.

FAITH RINGGOLD (1930-2024)

The Sunflower Quilting Bee at Arles, 1996

This lithograph is an impression of a story quilt by the same name. A story quilt is a hybrid form of painting and quilt making, referring to a practice where the quilt communicates a story or an aspect of the quilter's life. Ringgold is well known for her story quilts as part of her larger painting practice. Within the series, *The French Collection*, she imagines a place for Black people at European sites of art history, especially in the history of modernism. She depicts Madam C. J. Walker, Sojourner Truth, Ida B. Wells, Fannie Lou Hamer, Harriet Tubman, Rosa Parks, Mary McLeod Bethune, Ella Baker, and Vincent van Gogh in *The French Collection* story quilts.

In this recasting of the original story quilt, Ringgold has added the figure of the fictive Black woman Willia Marie Simone. According to the artist's narrative, Willia Marie Simone is on the heroic journey of pursuing art and life with her family while a transplant in Paris. She is among the great women who have gathered to quilt, doing "women's work" in the sunflower field of Van Gogh's inspiration outside Arles, France. Van Gogh stands to the side as a spectator, while presenting flowers to these impressive women.

Ringgold presents quilting as a community practice codified by the collective labor of Black women; this quilt is a microcosm for the world. In contrast, she places the image of Van Gogh to the right of the "Sunflower Quilters Society of America." He is representative of the solitary bravado of the European master. Van Gogh averts his eyes, but the offering of flowers suggests the gracious approach of his presence. Much is owed to Black women.

–KYLE B. CO.

LITERATURE: Farrington and Ringgold

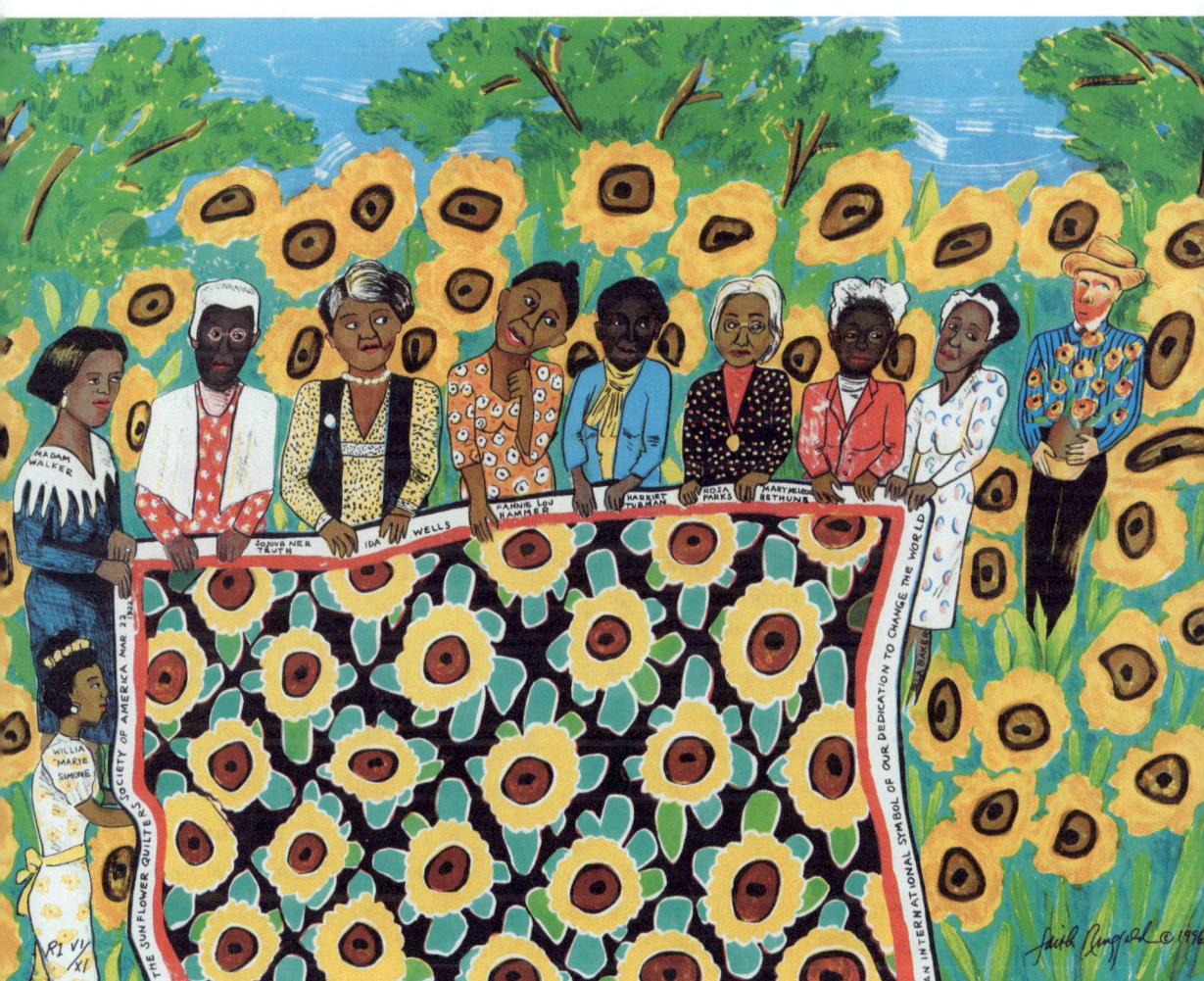

Fig. 5.1. Faith Ringgold, *The Sunflower Quilting Bee at Arles*, 1996. Color lithograph. 229/16×301/16 in. (57.3×76.4 cm). Collection Zimmerli Art Museum at Rutgers University. Gift of the Brodsky Center at Rutgers, The State University of New Jersey. 1996.0181. © 2026 Faith Ringgold / Artists Rights Society (ARS), New York. Courtesy ACA Galleries, New York.

EMMA AMOS (1937-2020)

My Mothers, My Sisters, 1992

My Mothers, My Sisters is a collage that honors the people who shaped Amos's life, career, and art making. She grew up in Atlanta, Georgia, where her parents often traversed the Black intellectual circles. Figures like the Harlem Renaissance writer Zora Neale Hurston, the sociologist and activist W.E.B. Du Bois, and the artist Hale Woodruff (her later colleague and mentor in the African American art collective Spiral) all frequented the Amos household. Surrounded by people who celebrated Black intellectualism and who were early advocates of her artistic journey, she was inspired and supported.

Portraits of her mother and her grandmother are present in the piece, but the sisters that she refers to in her title were not siblings by blood. Rather, Amos was a member of the feminist art collective Heresies, formed in 1976, which sought to generate discourse about the relationship between feminism, politics, and art. May Stevens, depicted in the center right, was a founding member and the editor of the *Heresies* journal. A side profile of Kay WalkingStick, the Cherokee painter, also appears at the top of the print. Both women are also included in Amos's acrylic portrait of forty women friends, artists, and colleagues, titled *The Gift*. Amos once said, "There's something powerful and strong about women artists, about womanhood."[1] By including portraits of these other women artists, she ties herself to a lineage of artistic excellence and creativity.

In addition to women artists, she also had an interest in depicting Black athletes. Her *Athletes and Animals Series* (1983–1985) explores the power, the flexibility, the physicality, and influence of Black athletes. At the center of *My Mothers, My Sisters* is an illustration of the entertainer, civil rights activist, and Rutgers University football player Paul Robeson, whom she very much admired. *Thank You Jesus for Paul Robeson (and for Nicholas Murray's Photograph—1926)* (1995) is another of her works that pays homage to Robeson. Alongside him are track athletes from Fisk University, the alma mater of her mother and a historically Black institution in Nashville, Tennessee. The placement of these figures in her work highlights how she centers herself within this illustrious line of Black heroes.

At the top and bottom of this print, Amos laid two pieces of yellow ochre fabric. A former weaver and designer for Dorothy Liebes, Amos had a lifelong love for textiles. She integrated Dutch wax print, handwoven and store-bought African kente and kanga cloths, and batik fabrics into the borders of many of her works. For Amos, the inclusion of these fabrics expresses her veneration for the material and a nod to the legacy of women and the African continent.

–EMILY HU

LITERATURE: Amos, Cotter 2020, Farrington "Emma Amos: Art as Legacy," 2007, Valentine 2016

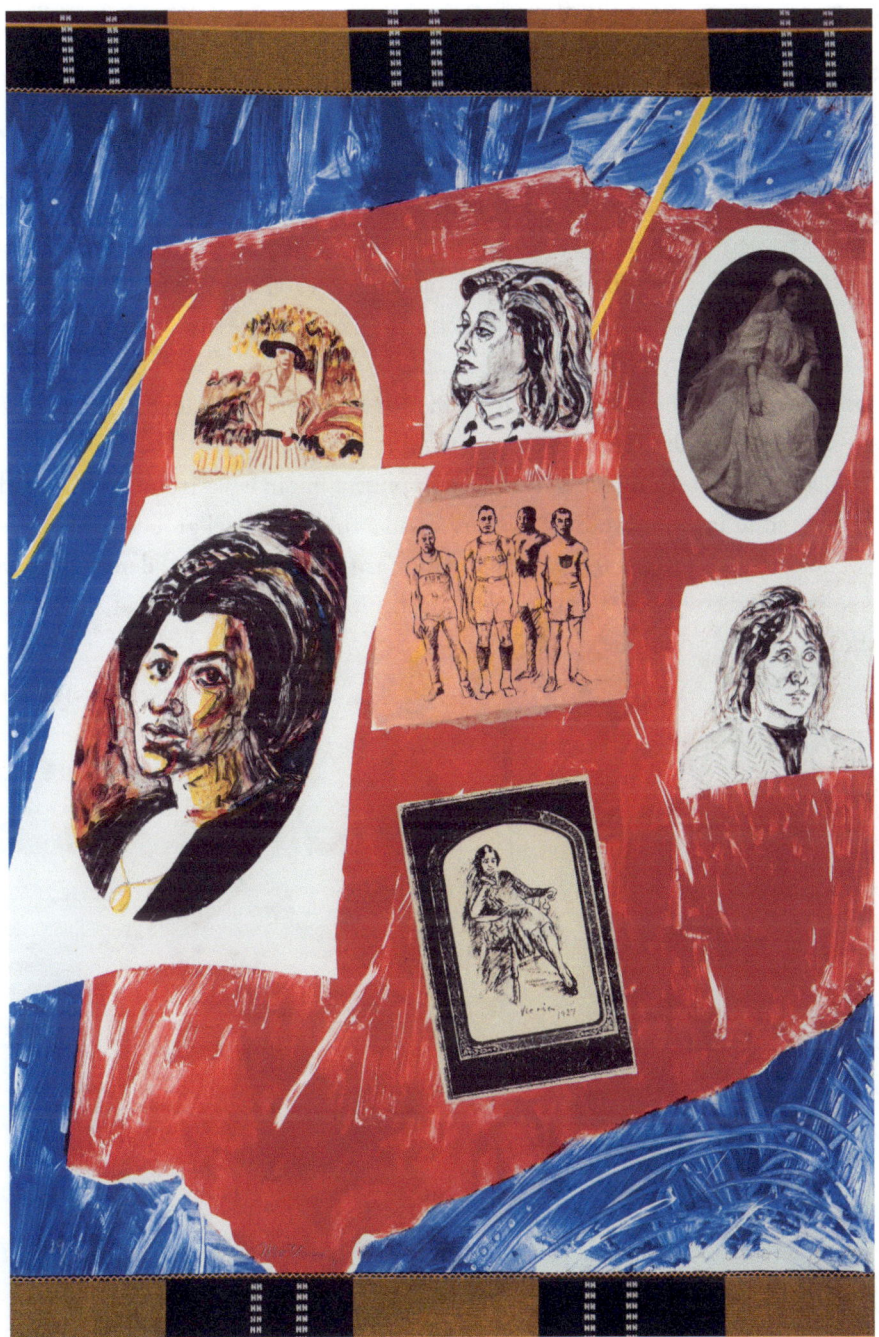

Fig. 5.2. Emma Amos, *My Mothers, My Sisters*, 1992. Color lithograph with fabric and handmade paper chine collé on Rives BFK and HMP paper. 445/16 × 303/16 in. (112.6 × 76.7 cm). Collection Zimmerli Art Museum at Rutgers University. Gift of the Brodsky Center at Rutgers, The State University of New Jersey. 1992.0515.001. © 2026 Emma Amos / Licensed by VAGA at Artists Rights Society (ARS), New York.

ELIZABETH CATLETT (1915-2012)

Danys y Liethis, 2005

A mother lovingly holds her baby. She attempts to shield them from the chaos of the racial discrimination they will endure as a Black child growing into adulthood in the United States. Catlett emphasized the bags under the mother's eyes by creating a high contrast between the black and white tones. The mother appears dignified yet exhausted by her responsibility. Her hand is gently holding and caressing the baby's head, offering full support and a gentleness that the child will not receive from the outside world. This is one of the baby's few safe havens, a place where they can be a child, naïve and innocent, without repercussions. This is the Black American struggle that begins in the womb, as symbolized by the child's blood red shirt.

Catlett creates meaning not only in what is present but in what is absent. The mother is the only adult in the picture. Her figure against the white background evokes a feeling of emptiness. Catlett captures the isolation this struggle brings, depicting it with a sensitivity and complexity that does not victimize the mother. Instead, she chooses to show us a regal strength.

–GRACE LYNNE HAYNES

LITERATURE: Herzog 2000 and 2005, Rosenberg

Fig. 5.3. Elizabeth Catlett, *Danys y Liethis*, 2005. Color lithograph on Somerset Velvet paper. 27 15/16 × 20 in. (70.9 × 50.8 cm). Collection Zimmerli Art Museum at Rutgers University. Gift of the Brodsky Center at Rutgers, The State University of New Jersey. 2007.0032. © 2026 Mora-Catlett Family / Licensed by VAGA at Artists Rights Society (ARS), New York.

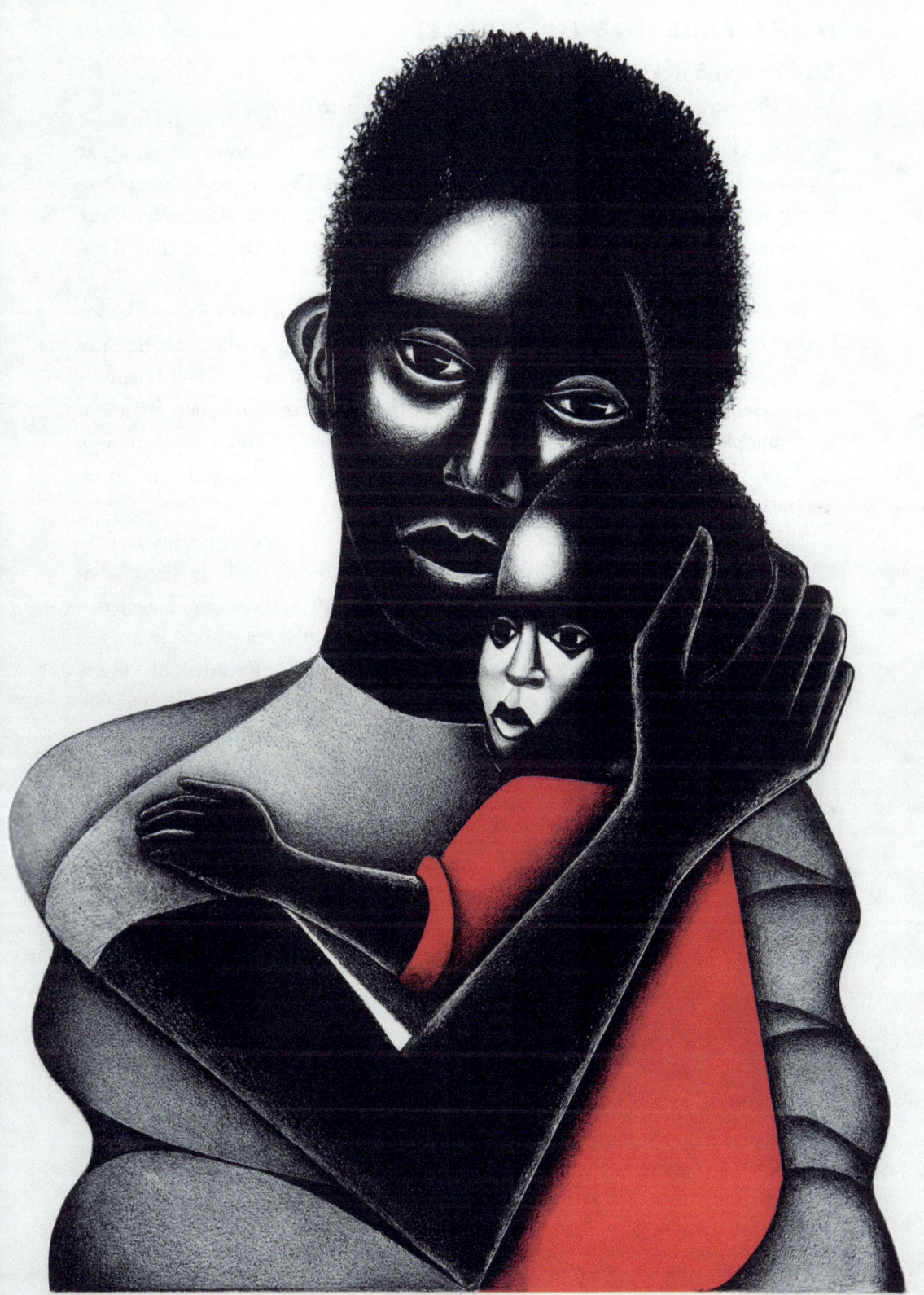

NONA FAUSTINE (1977–2025)

Scarlet and Black
from the Rutgers Print Collaborative portfolio, 2017

This piece builds on the series *White Shoes*, which portrays the history of slavery in New York City through a collection of nude self-portraits. Faustine took those photographs in former locations significant to the slave trade. The series also engaged with representation of the Black female body. She addressed not only the geographical history of slavery but the auctioning of the body as well.

Faustine produced this print in the Brodsky Center (housed in the Rutgers Mason Gross School of the Arts until 2018). Barbara Madsen led the graduate course Print Portfolio, in which she invited prominent contemporary artists to work collaboratively with students in the Brodsky Center facilities; Faustine was the 2017 guest artist. She used multiple printmaking techniques in this piece: silk screen (a common ink-transfer method), photopolymer etching (transferring an image with light), and hand painting the white shoes directly onto the surface of the print.

She took her signature aesthetic and applied an additional complex layer—acknowledging the problematic history of the institution with which she collaborated. Here she considered the relation of the work not only to the state of New Jersey but to Rutgers University specifically. She listed the names of enslaved people, aligned on both sides of the print. This list includes people the founding trustees of Rutgers enslaved, among them enslaved people who had a physical hand in the construction of the university.

—DESIREE MORALES

LITERATURE: Donoghue, Edwards, Fuentes and White, Holmes

Fig. 5.4. Nona Faustine, *Scarlet and Black* from the Rutgers Print Collaborative portfolio, 2017. Color screen print and polymer gravure with hand-painted shoes. 38×27 in. (96.5×67.4 cm). Collection Zimmerli Art Museum at Rutgers University. Gift of the Rutgers Print Collaborative. 2020.014.003.001. Courtesy of the artist.

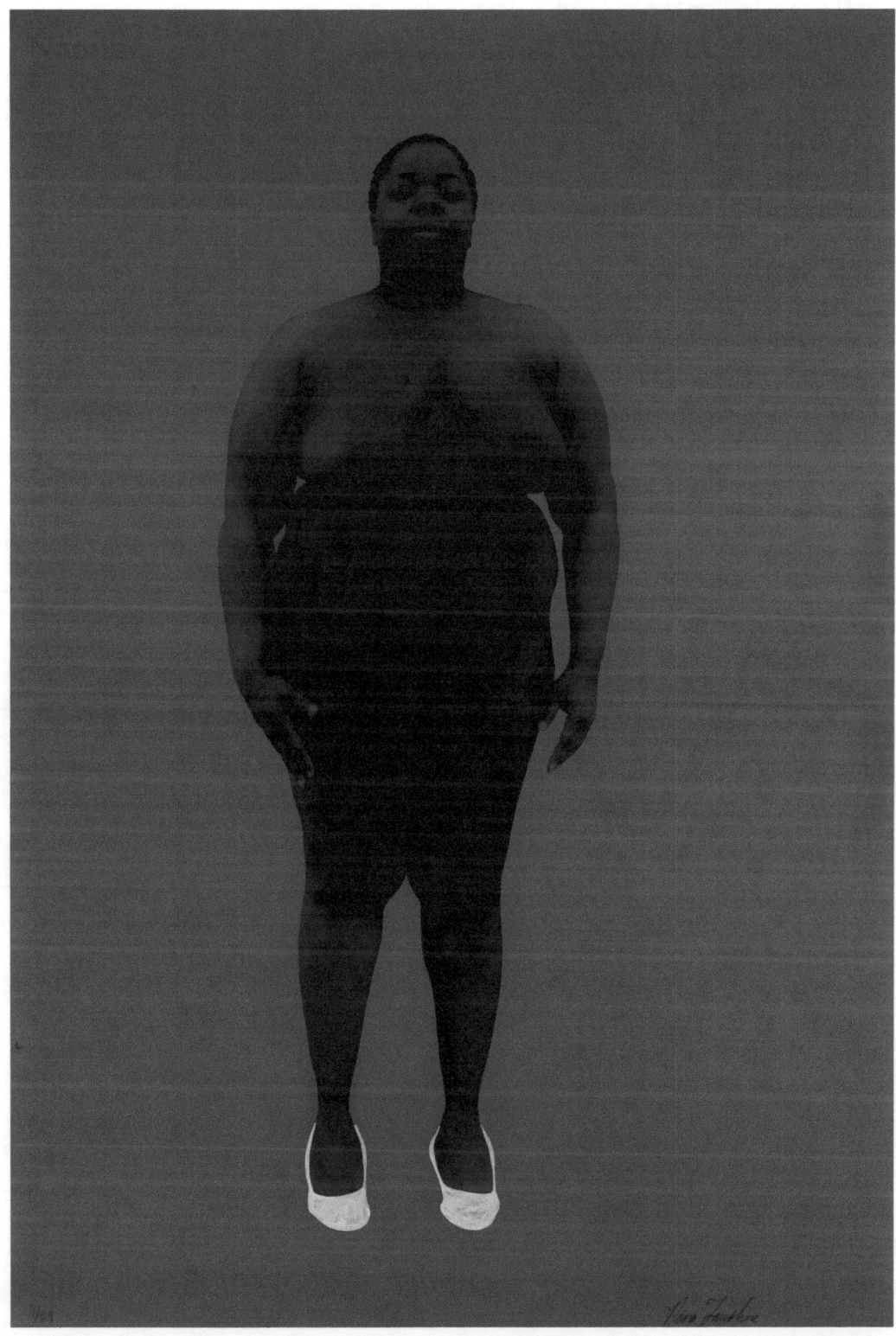

DAONNE HUFF (1983-)

Life Savers Are Red and Round (Sickle Cell)
from the Rutgers Print Collaborative portfolio, 2018

In this work, Huff engages the viewer in a conversation about an illness that weighs heavily on the Black community. She arranges words poetically across the page, overlaid on a reddish-brown surface. As a native of Alabama, her color choice references the heavy iron levels of the state's red clay. She also connects the colors with iron in the body and the anemic blood count of those with sickle cell. Her print pays homage to the people living with the sickle cell trait as well as those who have lost their battle with the illness.

The text describes a child entering the world with the possibilities of having sickle cell or being a trait carrier. The poem also describes historical traits passed on to children from Black parents, including words like *trauma* and *cotton*. There is a nod to Henrietta Lacks, a Black woman whose harvested cells have dramatically informed science and medicine.

Huff previously served as the graduate program coordinator and gallery manager for the Rutgers Mason Gross School of the Arts. In 2018, Barbara Madsen invited her to work alongside graduate students and the visiting artist Damien Davis in the Brodsky Center print facilities. This act reinforces the ethos of Mason Gross, showing the inherent value in engaging not only students but also faculty and staff and their artistic practices.

—DESIREE MORALES

LITERATURE: Angeleti and Carrigan, Huff 2021, Yasha

Fig. 5.5. Daonne Huff, *Life Savers Are Red and Round (Sickle Cell)* from the Rutgers Print Collaborative portfolio, 2018. Color polymer letterpress. 19×13 in. (48×33 cm). Collection Zimmerli Art Museum at Rutgers University. Gift of the Rutgers Print Collaborative. 2020.014.004.008. Courtesy of the artist.

Lifesavers are Red and Round (sickle cell)

Chubby cheeked with a full head of
hair, came to the world eyes swollen
shut nestled in fat. A red face cooled
to brown. A little girl, a little black
girl, a little Alabama black girl, a
little Alabama black girl that carries,
that carries a trait, that carries a
trait a trait a trait,
like millions.

life
these lives
                    Lives
        lives

                    Lost

                    breathe

*YOUR BABY
    IS NOT*

*YOUR INFANT
DOES NOT HAVE*

*WILL NEVER
DEVELOP THIS*

Hemoglobin	(Red)
Red	(Blood)
Blood	(Anemia)
Anemia	(Iron)
Iron	(Sickle)
Sickle	(Agriculture)
Agriculture	(Cotton)
Cotton	(Black earth)
Black earth	(Black hands)
Black hands	(Black lives)
Black lives	(Trauma)
Trauma	(Inheritance)
Inheritance	(DNA)

BREATHE

*try
for me, little ones, little little
                        ones*

*puff out, inflate, inflate inflate
                        til
            fully fully whole
                round round*

                round
                whole

but
you &
you &
you &&&&&&
&&&&&& you
do,   did.

Mutations
Genetics

Organs, they collapse
Life, be shortened

Henrietta, save
                me.

                Dice
                Blow
                Match the

            For
        SS SS
            SS SS SS
                SS

in episodes:
different night,
different time,
different day,
different day,
different time,
different night,
episodes in:

G E N E   G E N E   G E N E

THEN Connect the

M A R R O W M A R R O W M A R R O W

Take me to
        the

        AND

    HERE   Chance chance chances

                        25% 25% 25% 25% 25%
                                percent

    IS HOW

    IT WORKS: *Is that why
                    I'm drawn to
                    I'm compelled to
                    fall for
                    the color of
                    other other other
                    ness
                    ness
                    ness*

First comes love
Then comes

Dice
Blow
Match the

A   C   S

transfuse me

refresh me

cleanse me

baptize me me me in

*safety safety for my
future babies?*

Pain (relentless)

~~YOU ARE ALONE~~

clean

clean

THEN Connect the

Blessed be

Does anyone else have it?

No, just you.

You're special.

blessed be be
be the ones
who carry who

carry

CARRY the
burden in this

Blood Blood Blood
Blood Blood Blood
Blood Blood Blood
Blood Blood Blood
Blood Blood Blood

STEFANIE JACKSON (1961-)

Caged in the Circus of Civilization, 1994

This lithograph capitalizes on the power of the medium to deliver bold fields of color while simultaneously translating the sensitivity of the hand in the rendered line. On display are conceptions of Black life collapsed into the surreal architecture of Jackson's mapping. Surrealism refers to a movement in art and culture in the first half of the twentieth century. An interest in the bizarre, peculiar relationships between subjects and forms characterized the movement. André Breton, a pioneer of surrealism, stated that its purpose was to resolve the previously contradictory conditions of "dream and reality . . . into a kind of absolute reality, a *surreality*."[2] Jackson notes surrealism as an important influence, thus one must consider the framework of the surreal, the meeting place of the dream and reality within the space of this print.

A storefront's window box displays and the glass doors of an entryway demarcate the composition of the print. Behind each pane of glass are some rendering of reality captured by the architecture that frames each scene. Chained and hooded bodies of Black people wrap a column in the upper right corner—symbolizing slavery as a structural component of this building. The image to the center shows four bodies hung by their necks from ropes, making the violence even more graphic. Jackson adds the concentric circles of a shooting target and dresses the hanging Black men in clothing with images of bullets. This signifies how the death of the Black man seems inevitable.

In the upper left corner are allegories of the moral dilemmas facing Black life. A razor wire fence—a sign for incarceration—an advertisement for liquor, and the exquisite corpse of a body gambling without a mind. In place of that mind is a Black-faced Sambo or pickaninny—a racist depiction of a Black person previously circulated as popular media. Below these vices of the pop culture imaginary, to the lower left corner, Black people embrace one another, possibly in mourning, representing the Black family.

In the opposite corner, a group of men and women gather around a radio or are in conversation with one another, representing an informed community. These images of the family and community are to either side of the door, maybe even on the other side of it. The toy body of a Black woman is at the threshold of the storefront. While not in the architecture, the structure controls her body with red strings attached to her limbs, making her a marionette. The floor tiles come to resemble a circus ring at her feet.

On the ground is the cruel grin of a minstrel—the ringleader to this performance. Jackson places a whip to the right of the figure's foot. Collectively, these vignettes suggest how mundane the experience of racial violence has become. Anything can happen, even just walking to the store.

—KYLE B. CO.

LITERATURE: Rao and Stasio, Schneede, Welch

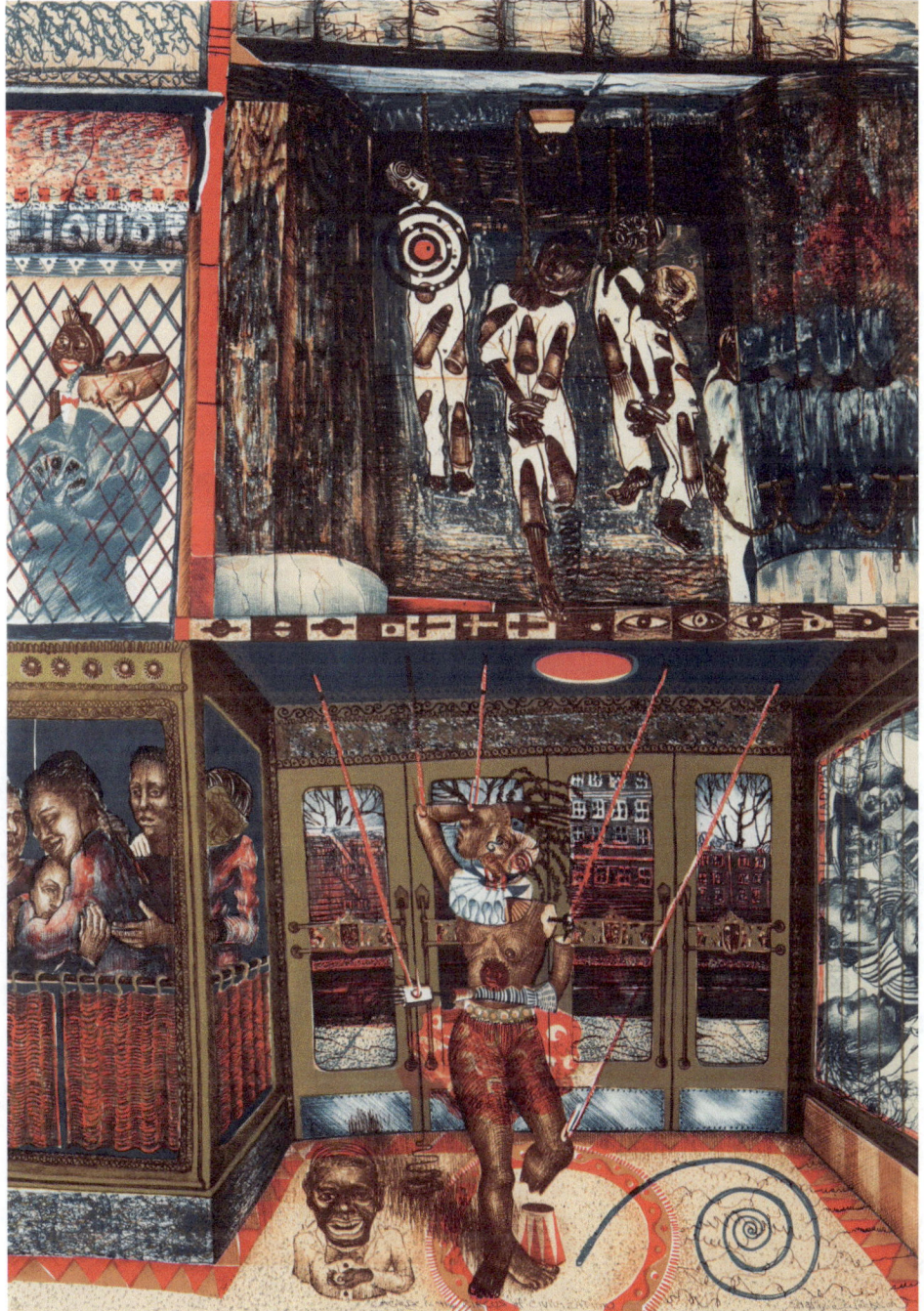

Fig. 5.6. Stefanie Jackson, *Caged in the Circus of Civilization*, 1994. Color lithograph with chine collé and metallic powder. 4115/16×295/8 in. (106.5×75 cm). Collection Zimmerli Art Museum at Rutgers University. Gift of the Brodsky Center at Rutgers, The State University of New Jersey. 1995.0133. © Stefanie Jackson.

I like to take hostility and turn it into something sweet for me
—you know, like the blues?
I think that's the story of Black people in America:
taking that bad stuff and making it into something good
—sing the blues over it.

—FAITH RINGGOLD,
2008

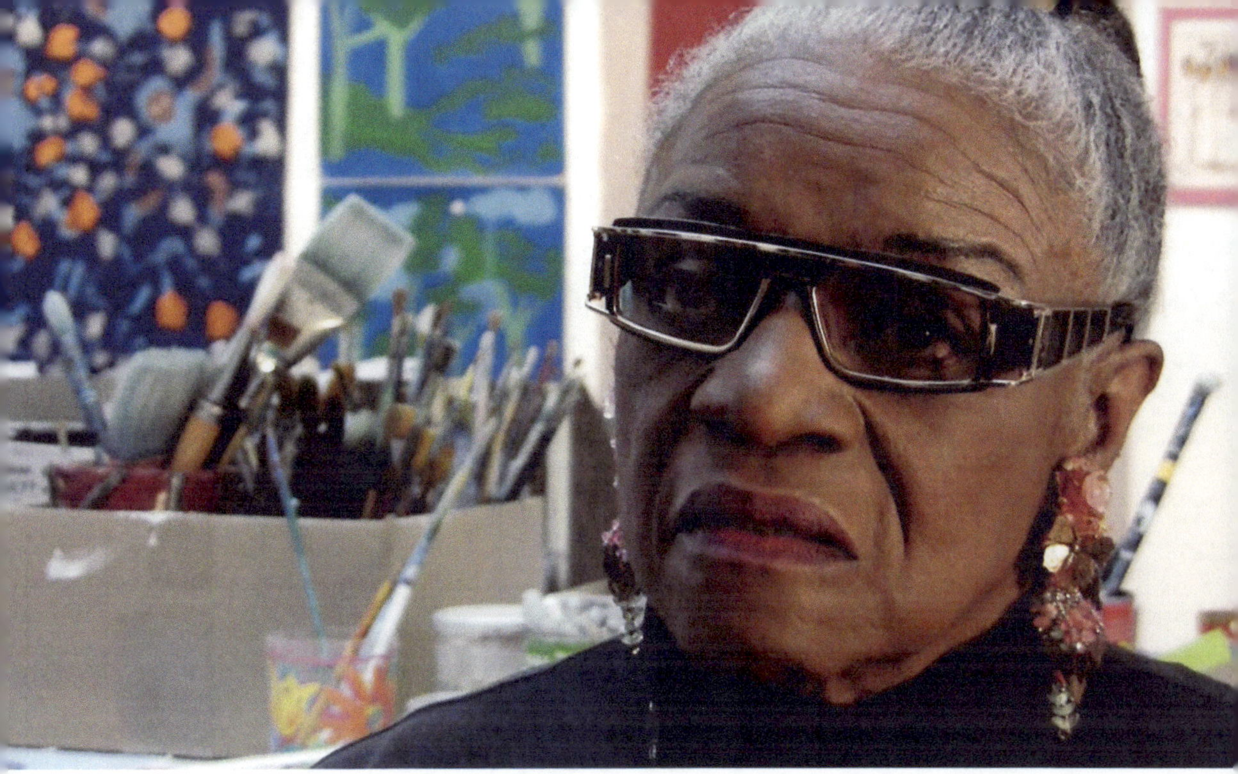

Fig. 5.7. Faith Ringgold in a still from *Taking Flight: An Interview with Faith Ringgold*, 2008.

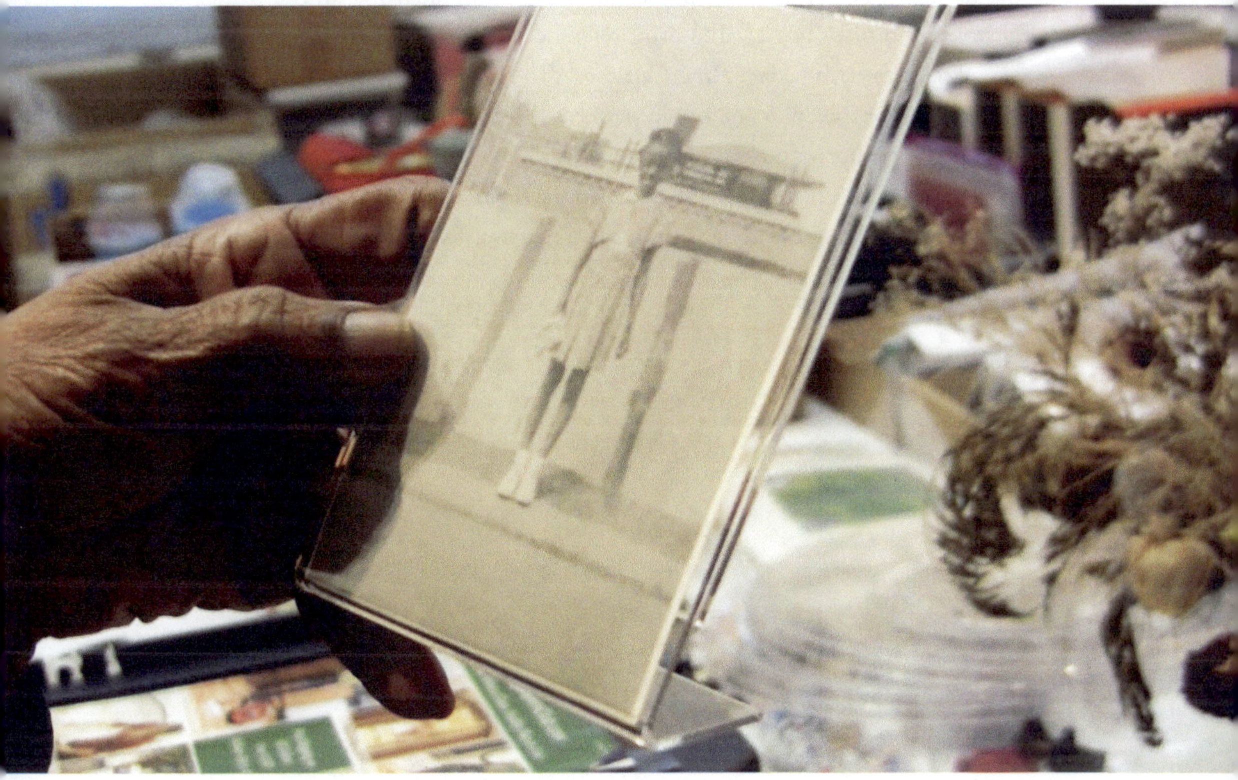

Fig. 5.8. Ringgold holding a picture of her younger self in a still from *Taking Flight: An Interview with Faith Ringgold*, 2008.

FAITH RINGGOLD (1930-2024)
Somebody Stole My Broken Heart, 2004

In this print, two Black women stand with their arms open in exchange with the band, the music, and the room. Each woman stands before her own band, brass instruments, and percussion. The bands may be playing with each other or just for the one woman they surround.

In the two groupings of figures, each woman is the center of a radiation of vibrant blue marks, reminiscent of a magnetic field. The patterning of a magnetic field is the result of magnetic materials exerting an influence on the surrounding electrical field. In this image, Ringgold has made these women magnetic forces, charged in the patterning of their dresses. The magnetic field forms at their polarities, at each woman's feet and hair, the top and bottom of their bodies, to consume the outlines of each band. The bold blue lines frame the faces of the women and the members of the band. Pushing out further, the blues is the band, is the music, is jazz. The border text narrates the scene: "Somebody stole my broken heart. Washed my tears down the drain. Sun shining through the rain. Chased the blues straight out the door. Don't hear me crying no more. Never used to see me smile. Now I'm laughing all the while. Somebody stole my broken heart." The print references a story quilt from Ringgold's series *Jazz Stories: Mama Can Sing, Papa Can Blow*. The borders of her story quilts are often filled with text or the colors of a bold pattern.

Ringgold was born and raised in New York City, and she recalls an education in jazz while growing up in Harlem. She also befriended the great saxophonist Sonny Rollins, who was the occasional nuisance to her mother when he came by her porch to play on the weekends.

−KYLE B. CO.

LITERATURE: Brodsky et al., Ringgold 1998

Notes

1. Lisa E. Farrington, "Emma Amos: Art as Legacy," *Woman's Art Journal* 28, no. 1 (Spring–Summer 2007): 9.
2. André Breton, "Manifesto of Surrealism" (1924), in *Manifestoes of Surrealism*, trans. Richard Seaver and Helen R. Lane (University of Michigan Press, 1972), 14.

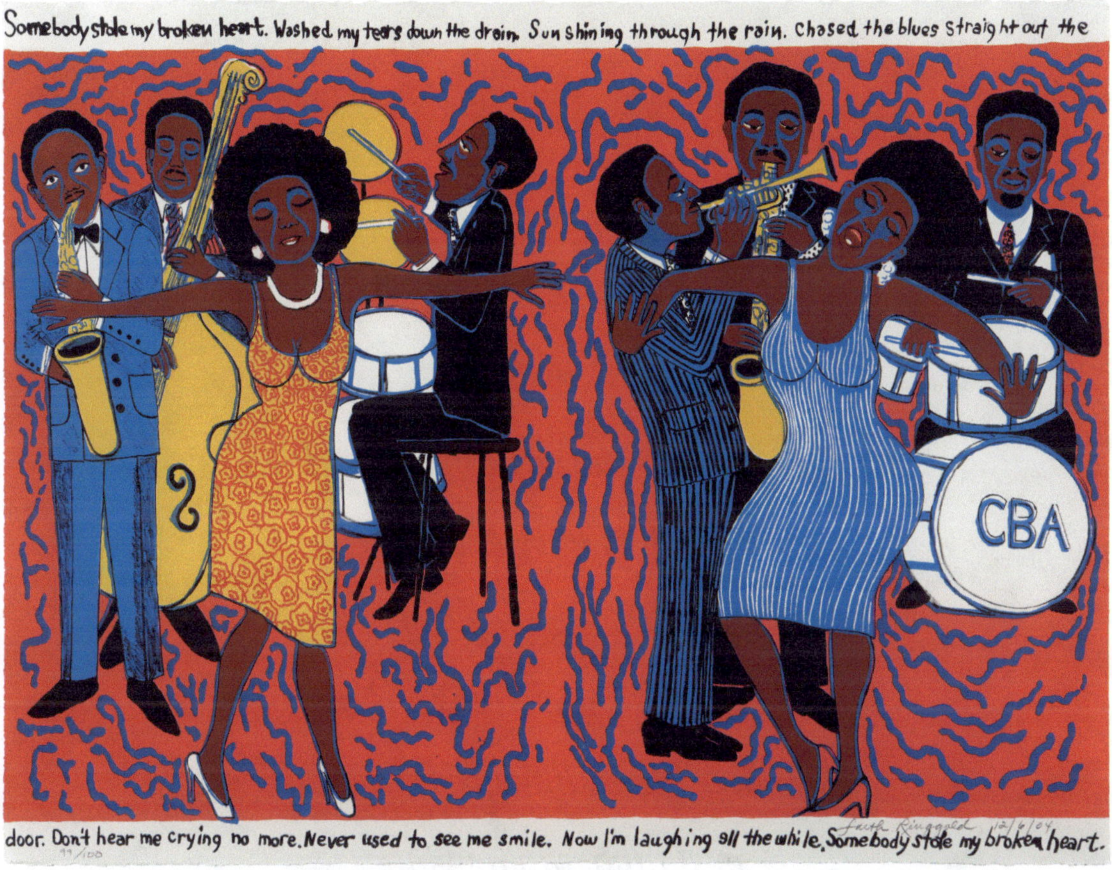

Somebody stole my broken heart. Washed my tears down the drain. Sun shining through the rain. Chased the blues straight out the

door. Don't hear me crying no more. Never used to see me smile. Now I'm laughing all the while. Somebody stole my broken heart.

Fig. 5.9. Faith Ringgold, *Somebody Stole My Broken Heart*, 2004. Color lithograph. 221/2 × 301/16 in. (57.1 × 76.4 cm). Collection Zimmerli Art Museum at Rutgers University. Gift of the Brodsky Center at Rutgers, The State University of New Jersey. 2007.0026. © 2026 Faith Ringgold / Artists Rights Society (ARS), New York. Courtesy ACA Galleries, New York.

There is a challenge in printmaking.

It is physical.

Understanding the chemistry

of an element that you're working on,

whether it be a lithographic stone

or a lithographic plate,

is like a science.

—MARGO HUMPHREY,
1995

6

Process and Materiality

JASMINE DARIA CANNON, HELEN GAO, EMILY HU, GRACE KIM, MICHAEL RANDALL, AND AUDREY ROCLORE

THE WORKS IN THIS EXHIBITION speak to the master craftsmanship of Black women artists. Printmaking is a laborious and meditative process that requires planning. The artists use a wide range of handmade and mechanical techniques, from traditional woodcuts to newer methods of digital printing. Each step requires the artist to directly engage with a new material. Wood and linoleum challenge the artist's hand with resistance as they carve into the material. Lithography is another lengthy process, from drawing the image on a plate, treating it with acid, and applying an oil-based ink. The artist then covers the level parts in ink and transfers the design to paper by running the carved materials and paper through a press.

> The birth of a print occurs in a single instantaneous moment
> when the ink meets paper.

Some major themes emerge from these artists' processes: time, in the sense of timeliness and legacy, and the construction and deconstruction of self. Elizabeth Catlett once said of her own prints, "Printmaking had to do with the moment. I thought of sculpture as something more durable and timeless."[1] Lorna Simpson challenges this notion with her sculpture *III*, which contains three wishbones made of indestructible bronze, bendable silicone rubber, and fragile ceramic. Simpson's final product holds multiple temporalities. This is also true of the works of many artists highlighted here.

Stitching fragments together becomes a way of revisiting childhood, of returning to one's roots, and of making sense of oneself. Exploring this catalog makes clear that the artistic process and chosen materials are vital to the artists' stories and messages.

–HELEN GAO AND EMILY HU

NELL IRVIN PAINTER (1942-)

Wise Woman Disappears, 2017

The mesmerizing and intricate background of this woodcut draws from a detail of a cloth that Painter bought in Nigeria in the 1960s. She loved that the fabric spoke to another origin, culture, and time. Repeated triangular and diagonal patterns and textures frame two silhouettes that face each other across a vertical axis. The diptych composition, which mimics a book closing in on itself, further emphasizes these repetitions. Both figures are indigo ink silhouettes. One is matte with no interior detail, while the other is overlaid with line drawing. The flat forms stand out against the patterned background. The right side of the image instantly draws viewers in, before they notice that the left side is "disappearing" in one dark shade of indigo.

The theme of disappearing resonates with Painter's personal experience as a second-career artist, a path she began at the age of sixty-four.[2] She argues that after a certain age women "seem to vanish—from our history books, off our screens, out of our corporate boardrooms," and she calls this phenomenon "getting disappeared."[3] The monotone color theme here emphasizes the phenomenon of disappearing, as if the silhouettes are literally vanishing into the darkness.

Painter created this piece as part of her residency at the Brodsky Center. She was especially interested in woodcuts because they retain traces of the artistic process. Her primary goal with this piece was to experiment with carving and to discover how to render a figurative image. She used as a reference a photograph of herself in 2016 from MacDowell, an artists' residency program in New Hampshire.

This was Painter's very first woodcut and her first attempt at depicting dark skin. During her previous academic career, she had made many paintings but had not worked with models with darker skin tones. She recognized the challenges in representing the Black body, which carries the weight of negative stereotyping rooted in American history. By creating this self-portrait, Painter did not worry about making the figure a battleground for commentaries on beauty and instead treats herself as an iconographic motif.

–HELEN GAO

LITERATURE: Painter, Painter and Morsiani, Schwob

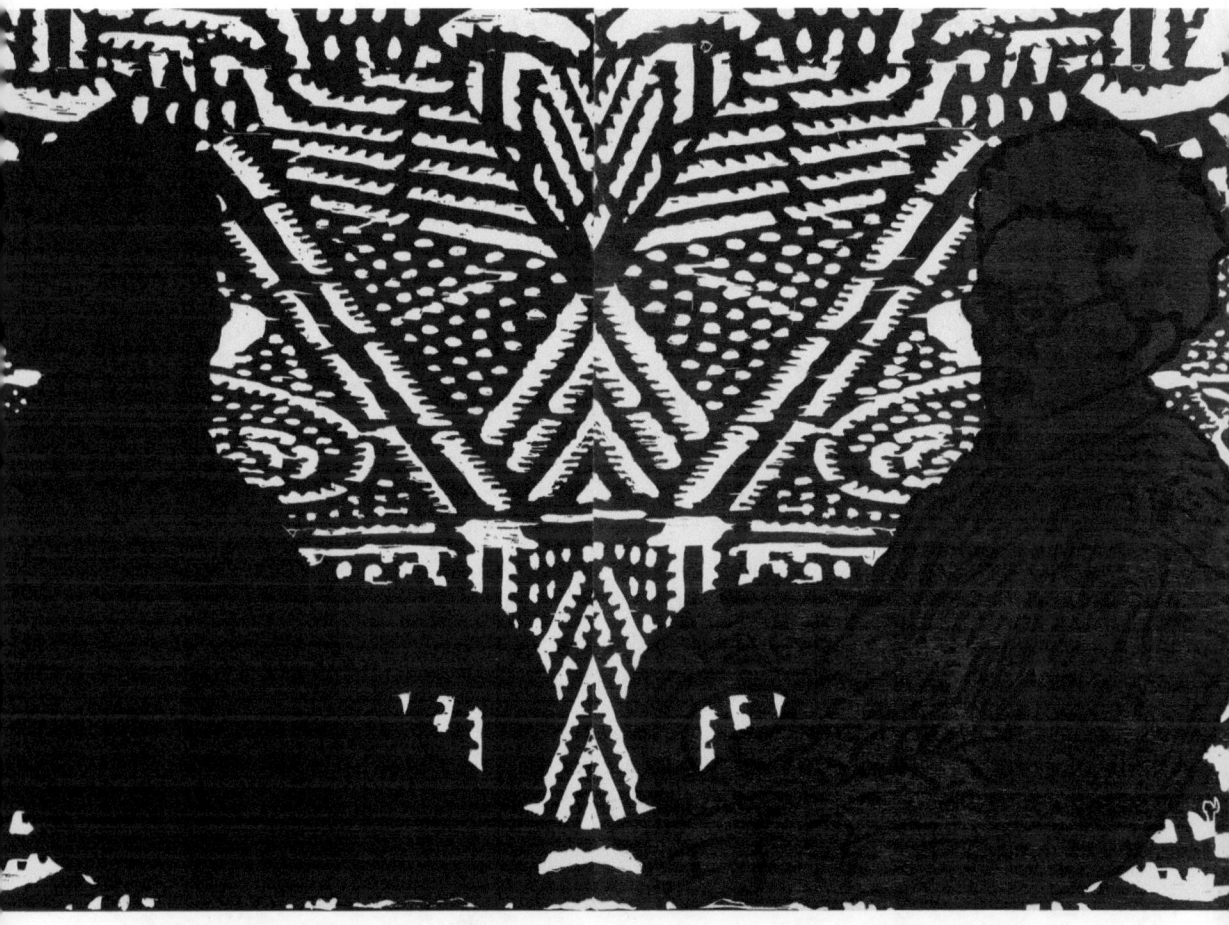

Fig. 6.1. Nell Irvin Painter, *Wise Woman Disappears*, 2017. Woodcut and polymer relief diptych on Sekishu white paper. 237/8×357/8 in. (60.7×91.2 cm). Collection Zimmerli Art Museum at Rutgers University. Gift of the Brodsky Center at Rutgers, The State University of New Jersey. 2018.034.001A,B. Courtesy of Nell Irvin Painter.

HOWARDENA PINDELL (1943-)

Kyoto (Positive Negative), 1980

Five beige rectangular grids appear like censor bars, framed by a thick *momiji* red border. The Japanese word symbolizes the color of fiery autumn leaves. In Japanese culture, *momiji* commands worship and respect. Pindell uses this special color and Japanese rice paper for this print to evoke her first trip to Japan in 1979. But the red color holds a double meaning. On a childhood road trip, a root beer stand operator gave Pindell and her father mugs with red circles on the bottom. The color was a way for the stand's operators to restrict that ware to Black Americans under Jim Crow laws. Even with this seemingly abstract piece, she drew from her personal memories to expose racism in her life and in the art world.

Confetti-like crimson dots scatter across the neutral strips. A close examination reveals that each dot is associated with tiny vectors and numbers, appearing as scars and scratches and giving the print's surface a bumpy texture. Though seemingly random, the dots have a highly symbolic and personal meaning. Pindell's father was a mathematician, who inspired her methodical approach to the artwork.

Pindell made this lithograph during a multiyear printmaking collaboration with Judith Solodkin of SOLO Impression. Solodkin was the first master printer with whom she collaborated. This experience solidified her interest in printmaking and abstraction.

–HELEN GAO

LITERATURE: Cahan, Franks and Steele, Pindell, Schor et al., Steinhauer

Fig. 6.2. Howardena Pindell, *Kyoto (Positive Negative)*, 1980. Color lithograph, etching, and chine collé on paper. 269/16 × 203/8 in. (66.7 × 51.7 cm). Collection Zimmerli Art Museum at Rutgers University. Gift of Doris Weintraub, Bristol Art Editions. 82.043.001. Courtesy of the artist and Garth Greenan Gallery, New York.

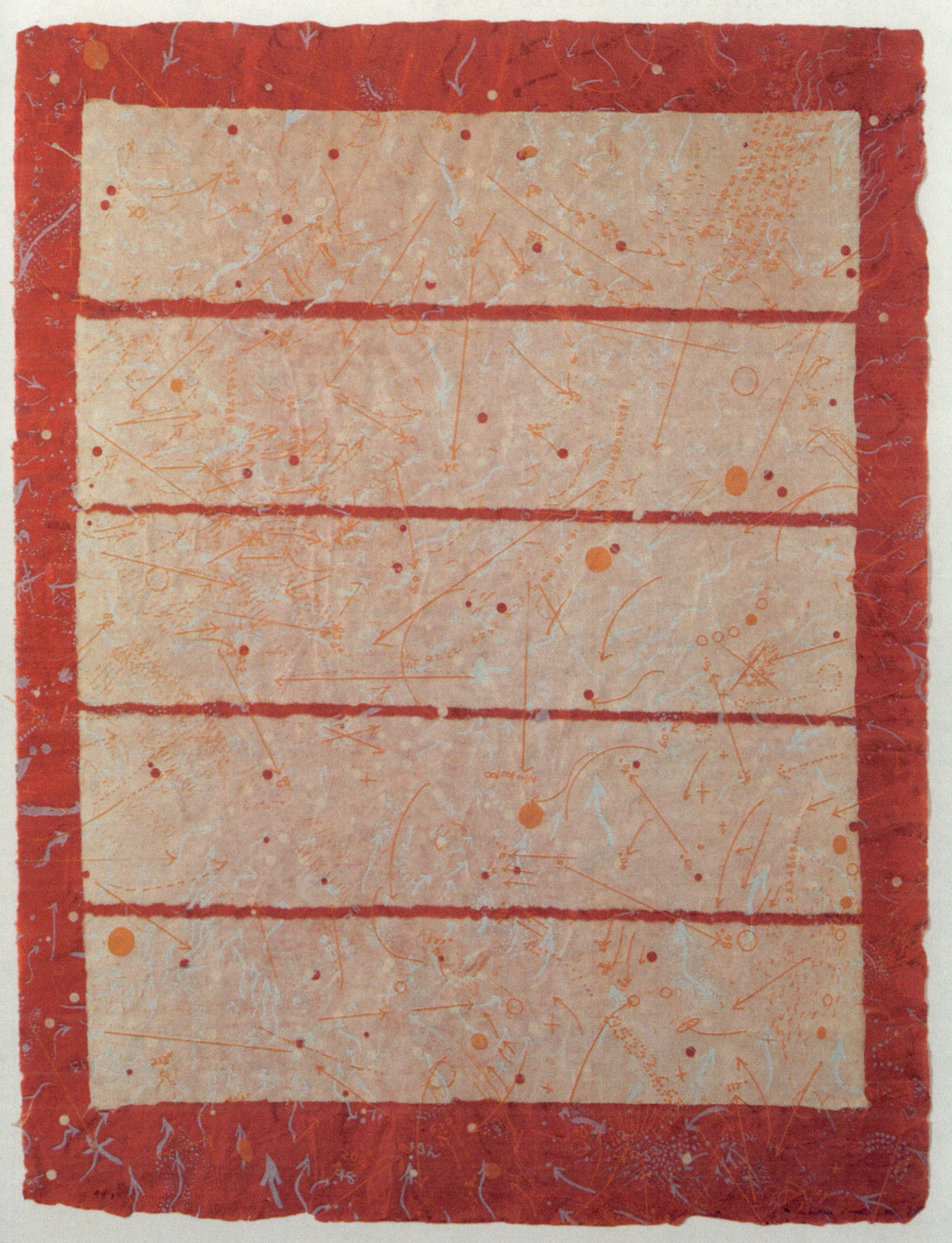

HOWARDENA PINDELL (1943-)

Flight/Fields, 1988-1989

In 1972, Pindell co-founded the A.I.R. Gallery, the first artist-run nonprofit art gallery for female artists in the United States. Located in Brooklyn, New York, the A.I.R. Gallery allowed female artists to curate their own exhibitions and step outside the boundaries set by traditional museums. Pindell's work in the 1970s and 1980s became increasingly abstract as she was exposed to artists at the gallery and at the Museum of Modern Art (MoMA). The collection of Akan batakari tunics on display at the MoMA's 1972 *African Textiles and Decorative Arts* exhibition deeply resonated with her and influenced her future artistic processes. Recalling a later trip to Ghana, Pindell described watching people weave kente cloth in a cultural center in Kumasi.

Her interest in African textiles led her to deconstruct canvases and reconstruct them by sewing the pieces back together. The laborious process of deconstruction and reconstruction is especially clear in this print. The piece's layering of different papers and combining of printing techniques with detailed etchings reflect Pindell's meticulous approach to design. The color blocking and squares that fit like a puzzle allude to quilt making.

The pattern in this print draws from Pindell's personal experience of flying over a grid-like field of pastures. She dislikes flying but has conquered that fear through her dedication to combating racism and discrimination, which has required her to travel frequently for lectures and art exhibits.

–HELEN GAO

LITERATURE: Pindell

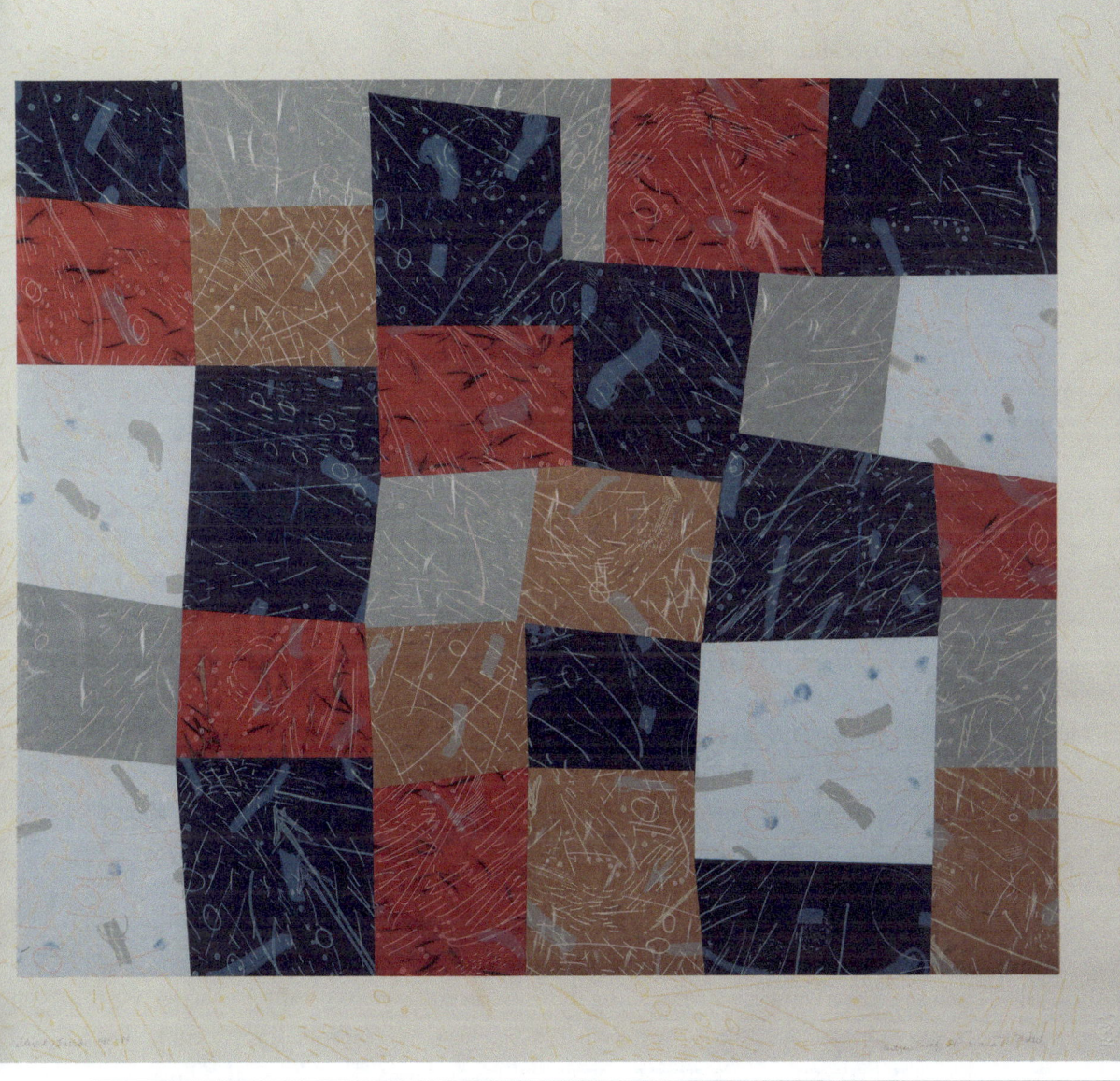

Fig. 6.3. Howardena Pindell, *Flight/Fields*, 1988–1989. Color lithograph, etching, chine collé on paper. 19 3/8 × 23 1/16 in. (49.2 × 58.6 cm). Collection Zimmerli Art Museum at Rutgers University. Gift of Judith Solodkin, SOLO Impression. 1989.0140. Courtesy of the artist and Garth Greenan Gallery, New York.

HOWARDENA PINDELL (1943-)

Video Drawing: Football Series, 1977

The *Video Drawings* series began when Pindell drew vectors and numbers, like those etched into the lithographs *Kyoto* and *Flight/Fields*, onto a sheet of acetate. She stuck the sheet on her television, using the static from the screen. Then she took photographs of the images that formed in front of her eyes and selected the most interesting ones to be a part of her portfolio. Defying typical expectations of how certain materials work together, she seamlessly integrated the static plastic sheet with a moving image to produce the final still image. Through the lens of the camera, the final image collapses the original materials such that the foreground and background are indistinguishable.

Creating video art is technically demanding. It requires repeated experimentation with shutter speed and exposure time. Pindell's *Video Drawings* pioneered work for succeeding artists who work with photographic manipulation and multimedia. These photographic works differ dramatically from her other works from the 1970s and 1980s. But they all involve a laborious process of production and manipulation of various media.

Pindell's travels to Africa inspired this series, and much of her other works. In many West African cultures, bodily adornment is a way to communicate with the spirits. She felt that this kind of aesthetic transcendence was lacking in Western contemporary art and strove to fill that gap. The plastic sheets in her *Video Drawings* are surfaces for her vector markings, much like how the body is a surface for ornaments. Juxtaposed against a TV screen, the materials transcend into another realm beyond traditional uses.

Her vectors and arrows in the *Football Series* resemble a coach's notes on the plays. These markers break down the structural rigidity of the images by underscoring the movement of figures across the TV. While the acetate sheet with its pre-drawn content suggests a certain way of reading the movements, they could also be abstractions from other analyses and other personal experiences. Thus, Pindell leaves spectators hanging between a predetermined order and randomness. The blur of the video further underlines this chaos. The final photographs retain marks of raster lines, image blur, and RGB (red, green, blue) discoloration.

–HELEN GAO

LITERATURE: Deveney, Tempini

Fig. 6.4. Howardena Pindell, *Video Drawing: Football Series*, 1977. Kodak color Cibachrome print. 45/8×65/8 in. (11.7×16.8 cm). Collection Zimmerli Art Museum at Rutgers University. Gift of Barbara Sunderman Hoerner. 2017.015.002. Courtesy of the artist and Garth Greenan Gallery, New York.

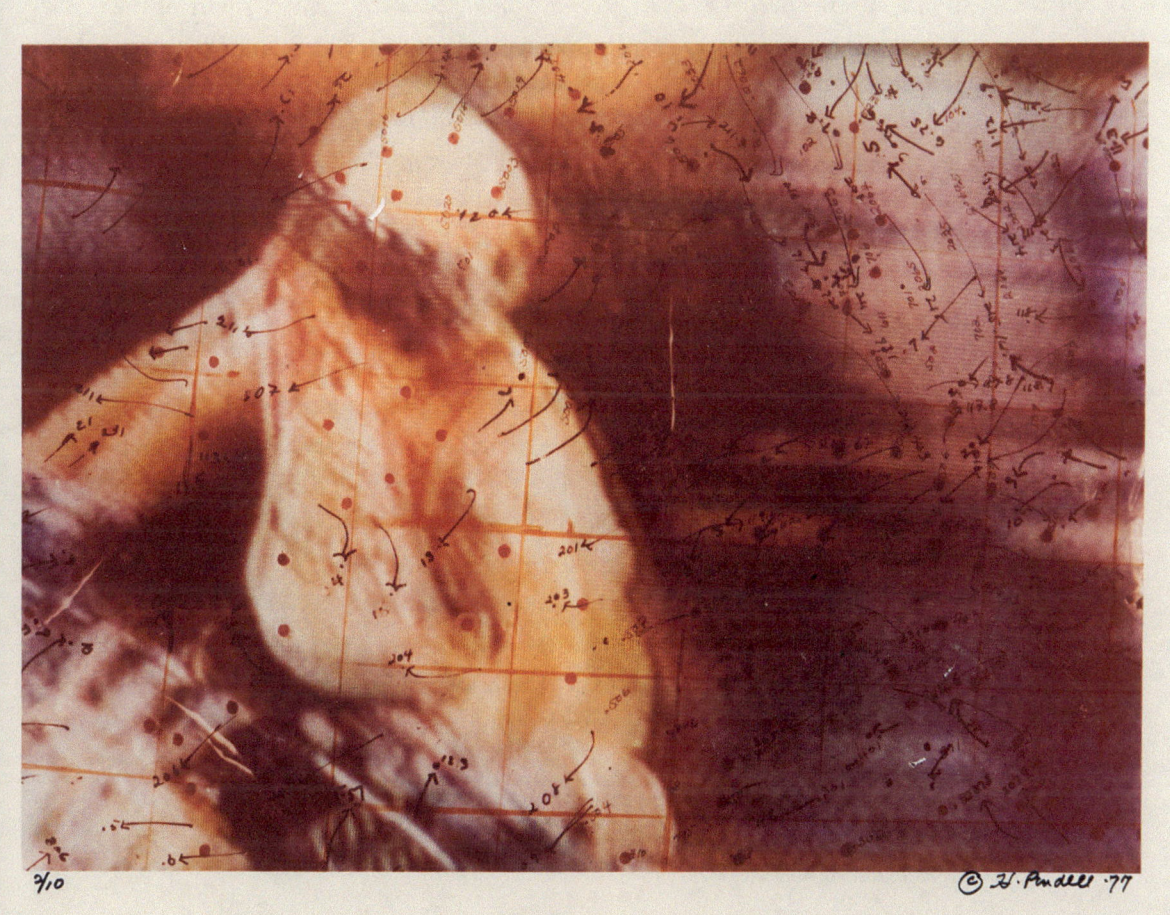

SHARON E. SUTTON (1941-)

Streets Paved in Moonlight and Candlelit Cafes from the American Portfolio, 1980

Sutton deconstructs the view of a street with geometric abstraction in her work. Through uniformity and repetition, the eye melds the warm hues to create a solid reflection of lights. In this way, viewers hold a still image that also moves with the eye and draws into question the human eye's perception of everyday views such as lights reflected on a street. *Streets Paved in Moonlight and Candlelit Cafes* is a part of the *American Portfolio*, which features works from other artists such as Romare Bearden, Lester Johnson, Alice Neel, Henry Pearson, and Will Barnet, and touches on the experiences and quotidian aspects of American life. Karl Lunde, who wrote the introduction to the *American Portfolio*, describes this work as a "spiritual painting, declaring the reality of intangibles and the omnipresence of energy and light."[4] Thus, the energy of this work, rather than a visual likeness to objects in the physical world, pushes viewers to consider a world they cannot see, that of music.

Sutton was a professional musician in New York City before becoming an architect, and most of her artworks display aspects of musicality. Here, she uses patterns that resemble, in part, a music sheet in which dots, like music notes, float. The visual integration of motion and rhythm also mimics the act of reading a music sheet, which becomes an audio-visual immersive experience. In an interview, she commented on the kinship of space and music: "If you go into a hall that has great acoustics, you're a better performer, so I was very aware of the importance of space."[5] She even considers how a viewer in a gallery space might interact with this two-dimensional wall piece by slightly staggering her columns so that they mimic the natural wave in walking. Sutton's work is thus the amalgamation of her combined professional training and personal interests in architecture, music, psychology, philosophy, and art.

–GRACE KIM

LITERATURE: Akigbogun, Columbia University GSAPP, Lunde, University of Washington

Fig. 6.5. Sharon E. Sutton, *Streets Paved in Moonlight and Candlelit Cafes* from the *American Portfolio*, 1980. Color lithograph on paper. 285/8 × 211/8 in. (72.7 × 53.7 cm). Collection Zimmerli Art Museum at Rutgers University. Gift of Gordon Meisner. 81.036.002. Image courtesy of Sharon Egretta Sutton.

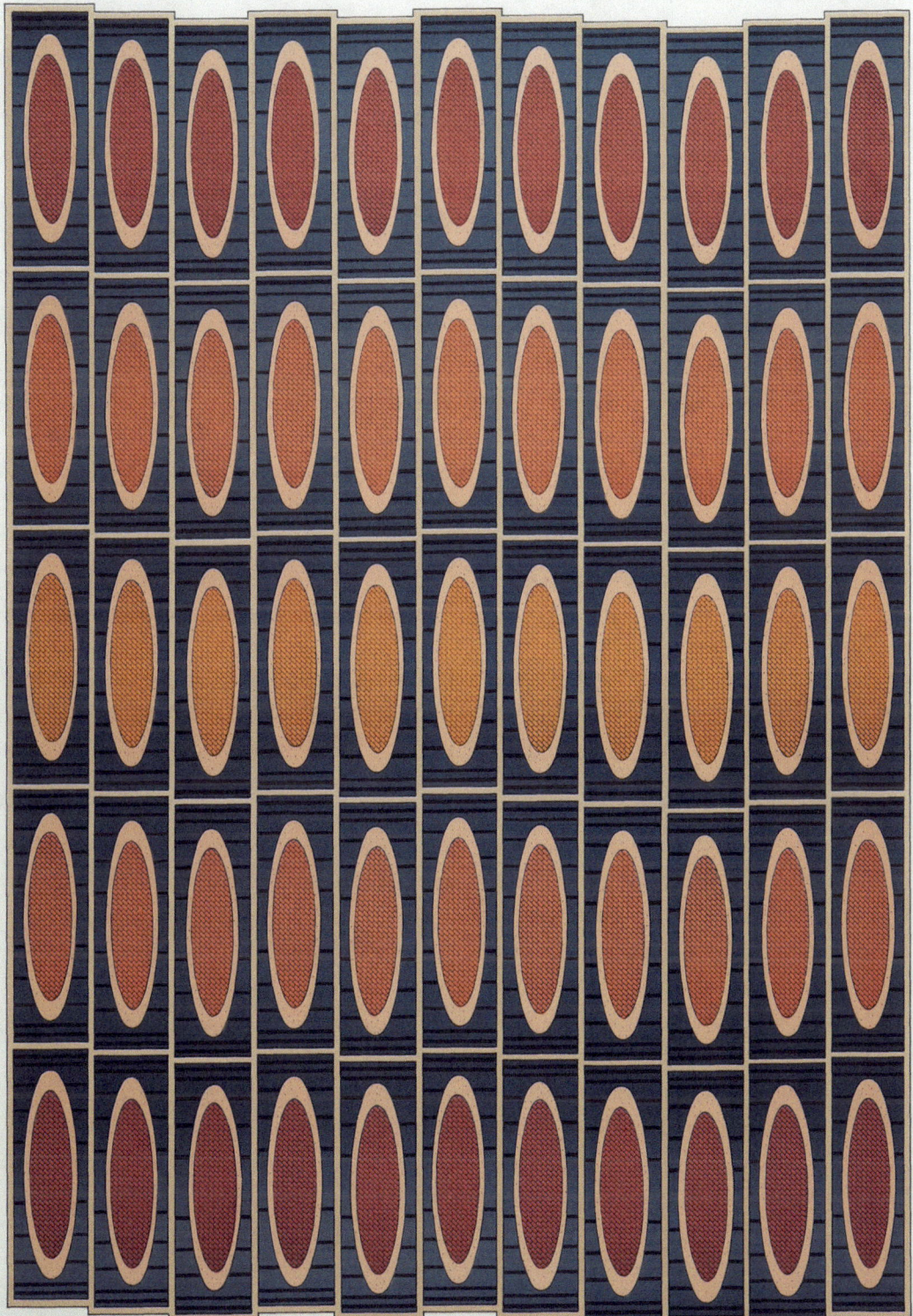

SHINIQUE SMITH (1971-)

Salt & Pepper from the Ecstasy: Exit Art portfolio, 2010

This print is part of an Exit Art portfolio that features six other prints by the artists Rina Banerjee, Willie Cole, Papo Colo, James Nares, Kenny Scharf, and Stephen Talasnik. Exit Art was a nonprofit cultural center and art gallery. From 1982 to 2012, the gallery, which focused on representing the underdog, offered contemporary visual art, performance art, theater, and installations. Situated in various locations across Manhattan, its last space was a two-story gallery in Hell's Kitchen.

Over the past twenty years, Smith developed a visually poetic style inspired by her travels and early graffiti roots in Baltimore. In this piece, one can see a label with the words *Salt & Pepper* interspersed among magazine cutouts. Some cutouts have repeating patterns, others have similar forms. Smith pieced together additional shapes in more abstract and experimental ways. The different black-and-white patterns meld together.

Arranging the cutouts in a collage, she then took a paintbrush and made a deft stroke across the canvas that connected all the collage elements. Looking closely behind the bold black brushstrokes are scribbles that resemble calligraphy. Thus, the artwork evokes her unique graffiti-like, flowing art style. Through her process of collaging and painting, Smith builds a complex vocabulary that interweaves brushwork with graphic materials.

–HELEN GAO

LITERATURE: Gopnik, Exit Art Archive, MICA, Pinder 2008

BARBARA BULLOCK (1938-)

Water Spirit, 1992

This mythical lizard-like creature consists of bold colors and patterns juxtaposed with black tones, creating visual and figurative depth. The use of the color black is spiritually evocative and holy. Black symbolizes natural elements, including creatures both real and imagined, or a combination of both, as in the case of the *Water Spirit*.

The paper sculpture investigates the dichotomous and inherently feminine nature of water in its ability to simultaneously create and destroy life. This belief and its associated imagery of water deities is manifest in West African Vodun, as well as Haitian Vodou and folk Catholicism. Bullock explores elements of African spiritual, cultural, and artistic practices in her work, while also articulating her own experience as a Black woman in America.

This piece remains striking in its dynamism and firmness, despite its fragile paper materiality. The dramatic movement within the collage might allow the central feminine spirit figure, draped in purple and blue tones, to go unnoticed. The colorful surface is enough to both capture and captivate any beholder.

–AUDREY ROCLORE

LITERATURE: National Museum of African Art, Petrucci Family Foundation Collection

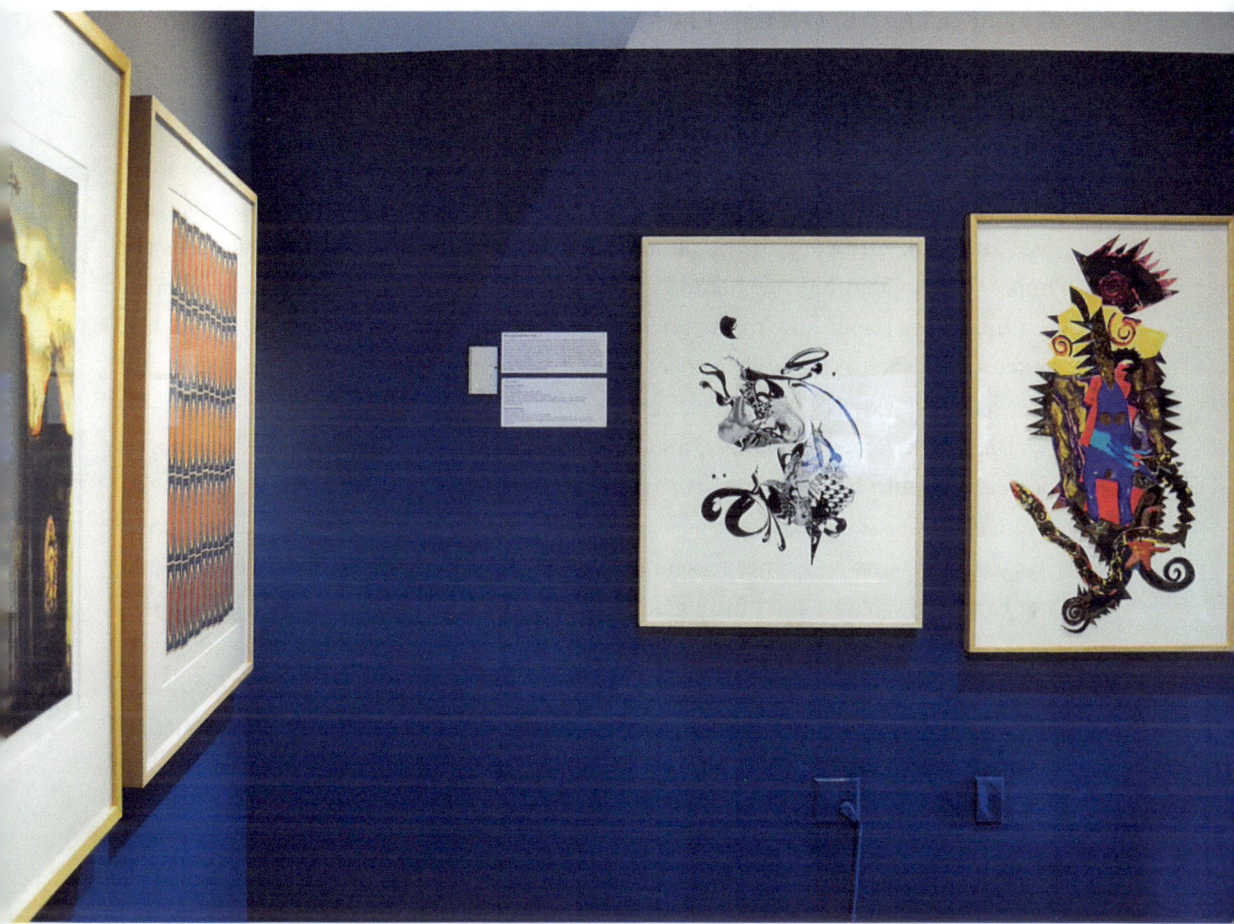

Fig. 6.6. Installation view of Gallery 104A of the DWAS. Shinique Smith, *Salt & Pepper* (front left) from the *Ecstasy: Exit Art* portfolio, 2010. Screen print with collage and hand additions. 301/16×223/16 in. (76.3×56.3 cm). Collection Zimmerli Art Museum at Rutgers University. Gift of Exit Art. 2013.001.004.05. Barbara Bullock, *Water Spirit* (front right), 1992. Color lithograph with chine collé and collage on handmade and Rives white paper. 263/4×421/2 in. (67.9×107.9 cm). Collection Zimmerli Art Museum at Rutgers University. Gift of the Brodsky Center at Rutgers, The State University of New Jersey. 1993.0369. Renée Stout, *Waiting for Jimi* (side wall, left), 2006; Sharon E. Sutton, *Streets Paved in Moonlight and Candlelit Cafes* (side wall, right), 1980. 2022. Nicole Ianuzelli, photographer.

CHAKAIA BOOKER (1953-)

Quality Time
from *Six×Four: Exit Art* portfolio, 2004

Quality Time explores the role of family and intergenerational knowledge. Booker intricately wove and manipulated rubber to create the two repeating images of a youthful face and milk cartons with the phrase "Say no to drugs." The piece emphasizes the importance of sharing information with young people, who are navigating competing messaging about how to interact with the environments in which they live. Her other works, such as the widely collected and circulated *Mother and Child* (1994) and *Not That Daughter* (1998), also explore the role of family.

The numbers three, six, nine, and twelve score the image, suggestive of the hands of a clock, signifying real time, its passing, and the importance of spending time with younger, impressionable loved ones. Since Booker often works with rubber materials recycled from cars and other machinery, she is also signaling the importance of taking care of the planet for future generations. Time is ticking, albeit silently, in this work, and the time for saving the planet for future generations is running out.

The alternative arts space Exit Art produced the work as part of the *Six x Four* portfolio. Founded in 1982 and closed in 2012, Exit Art was a New York City gallery that prided itself on exhibiting complex art pieces by underdog artists in the art world—underrepresented communities, women, non-mainstream practitioners.

–JASMINE DARIA CANNON

LITERATURE: Booker, Corbett, Cotter 1998, Genocchio

Fig. 6.7. Chakaia Booker, *Quality Time* from the *Six×Four: Exit Art* portfolio, 2004. Vulcanized synthetic rubber relief. 261/8×203/8 in. (66.3×51.7 cm). Collection Zimmerli Art Museum at Rutgers University. Gift of Peter Frey. 2008.015.003.01. Courtesy of the artist and David Nolan Gallery, New York.

LORNA SIMPSON (1960-)

III, The Peter Norton Family Christmas Project, 1994

Though more commonly known for her elusive approach to photography, in this piece Lorna Simpson utilizes sculpture to explore the popular trope of "three wishes." One first confronts a cedar box featuring a Roman numeral three (III) on the top. When one removes the lid, the box reveals a Christmas card that reads "We Wish You a Merry Christmas and a Happy New Year" and displays a photo of Peter and Eileen Norton along with their children, Diana and Michael. Each year, the Norton family commissions an original piece of art as their holiday greeting, and so Simpson crafted *III* for them in 1994.

Further in the box, just past the Christmas card, is a layer of felt with an image of a wishbone printed on it along with the words *Wish #1*, *Wish #2*, and *Wish #3* centered vertically. Beneath that are three physical wishbones, organized vertically and crafted from unique materials inset in their own layer of felt. The first bone is ceramic, the second is silicone rubber, and the third, bronze.

The wishbone is familiar as a representative symbol of the "wish." Anatomically known as the furcula (a fusion of two clavicle bones found in many birds), it is pulled apart in the tradition of two persons making wishes, which can be traced back to ancient Rome. Legend holds that the person who pulls the longer fragment of the bone when making the wish will have their wish granted. The wishbone has played a role in several other works by Simpson. Here, it brings the Christmas "wish" of the Norton family to the forefront of the message.

The bones are both an analysis of tradition and an exploration of material. If one were to pull apart the ceramic bone, it would break and possibly shatter. The rubber bone would stretch and bend but ultimately return to its original form. With great difficulty, one could potentially bend the bronze bone, but it would remain intact, though misshapen. There is an irony in this experimental approach to material; Simpson offers three wishes and at once denies them by making the wishbone ritual impossible to complete.

–MICHAEL RANDALL

LITERATURE: Armand, Belisle, Boone, Ode

Notes

1. Michael Brenson, "Form That Achieves Sympathy: A Conversation with Elizabeth Catlett," *Sculpture*. April 1, 2003, https://sculpturemagazine.art/form-that-achieves-sympathy-a-conversation-with-elizabeth-catlett/.

2. Nell Painter, *Old in Art School: A Memoir of Starting Over* (Counterpoint Press, 2018), 12–13.

3. Rebecca Brown, "Disappearing Women: Nell Painter and Christine Lahti," GBH Forum Network, August 15, 2018, https://gbhforumnetwork.medium.com/disappearing-women-nell-painter-and-christine-lahti-e508da6b5271.

4. Karl Lunde, introduction to *American Portfolio* (Joseph Kleinman Fine Arts Printing, 1980).

5. Sarah Akigbogun, "In Conversation . . . Sharon Egretta Sutton," Parlour: Gender, Equity, Architecture, October 6, 2019, https://archiparlour.org/in-conversation-with-sharon-egretta-sutton/.

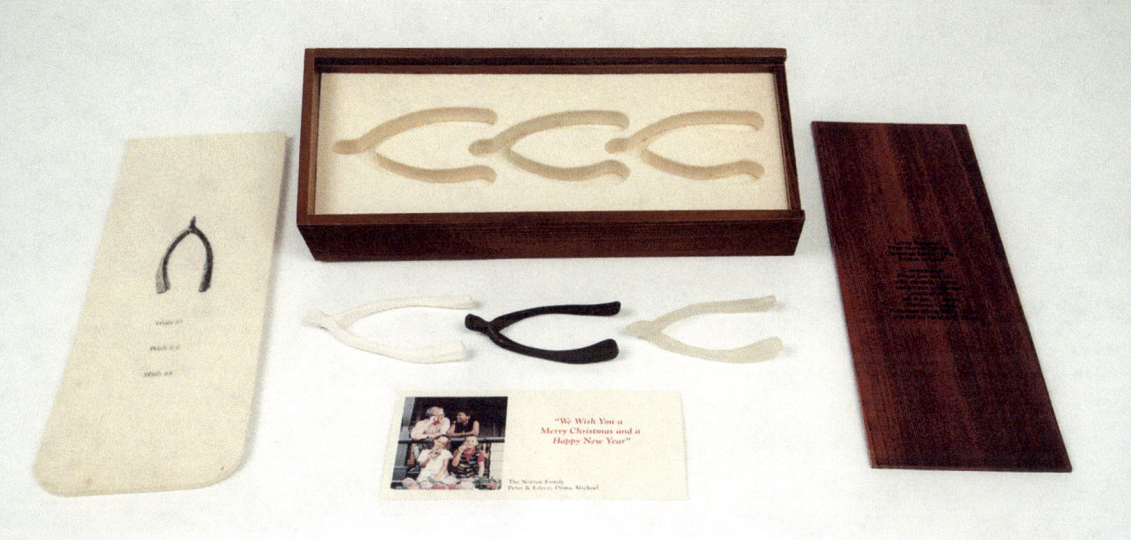

Fig. 6.8. Lorna Simpson, *III, The Peter Norton Family Christmas Project*, 1994. Mixed media, ceramic, bronze, rubber, and felt in wood box. Box: 13 5/8 x 5 3/8 x 1 1/8 in (34.6 x 12.7 x 2.8 cm). Collection Zimmerli Art Museum at Rutgers University. Gift of Phillip Dennis Cate. 1994.0665A–G. © Lorna Simpson. Courtesy of the artist and Hauser & Wirth.

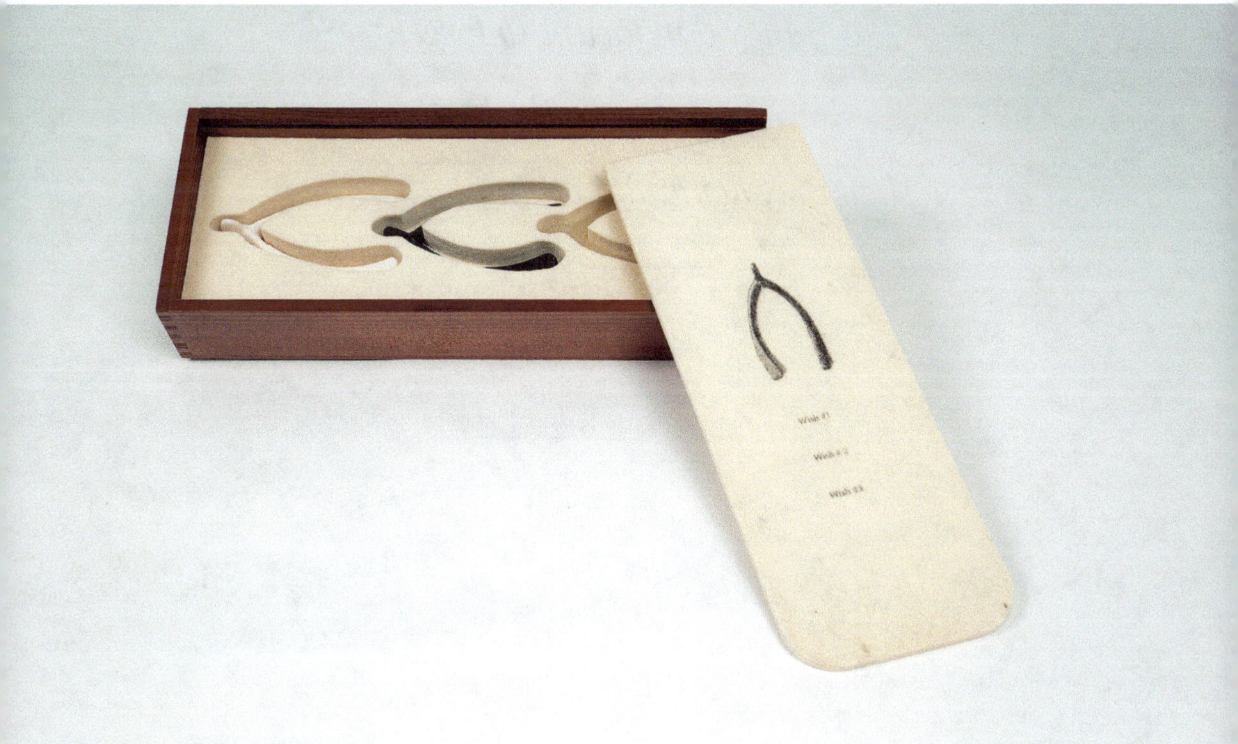

Fig. 6.9. Close-up of Lorna Simpson, *III, The Peter Norton Family Christmas Project*, 1994, depicting three wishbones and a felt print, 1994. © Lorna Simpson. Courtesy of the artist and Hauser & Wirth.

Now, women forget all the things

they don't want to remember,

and remember everything

they don't want to forget.

The dream is the truth.

Then they act and do things accordingly.

—ZORA NEALE HURSTON,
1937

7

The Art of Storytelling

JASMINE DARIA CANNON, GRACE LYNNE HAYNES,
EMILY HU, GRACE KIM, DESIREE MORALES,
AND AMBER N. WILEY

HISTORICALLY IN THE UNITED STATES, Black women were denied access and opportunity to tell their own stories and be the author of their own image. Storytelling gives us a lens into the radical imagination that invites the creation of our own alternate universe through complex narratives that redefine our realities and shape our existence. This exhibition put the Black woman's gaze at the forefront and allowed the audience to see the internal world of Black women and the creative stories they produce when given agency. Their narratives take on a multitude of forms, from folklore and mythology to spirituality.

Works such as Faith Ringgold's *Letter from Birmingham City Jail* address notable events of the classical Civil Rights Movement. In this piece, Ringgold utilizes the book format, presenting Dr. Martin Luther King's story in a form familiar to her audience. Ringgold adds a distinct twist by not binding us to one "reading" of history. Instead, she creates a series of eight prints, each one a vignette that we can understand on its own, as well as part of a larger narrative. In a similar vein, Kara Walker creates a pop-up book, a format often used to instruct young scholars. Using this familiar children's literary tool, she depicts the realities of racism and gender discrimination in the life of a formerly enslaved woman through a Black feminist lens.

The act of storytelling allows space for fantasy to merge with reality, inspiring Black women to rewrite their own versions of history and share their distinct perspective with wider audiences. Storytelling is a powerful mechanism that promotes the richness and fullness of our imagination. Black imagination historically has been an instrument for survival, and with radical intention we can dare to use it as means for thriving. This catalog allows us to examine the past to enable a more equitable future.

–GRACE LYNNE HAYNES AND GRACE KIM

CARRIE MAE WEEMS (1953-)

Hush of Our Silence
from the In the Year Three: Exit Art portfolio, 2003

Hush of Our Silence exemplifies Weems's renowned multimedia combination of photography, print, and text. She often uses riddles and poetic discourse to interrogate heteronormative relationships from her distinct perspective as a Black woman. Here a phonograph horn is supported by a marble slab, elevating an everyday object into sculpture. The text discusses a relationship that has faded into the void. The presence of the phonograph horn, which typically transmits music out like a speaker, amplifies the emptiness. Weems uses the horn to express her unique sound through visual imagery. An object typically used to record "noise" now falls silent, representing her muted voice.

We can hear Weems's frustrations within heteronormative relationships that often derive from Western patriarchy and sexism. Historically, slavery disrupted traditional gender roles and familial dynamics for Black men and women. Black women experience an extremely specific struggle at the harsh intersection of racism and sexism. Weems is known to express her activism for women's rights through her camera lens, arguing, "Photography can be used as a powerful weapon toward instituting political and cultural change."[1] *Hush of Our Silence* is a Black woman's cry as her coveted safe space with her partner becomes stagnant and quiet. Relationships change and take on new forms as time progresses, and Weems highlights the pain that accompanies this transitional journey.

–GRACE LYNNE HAYNES

LITERATURE: Drew, O'Grady, Weems 2015 and 2019

Fig. 7.1. Carrie Mae Weems, *Hush of Our Silence* from the *In the Year Three: Exit Art* portfolio, 2003. Chromogenic print. 2315/16×1915/16 in. (60.8×50.6 cm). Collection Zimmerli Art Museum at Rutgers University. Gift of Peter Frey. 2008.015.002.05. © Carrie Mae Weems. Courtesy of the artist and Gladstone Gallery, New York; Fraenkel Gallery, San Francisco; and Galerie Barbara Thumm, Berlin.

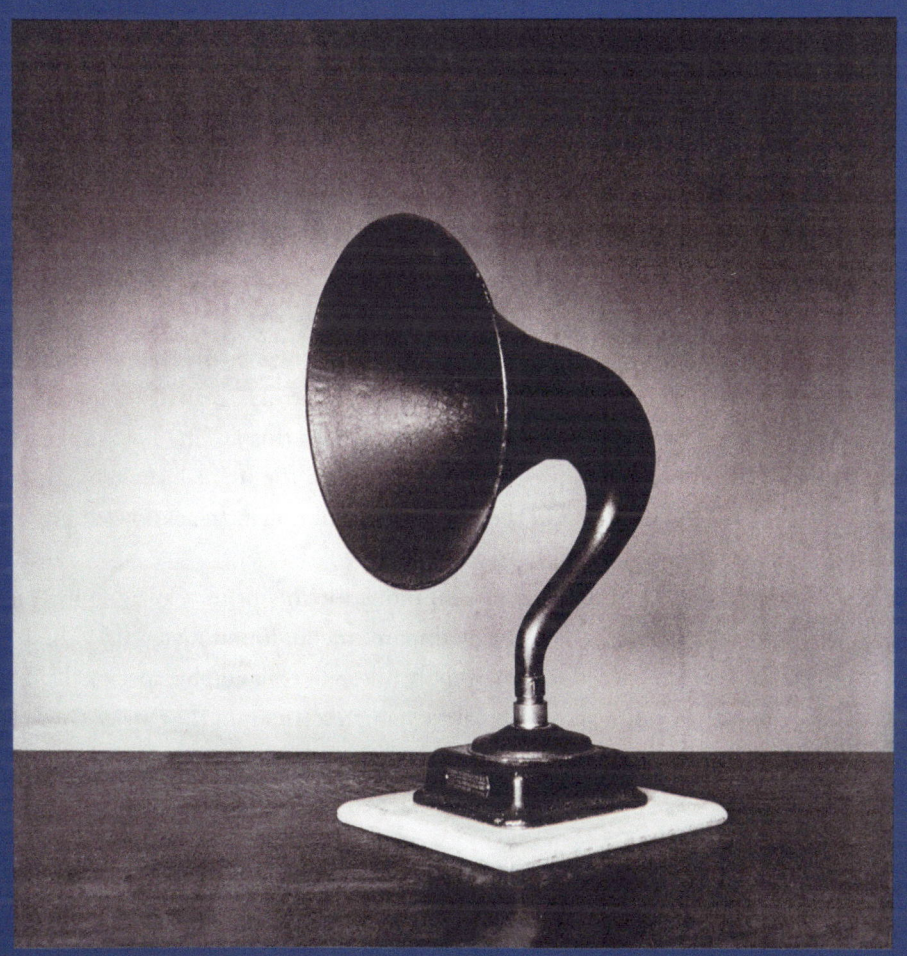

I REMEMBER LONG NITES AND ENDLESS DISCUSSIONS WITH YOU, WHEN WE WERE NOT AFRAID TO SPEAK OUR MINDS, AND NOW I ONLY FEEL THE HUSH, HUSH, HUSH OF OUR MUTUAL SILENCE.

EMMA AMOS (1937-2020)
Red Fish
from the *Aquarium Series*, 1987

Bright, scarlet red fish dart through the contrastingly dark, blue water in front of the viewer as the faint white shapes of indigo fish surge upward through the water in the background. Sharp white lines and blurry pale foam around their small slick bodies show their movement through the heavy water around them. These red fish, which have spent their entire lives in the water, speed through it with ease. The fish in the bottom left corner even opens its mouth in a gleeful grin at the viewer.

Anchored in the underwater world, this dynamic, yet simultaneously serene, scene of aquatic life is a therapeutic answer to Amos's lifelong fear of water. Amos was inspired to create the *Aquarium Series* after she noticed the lack of Black athletes in water sports at the 1984 Los Angeles Summer Olympics. She was fascinated with water, with the way water made her anxious and fearful not knowing how to swim, but also with the freedom and liberation that comes with losing full control. Created in concurrence with Amos's *Water Series*, the *Aquarium Series* addresses this fascination and her disorienting fear. Like the figures in Amos's *Falling Series*, the red fish invite viewers to ponder the joy that can be found in the frightening unknown. In acknowledging this fear and the uncertainty of it, Amos can find peace.

Amos employed the silk collagraphy technique for this print. Collagraphy, more generally, uses various materials (paper, cardboard, metal, found materials), which an artist collages on a plate, onto which they apply ink. Silk collagraphy, specifically, consists of applying acrylic paint across silk fabric, which settles into the crevices between the threads of silk and creates a barrier that the ink cannot seep through when dried. This produces the image of the fish that appears on the paper.

–EMILY HU

LITERATURE: Dawson, Valentine 2016 and 2020

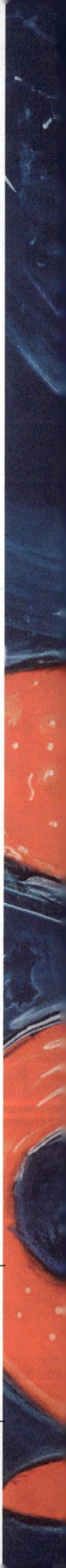

Fig. 7.2. Emma Amos, *Red Fish* from the *Aquarium Series*, 1987. Color silk collagraph with glitter on Arches Cover paper. 457/8 × 319/16 in. (116.5 × 80.2 cm). Collection Zimmerli Art Museum at Rutgers University. Purchased in part with a grant from the National Endowment for the Arts. 1990.0508.001. © 2026 Emma Amos / Licensed by VAGA at Artists Rights Society (ARS), New York.

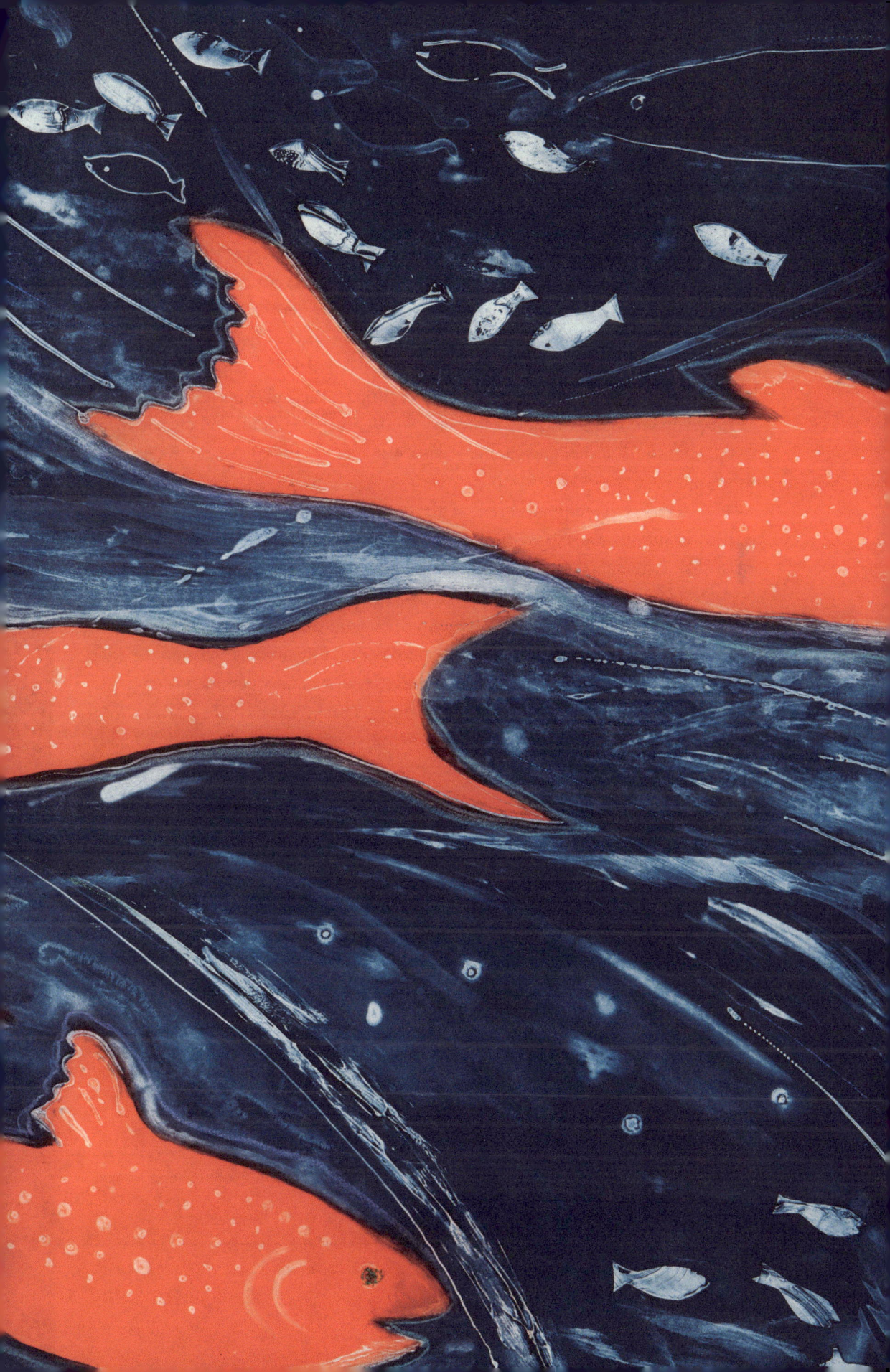

EMMA AMOS (1937-2020)

Water Wonder Woman
from the *Aquarium Series*, 1987

A woman takes a breath as she emerges between swirling waves of deep, blue water. The ghostly pale silhouettes of indigo fish swim alongside her. Amos uses her own likeness to depict the "Water Wonder Woman," a characteristic of many of her later works, such as the 1994 painting *Tightrope*, which features the artist in a Wonder Woman costume. By taking on the identity of a "Wonder Woman" in an aquarium where the world perceives and judges her, she critiques societal conceptions of women as superhuman and invincible, while also confronting her childhood fear of swimming. She is both scared and strong: she is a testament to bravery under the colonialist gaze.

Her larger oeuvre responds to colonialist notions in the art historical canon. Amos wanted to subvert the exploitation of women and brown bodies by male European artists like Paul Gauguin, whose depictions of nude women diving into and near the ocean were rooted in racist ideas of primitivism. By taking on the subject herself, she can breathe autonomy and a reclamation of power into these types of imagery. The white *X*'s created by the water's movement indicate cancellation, refusal, and defiance. Amos has remarked about the *X*'s in her work, "I cross out my comments, my noticing, my daring to comment, as if to take my images back."[2] As the titular Water Wonder Woman, she refuses to meet the patronizing male gaze, turning her head away. Instead, she swims onward and reaches forward.

–EMILY HU

LITERATURE: hooks 1995, Patton 2002, Wolfskill 2016

Fig. 7.3. Emma Amos, *Water Wonder Woman* from the *Aquarium Series*, 1987. Color silk collagraph on Arches Cover paper. 463/16 × 311/2 in. (117.3 × 80 cm). Collection Zimmerli Art Museum at Rutgers University. Purchased in part with a grant from the National Endowment for the Arts. 1990.0508.002. © 2026 Emma Amos / Licensed by VAGA at Artists Rights Society (ARS), New York.

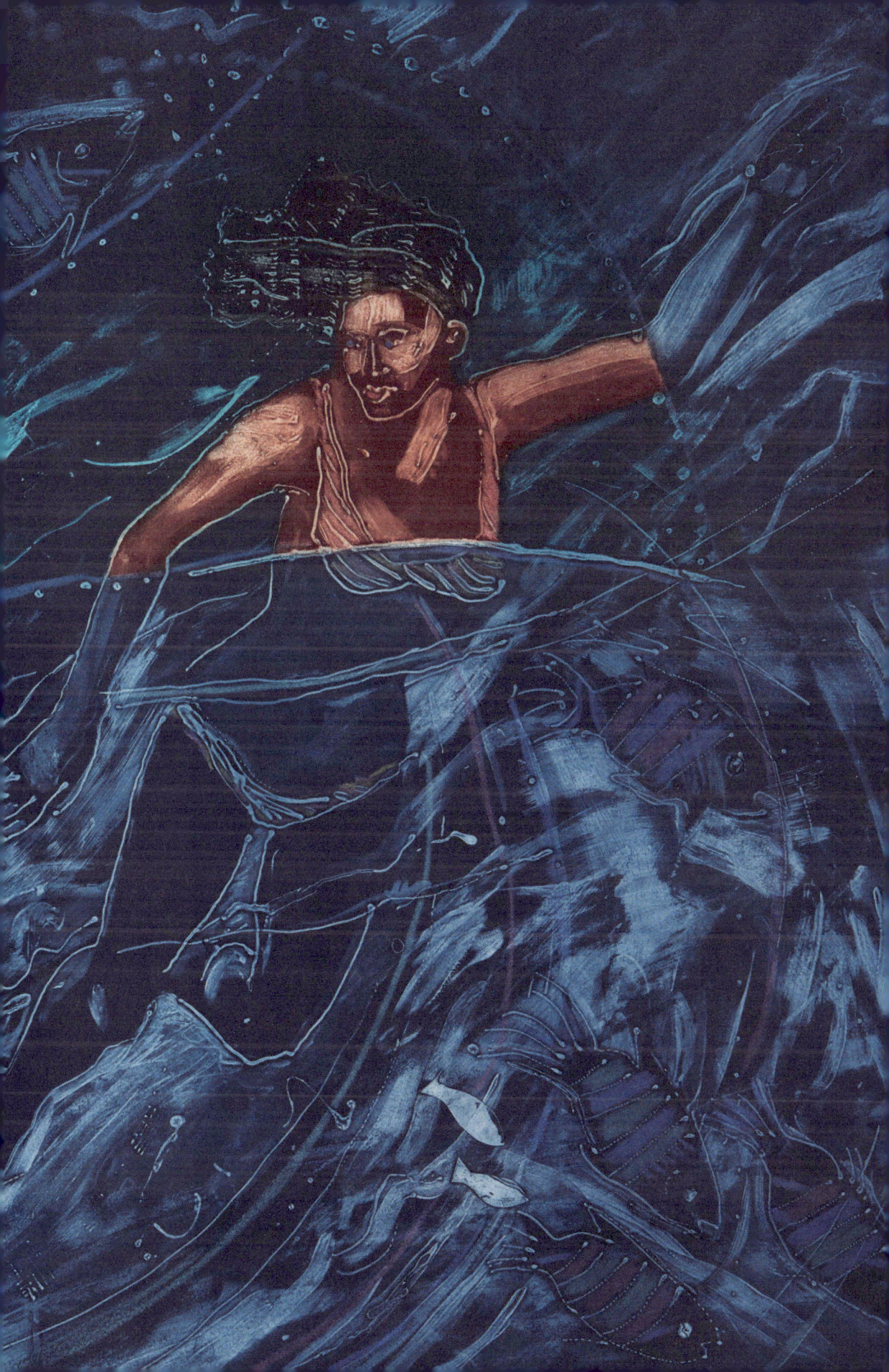

EMMA AMOS (1937-2020)

Octopus
from the *Aquarium Series*, 1987

Slithery and mysterious, fascinating yet repulsive, the octopus has captivated seafaring communities across time and space. The cephalopod is a common motif of Minoan and Mycenean pottery, the basis of the vicious Kraken of seventeenth century Norse legends, a familiar character in eighteenth and nineteenth century Japanese woodprints, and the inspiration behind twentieth century cinematic sea monsters. The root of much lore, ancient and modern civilizations created stories of its ferocity, agility, adaptability, intelligence, and regenerative characteristics. These seemingly contradictive aspects are part of the creature's enigmatic appeal.

Here Amos depicts a glowing solitary octopus whose translucent body picks up hints of the red fish referenced in another print from her *Aquarium Series*. Its glittery yellow eye peers suspiciously at the viewer. The large lone creature is rendered in contrast to the shadowy schools of fish in the background.

Why did Amos decide to include this particular sea creature in her series? On the one hand, the decision could be based on her practice of referencing traditional Eurocentric motifs in her work to break and transform them. Yet this iconographic figure transcends the categorically classical Western European canon. On the other hand, the choice might have been self-referential. The octopus is known to have the ability to adapt to a variety of environments, camouflaging itself to hide from predators and to lure in prey. These metamorphic qualities make it both resilient and enduring.

—AMBER N. WILEY

LITERATURE: Bates and Schnier

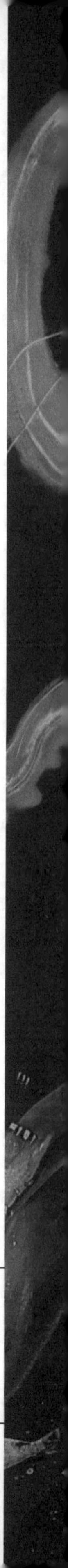

Fig. 7.4. Emma Amos, *Octopus* from the *Aquarium Series*, 1987. Color silk collagraph with glitter. 465/16 × 311/2 in. (117.6 × 80 cm). Collection Zimmerli Art Museum at Rutgers University. Purchased in part with a grant from the National Endowment for the Arts. 1990.0508.005. © 2026 Emma Amos / Licensed by VAGA at Artists Rights Society (ARS), New York.

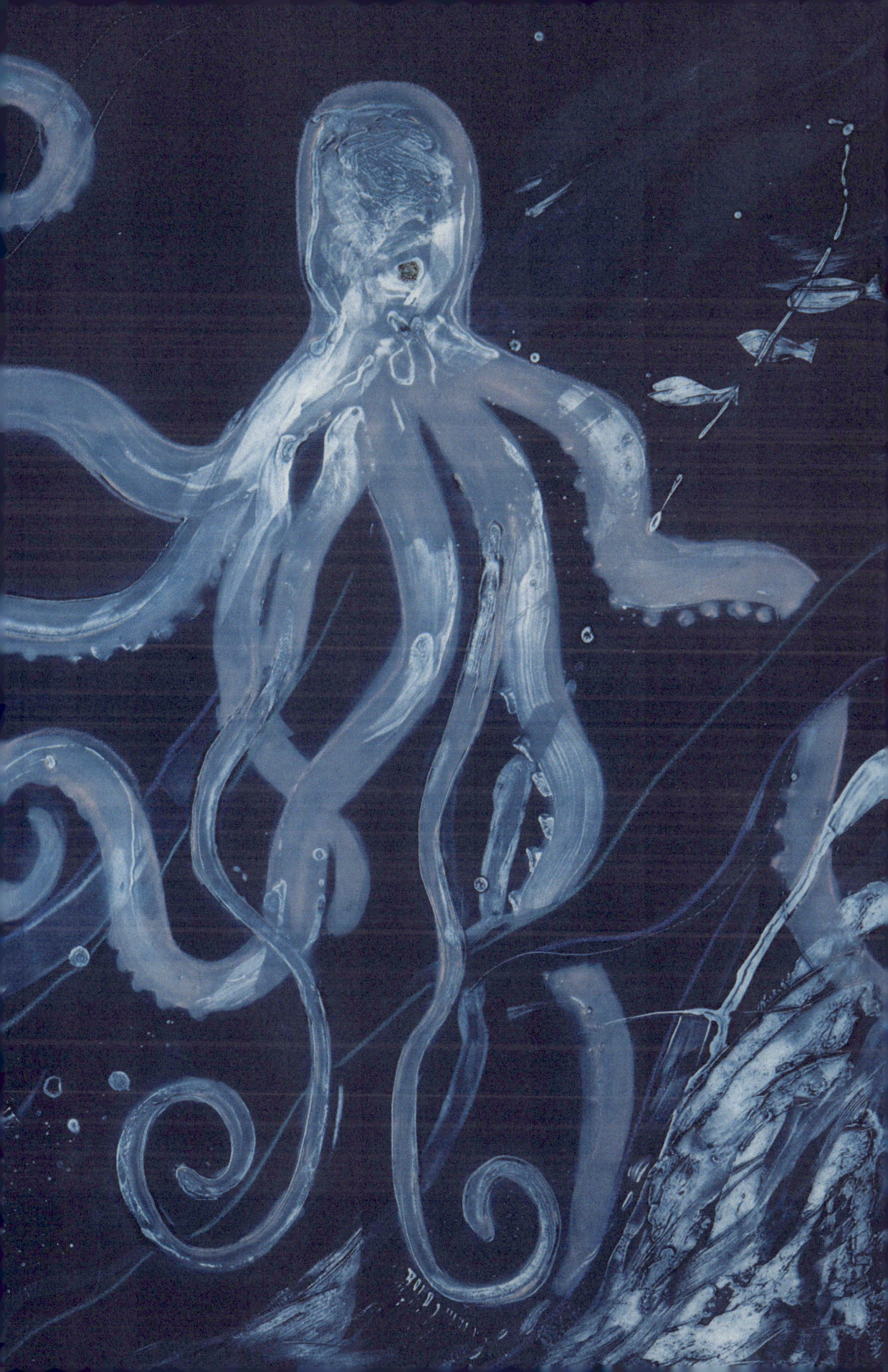

EMMA AMOS (1937-2020)

Diver
from the *Aquarium Series*, 1987

The titular diver in this piece is expressing a combination of confidence and freedom that Amos herself did not feel in her relationship to water. Amos portrays the diver with strong legs and a bare abdomen. Leaving the monotone world of air to enter the upside-down world of the ocean, our subject comes alive. Her body is rendered in energetic full color once she is submerged in the water. Her brown skin reveals kinetic dynamism, yet her face relays serenity and a sense of peace.

The vertical entry into the water suggests mastery over the technique. There is no indication of a splash on surface of the water. The force of the diver's entry is represented through the strong directionality of the underwater ripples emanating from her body. She is calm, powerful, and confident.

Amos created this piece in tandem with other explorations of the human figure in motion. Inspired by the 1984 Los Angeles Summer Olympics, Amos's mid-to-late 1980s catalog includes several depictions of divers gracefully entering bodies of water. In those pieces, she utilizes various media including acrylics, fabric, print and collage.

—AMBER N. WILEY

LITERATURE: Farrington "Emma Amos: Bodies in Motion" 2007

Fig. 7.5. Emma Amos, *Diver* from the *Aquarium Series*, 1987. Color silk collagraph with glitter. 467/16 × 3113/16 in. (117.9 × 80.8 cm). Collection Zimmerli Art Museum at Rutgers University. Purchased in part with a grant from the National Endowment for the Arts. 1990.0508.006. © 2026 Emma Amos / Licensed by VAGA at Artists Rights Society (ARS), New York.

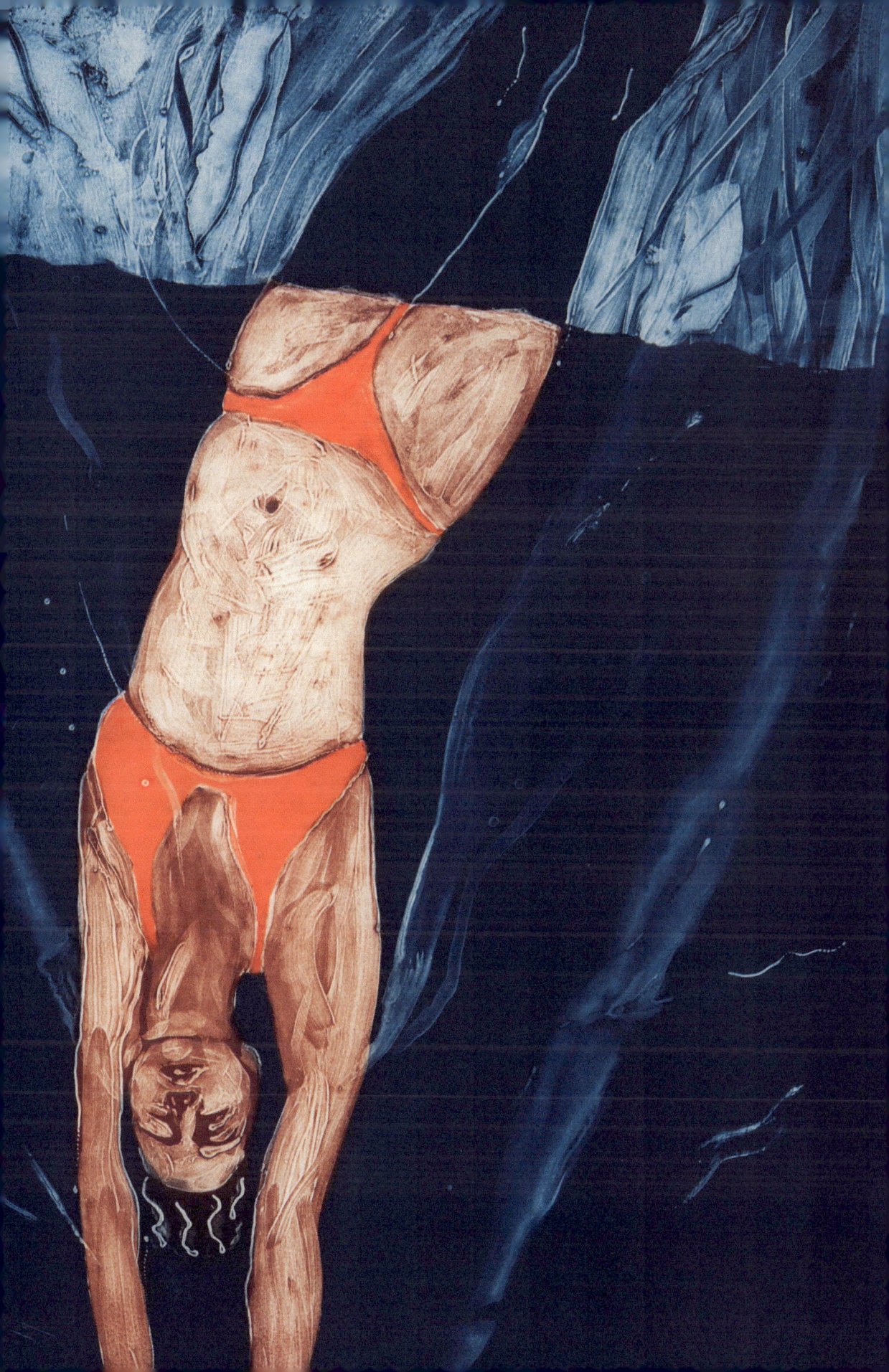

FAITH RINGGOLD (1930-2024)

A Letter from Martin Luther King
from the *Letter from Birmingham City Jail* portfolio, 2007

Ringgold was an artist and activist whose work deeply engaged both civil and women's rights. She had a long history of confronting issues of diversity in her art and in the museum world. In addition to creating imagery highlighting the country's race relations, she led protests demanding inclusion of both Black and women artists in museum spaces. She seamlessly combined her political beliefs and art making within her practice.

In 2007, Ringgold published *Letter from Birmingham City Jail*, a book of colored screen prints based on the iconic 1963 letter written by Dr. Martin Luther King Jr. while jailed in Alabama. He wrote the letter in response to eight white clergymen who had called for "peaceful obedience" of the segregation law. The white clergymen also chastised the "confrontational" nature of King's civil rights movement tactics. King argued that silencing the oppressed required a position of privilege that was not accessible to all. He instead called for commendation of protesters for their dedicated work.

—DESIREE MORALES

LITERATURE: King 1963 and 2008

Fig. 7.6. Faith Ringgold, *A Letter from Martin Luther King* from the *Letter from Birmingham City Jail* portfolio, 2007. Color screen print. 119/16×811/16 in. (29.4×22 cm). Collection Zimmerli Art Museum at Rutgers University. Gift of Ralph Voorhees. 2009.001.002.01. © 2026 Faith Ringgold / Artists Rights Society (ARS), New York. Courtesy ACA Galleries, New York.

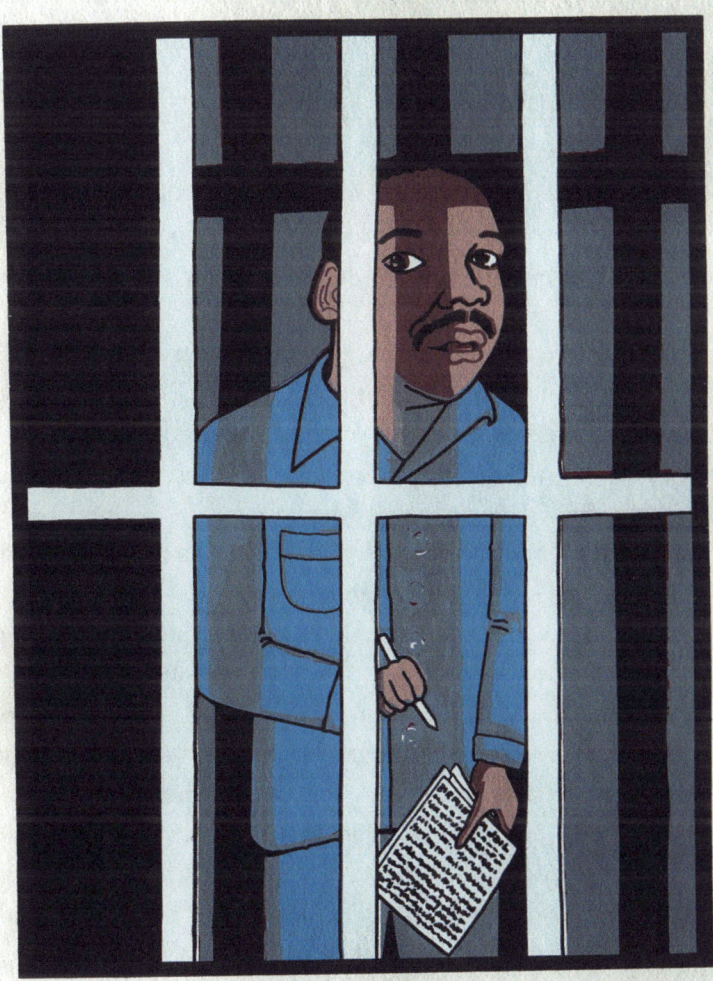

13/45   Faith Ringgold 2007

FAITH RINGGOLD (1930-2024)

Four Little Girls Bombed in a Church
from the *Letter from Birmingham City Jail* portfolio, 2007

This print references the horrific bombing of the Sixteenth Street Baptist Church in Birmingham on September 15, 1963. Martin Luther King Jr. does not address the event in his letter, which he wrote in April of that same year; however, it is reflective of the dangers that King warned the public about while imprisoned. In his letter, King writes "There have been more unsolved bombings of Negro homes and churches in Birmingham than in any other city in this nation. These are the hard, brutal, and unbelievable facts."[3] One of the most notorious would be the Sunday morning bombing of the church by four cowardly Klansmen.

Two dozen church members sustained injuries from the blast, while four schoolgirls were claimed as fatalities: fourteen-year-old Addie Mae Collins, eleven-year-old Carol Denise McNair, fourteen-year-old Carole Rosamond Robertson, and fourteen-year-old Cynthia Dionne Wesley. A fifth victim, Addie Mae Collin's younger sister, twelve-year-old Sarah Collins, survived the basement explosion but suffered from twenty-one pieces of glass embedded in her face, and was blinded in one eye. The terrible carnage wrought at the scene stands in stark contrast to the youthful glory of the girls, who were readying themselves for a Sunday school choir performance. My own mother was an eleven-year-old schoolgirl living in Washington, DC, when this horrific act of domestic terrorism occurred. Putting the event into perspective, these little girls should have had the opportunity to grow into women and have little girls of their own.

In Ringgold's depiction, the four little girls are in all white dresses, flying above the church. They are angels, free from worldly prejudice and violence. They have made their escape. Ringgold often uses the act of flying as a motif in her story quilts and children's books, a superpower afforded to children with big imaginations and curiosity to explore. It is also an allegorical callback to "the flying African," a theme prevalent in stories passed down in Afrodiasporic oral tradition. Historian Jason R. Young noted that in some scholarly interpretations, "In the case of flying Africans, freedom is attained not through literacy, escape, or arrival in the free North, but rather through death."[4]

The four Klansmen are also in all white, their faces obscured by their masks. They are juxtaposed with the angelic girls—stuck on earth, devoid of the human condition, phantom versions of sentient beings. They are but specters. They remain on the ground, consumed in the fire from the fifteen sticks of dynamite they planted under the church. Theirs is an ever-present, living hell. It is self-created, born of their own hate.

—AMBER N. WILEY

LITERATURE: Jenkins, King 1963, Young

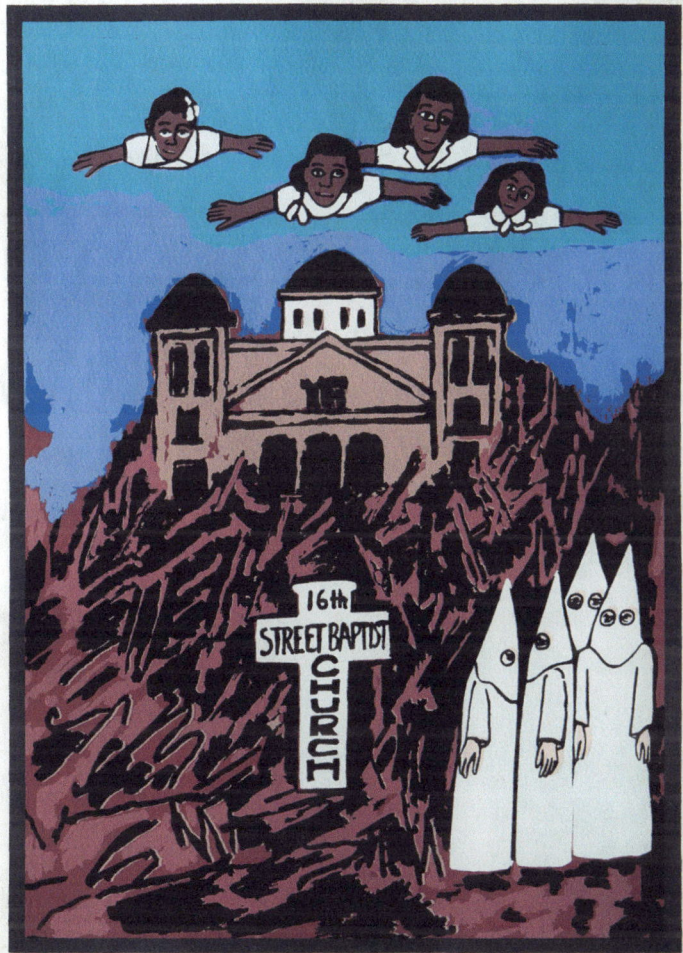

13/45

faith Ringgold 2007

Fig. 7.7. Faith Ringgold, *Four Little Girls Bombed in a Church* from the *Letter from Birmingham City Jail* portfolio, 2007. Color screen print. 177/8×141/8 in. (45.4×35.9 cm). Collection Zimmerli Art Museum at Rutgers University. Gift of Ralph Voorhees.

FAITH RINGGOLD (1930-2024)

For Whites Only from the Letter
from Birmingham City Jail portfolio, 2007

When you suddenly find your tongue twisted and your speech stammering as you seek to explain to your six year old daughter why she can't go to the public amusement park that has just been advertised on television, and see tears welling up in her eyes when she is told that Funtown is closed to colored children, and see ominous clouds of inferiority beginning to form in her little mental sky, and see her beginning to distort her personality by developing an unconscious bitterness toward white people . . . then you will understand why we find it difficult to wait.

—DR. MARTIN LUTHER KING JR.,
1963

Fig. 7.8. Faith Ringgold, *For Whites Only* from the *Letter from Birmingham City Jail* portfolio, 2007. Color screen print. 177/8×14 in. (45.4×35.6 cm). Collection Zimmerli Art Museum at Rutgers University. Gift of Ralph Voorhees. 2009.001.002.03. © 2026 Faith Ringgold / Artists Rights Society (ARS), New York. Courtesy ACA Galleries, New York.

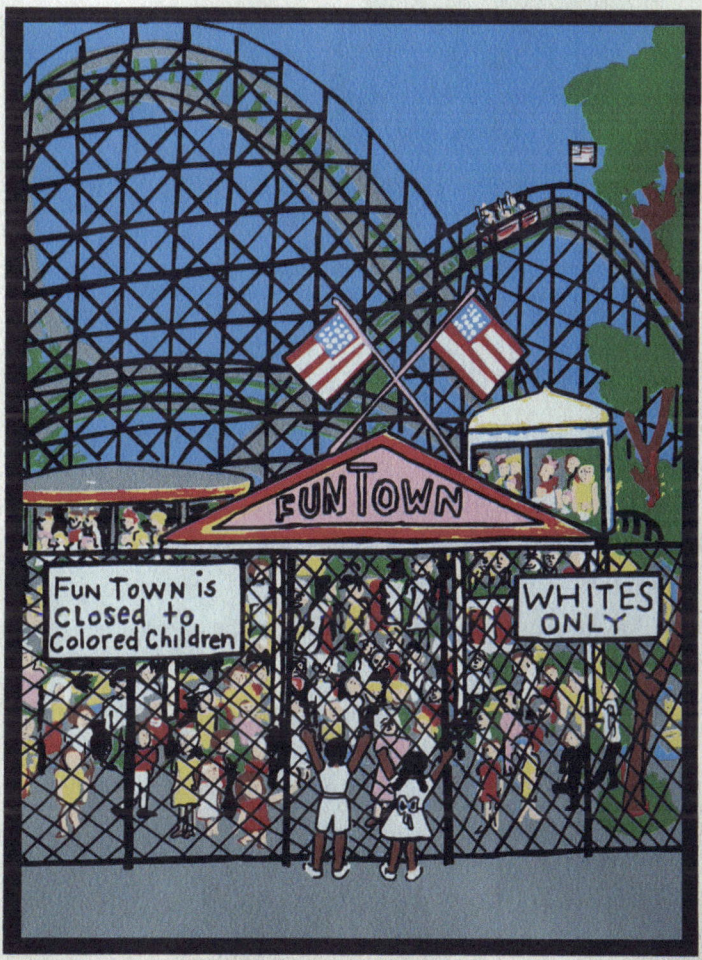

13/45   Faith Ringgold 2007

FAITH RINGGOLD (1930-2024)

Brown Versus Board of Education 1954
from the Letter from Birmingham City Jail portfolio, 2007

The red brick schoolhouse is an image seared into the public consciousness across generations of Americans. It is a space of self-improvement, socialization, and community. Students learn the basics of analytical thought and ultimately, independent thinking. They forge friendships within the warm and inviting schoolhouse walls.

Alternatively, the red brick schoolhouse is a metaphor, especially for Black Americans, of the American Dream. A place where literacy equals liberation. The push to integrate public schools was a result of the separate but unequal nature of resources given over to segregated Black and white school systems across the nation. The Supreme Court ruled segregation illegal in all fifty states and the District of Columbia in 1954, yet powerful white segregationists violated federal law by retaining separate facilities for Black and white students for almost two decades after the ruling. At the frontlines of the battle for equal educational access and opportunity in the United States were young children, and in particular, Black schoolgirls.

In this print, Ringgold illustrates a familiar scene of the classical Civil Rights era. Captured extensively in the popular press through photography and TV broadcasts, intrepid Black girls confronted angry crowds while attempting to desegregate white schools. The irony here, and in many of the widely circulated media images, is that the main antagonists are white adult women, presumably demure housewives protecting the extended boundaries of their domesticity—from the home to the school. We see the cult of white womanhood turned on its head, with white women hurling ugly racial epithets to girls a fraction of their age and size.

Ringgold's composition leads the viewer's eyes in a triangular motion, from the outstretched combative arms of the white women, pointing down to the face of the young Black schoolgirl looking back at them with a mix of curiosity and innocence. In the bottom right corner, a red-headed white youth picks up a sign that reads "**GGER STAY OUT Of OUR School." That sign is mirrored by another hoisted above the heads of the crowd of all-white women aggressors. The next generation of white youth are learning the tenets of racial prejudice from their parents, in this case, their mothers. A federal guardsman is ineffectual, reduced to a prop in the background.

—AMBER N. WILEY

LITERATURE: Devlin, Wiley 2025

Fig. 7.9. Faith Ringgold, *Brown Versus Board of Education 1954* from the *Letter from Birmingham City Jail* portfolio, 2007. Color screen print. 1713/16×1315/16 in. (45.2×35.4 cm). Collection Zimmerli Art Museum at Rutgers University. Gift of Ralph Voorhees. 2009.001.002.04. © 2026 Faith Ringgold / Artists Rights Society (ARS), New York. Courtesy ACA Galleries, New York.

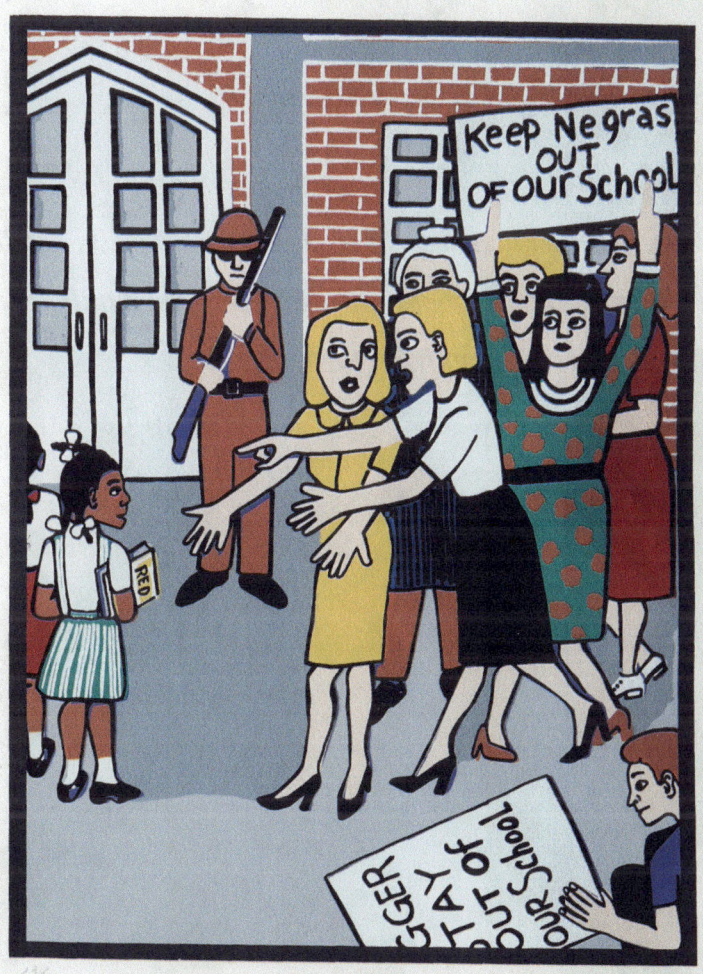

faith Ringgold 2007

FAITH RINGGOLD (1930-2024)

The Right to Vote
from the Letter from Birmingham City Jail portfolio, 2007

The Right to Vote, depicts the chaotic scene of a protest unfolding in the streets. Three white police officers frame the image. One sits on a horse above the crowd, signaling his physical and worldly elevation. The other officers flank a Black woman who is under arrest. Black men are in the background with looks of concern. Other protesters fill the scene in crowded proximity, evoking a sense of solidarity, yet helplessness.

–DESIREE MORALES

Nonviolent direct action seeks to create such a crisis and foster such a tension that a community which has constantly refused to negotiate is forced to confront the issue.

–DR. MARTIN LUTHER KING JR.,
1963

Fig. 7.10. Faith Ringgold, *The Right to Vote* from the *Letter from Birmingham City Jail* portfolio, 2007. Color serigraph. 18×14 in. (45.7×35.6 cm). Collection Zimmerli Art Museum at Rutgers University. Gift of Ralph Voorhees. 2009.001.002.05. © 2026 Faith Ringgold / Artists Rights Society (ARS), New York. Courtesy ACA Galleries, New York.

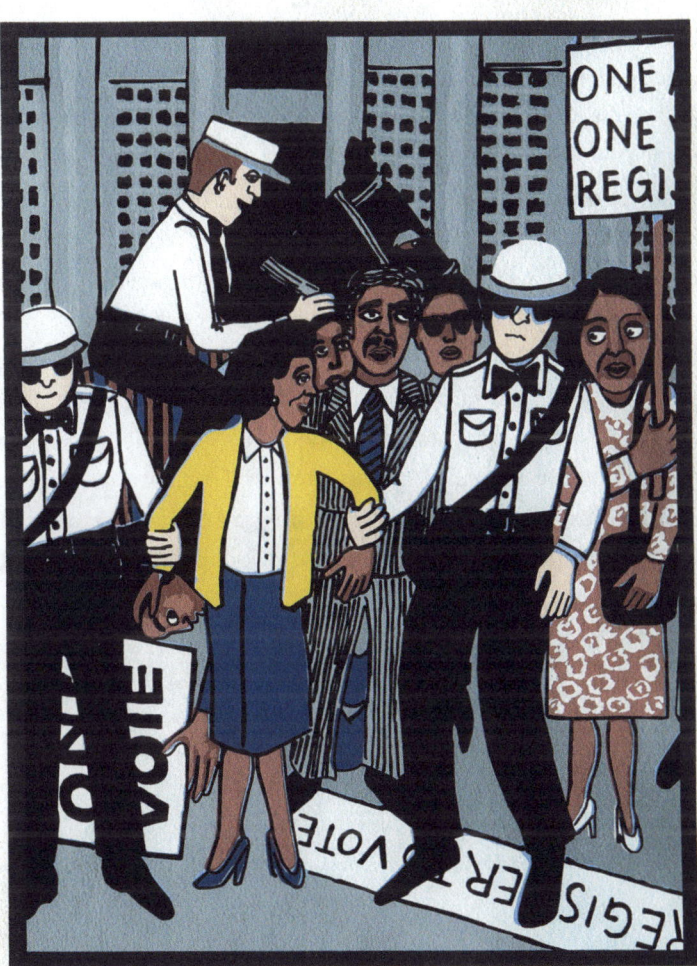

13/75   faith Ringgold 2007

FAITH RINGGOLD (1930-2024)

Police Brutality Viewed thru Stained Glass Windows from the Letter from Birmingham City Jail portfolio, 2007

Martin Luther King Jr. believed deeply in the church's responsibility to move forward human rights, not just for Black Americans, but for all oppressed people. King also repeatedly lamented that "11 o'clock on Sunday morning is one of the most segregated hours, if not the most segregated hour, in Christian America."[5] One of his greatest disappointments, as expressed in his letter from jail, was the stoic response of the white moderate and white clergy to the injustices inflicted upon the Black citizens of Birmingham. In King's letter, he refutes the notion expressed by eight white Birmingham religious leaders that local law enforcement officials handled the public demonstrations against segregation with restraint and calm.[6] Indeed, King proclaims that in the face of repeated police brutality against fellow citizens, white religious leaders and their congregations were "more cautious than courageous and have remained silent behind the anesthetizing security of stained-glass windows."[7]

Here Ringgold brings those two observations together, showing a segregated all-white congregation and their faithful leader in communion with one another. In the pristine and sacred sanctuary, they are oblivious to the violent scenes portrayed in stained glass designs beside them. Against the turquoise, lavender, and salmon pink window panels, black silhouettes illuminate firemen crushing some protesters with high pressure firehoses, and policemen using attack dogs to dominate others.

—AMBER N. WILEY

Fig. 7.11. Faith Ringgold, *Police Brutality Viewed thru Stained Glass Windows* from the *Letter from Birmingham City Jail* portfolio, 2007. Color screen print. 1713/16×14 in. (45.2×35.6 cm). Collection Zimmerli Art Museum at Rutgers University. Gift of Ralph Voorhees. 2009.001.002.06. © 2026 Faith Ringgold / Artists Rights Society (ARS), New York. Courtesy ACA Galleries, New York.

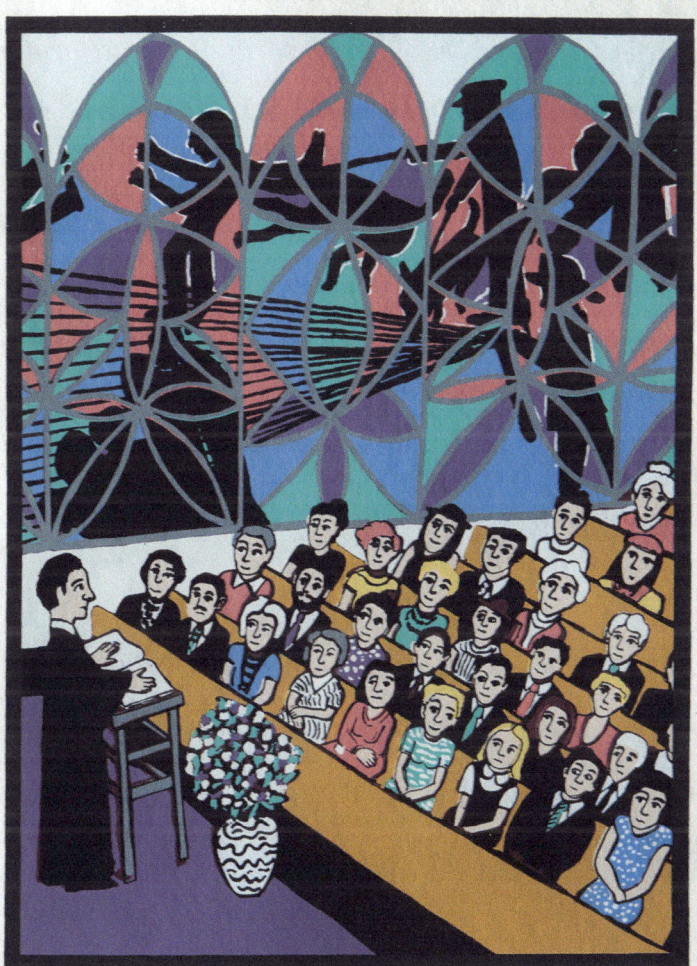

13/35   Faith Ringgold 2007

FAITH RINGGOLD (1930-2024)

Slavery
from the *Letter from Birmingham City Jail* portfolio, 2007

Before the pilgrims landed at Plymouth, we were here. Before the pen of Jefferson etched the majestic words of the Declaration of Independence across the pages of history, we were here. For more than two centuries our forebears labored in this country without wages; they made cotton king; they built the homes of their masters while suffering gross injustice and shameful humiliation—and yet out of a bottomless vitality they continued to thrive and develop.

—DR. MARTIN LUTHER KING JR.,
1963

For hundreds of years, Black people have passed down this collective yearning for freedom from one generation to the next. We are doing now what should have been done in the aftermath of slavery.

—ANGELA DAVIS,
2020

Fig. 7.12. Faith Ringgold, *Slavery* from the *Letter from Birmingham City Jail* portfolio, 2007. Color screen print. 1711/16×137/8 in. (44.9×35.2 cm). Collection Zimmerli Art Museum at Rutgers University. Gift of Ralph Voorhees. 2009.001.002.07. © 2026 Faith Ringgold / Artists Rights Society (ARS), New York. Courtesy ACA Galleries, New York.

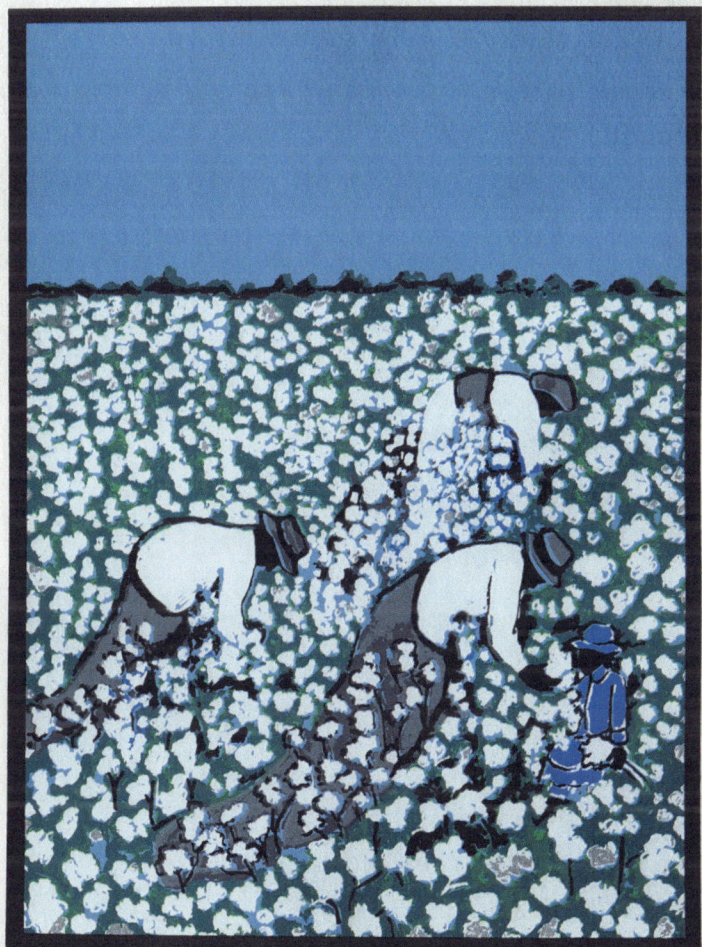

13/75   Faith Ringgold 2007

FAITH RINGGOLD (1930-2024)

Montgomery Bus Boycott
from the *Letter from Birmingham City Jail* portfolio, 2007

Montgomery Bus Boycott shows a visual re-creation of a protester King described as "a seventy two year old woman in Montgomery, Alabama, who rose up with a sense of dignity and with her people decided not to ride segregated buses, . . . [proclaiming,] 'My feets is tired, but my soul is at rest.'"[8] The white-haired woman is in the foreground, walking with a cane, beside a bus. Four Black protesters, who get younger further down the line, follow her in solidarity. Only white people ride the bus in the background. The rear of the bus, where Black people were forced to sit during segregation, is empty.

–DESIREE MORALES

Fig. 7.13. Faith Ringgold, *Montgomery Bus Boycott* from the *Letter from Birmingham City Jail* portfolio, 2007. Color screen print. 1713/16×137/8 in. (45.2×35.2 cm). Collection Zimmerli. Art Museum at Rutgers University. Gift of Ralph Voorhees. 2009.001.002.08. © 2026 Faith Ringgold / Artists Rights Society (ARS), New York. Courtesy ACA Galleries, New York.

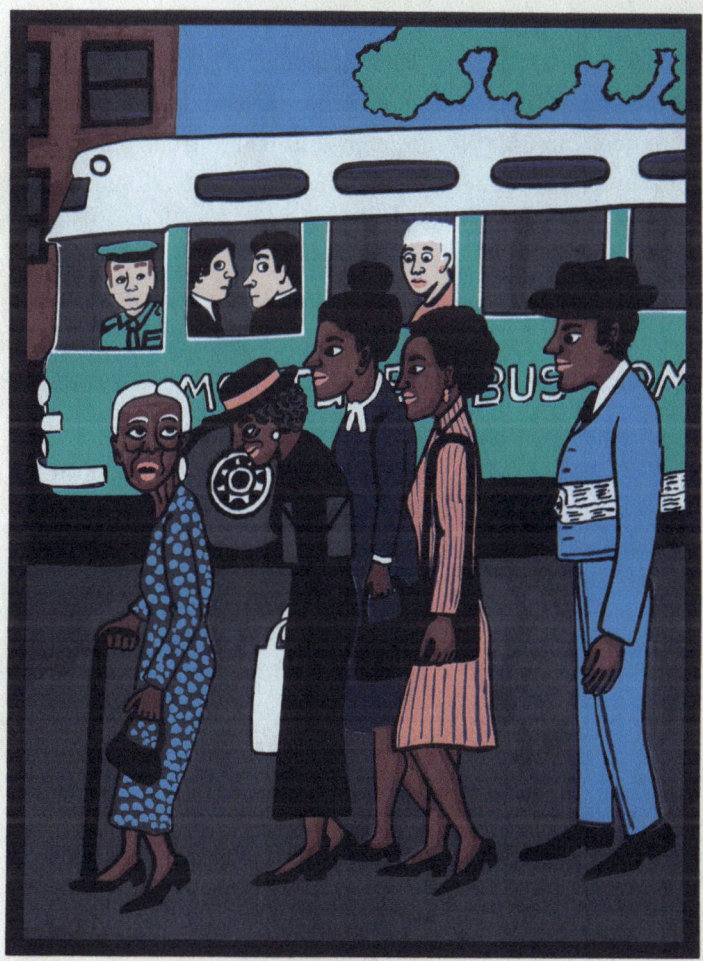

Faith Ringgold 2007

FAITH RINGGOLD (1930-2024)
Yes I Can Playing Cards, 2009

In 2009, Rutgers hosted a retrospective of Ringgold's work. Curated by Judith Brodsky and Ferris Olin, the exhibition was a program of the Institute for Women and Art, a predecessor to the Center for Women in the Arts and Humanities. Ringgold designed the *Yes I Can* playing cards for this occasion and in observance of the historic election of Barack Obama as the first Black president of the United States. Consisting of four suits, the cards represented the White House, the Light, the Money, and Uncle Sam's Hat. Ringgold argued that the items were "symbolic of the presidency, enlightenment, power, and patriotism, respectively—'everything Obama needs to prove He Can.'"[9]

The impetus to create the playing cards also came from Ringgold's own story, repairing a deep hurt she experienced at the hands of her freshman-year classmates at the City College of New York. Those students purposefully left her, the only Black person and one of the few women in the class, out of a group collaboration on an assignment to design a single playing card. Though she completed the assignment alone, she never forgot the sting of exclusion in the class. Here, she was able to create her own full deck of cards as a means of reclaiming her autonomy, power, and freedom.

—AMBER N. WILEY

LITERATURE: Brodsky et al.

Figs. 7.14-7.19. Faith Ringgold, *Yes I Can Playing Cards,* 2009. Top row: Jack of Money, Jack of Uncle Sam's Hat. Middle row: Male Joker, Female Joker. Bottom row: King of the White House, Queen of the Light. Full color photo reproduction on laminated card paper. 37/16 × 21/2 in. (8.7 × 6.3 cm). Collection Zimmerli Art Museum at Rutgers University. Gift of the Center for Women in the Arts and Humanities. TR102977.001A-CCC. © 2026 Faith Ringgold / Artists Rights Society (ARS), New York. Courtesy ACA Galleries, New York.

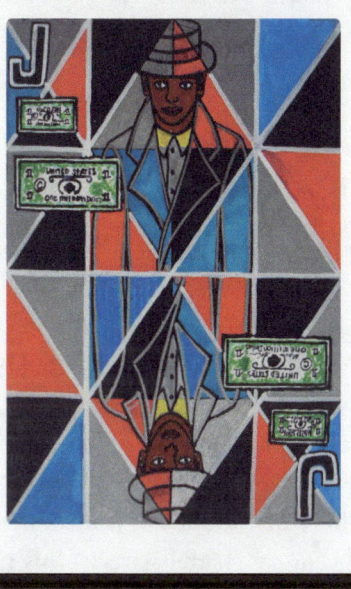
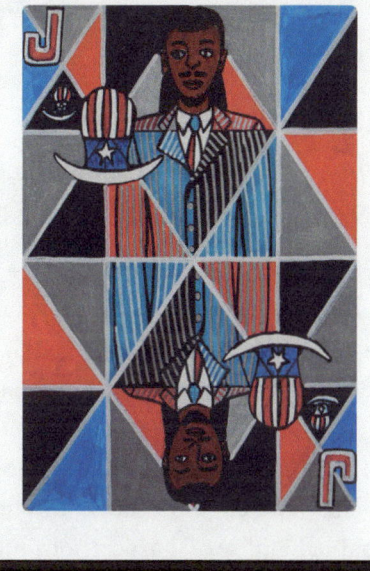
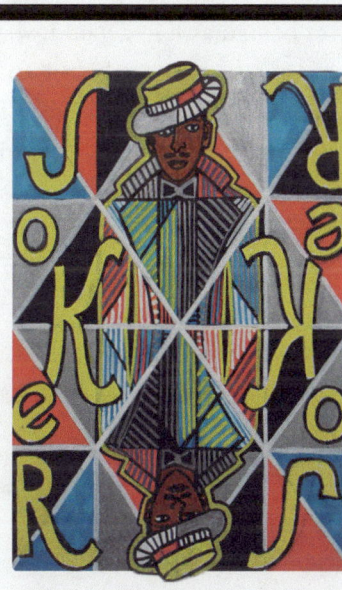
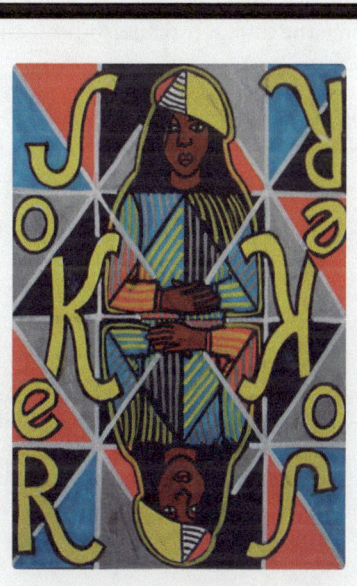
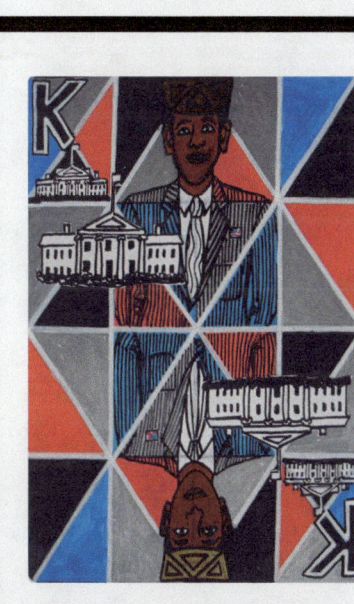
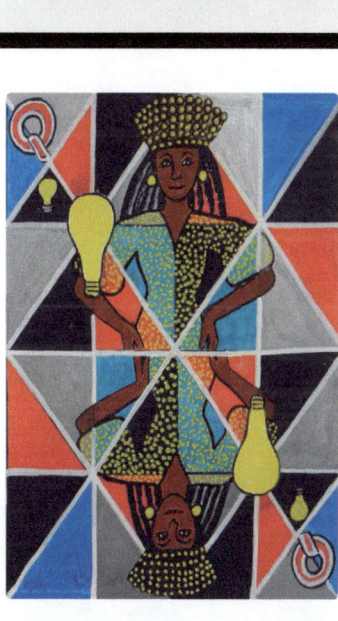

KARA WALKER (1969-)

Freedom, a Fable: A Curious Interpretation of the Wit of a Negress in Troubled Times, 1997

Walker presents *Freedom, a Fable* as a slave narrative children's book. This format, which blends the horror of an enslaved person's saga with playful storytelling intended for young audiences, offers readers a challenging paradox for the meaning of freedom for a Black woman during the nineteenth century.

"N," the story's main character, is not given the specificity of a name, origin story, or homeland, as she typically would not in any archive. The book is only offering her temporality and circumstances. Throughout this story, Walker is fearless in sharing the libidinal and sexual aspects of nineteenth-century chattel slavery. This trickster tale is meant to teach readers about the dangers of being naïve in a world where one is unfree, as well as how our own imagination can limit how we envision freedom.

Books and the stories they tell can last for generations. The enduring nature of books is indicative of Walker's desire for the lesson of this book to last a long time. Her versatility in style and medium underscores the variety of ways she can use her art to explore the grotesque and terrible experiences of American chattel slavery.

—JASMINE DARIA CANNON

LITERATURE: Kent, Oh, Walker 2011 and 2014

Fig. 7.20. Kara Walker, *Freedom, a Fable: A Curious Interpretation of the Wit of a Negress in Troubled Times*, 1997. Pop-up silhouette book. 97/16×81/4 in. (24×21 cm). Collection Zimmerli Art Museum at Rutgers University. Gift of Phillip Dennis Cate. 1997.0767. Artwork © Kara Walker.

In it she knows she need not fear
an insurrection. "Why, surely my people will
understand that my knowledge of pairs
in opposition and their operation in
America will make
me great."

She thinks.

She has taken to referring
to these unknown Africans as her people.
She would like to claim ownership,
"But not with papers or deeds or laws or
such-like, but with undying devotion,
and when I've earned myself that then I'll
work on the White people
as well!"

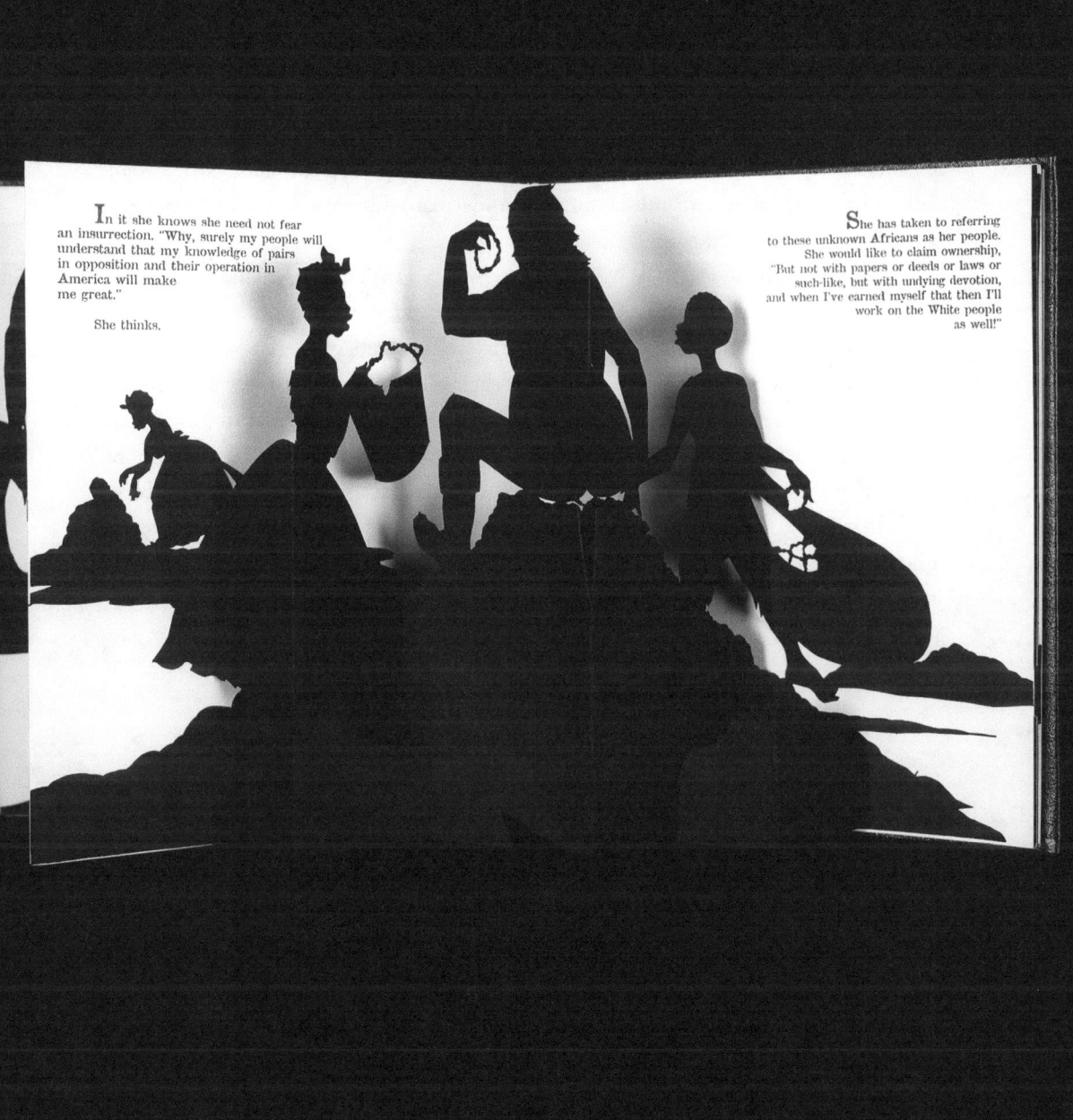

KARA WALKER (1969-)

Excerpt, 2014

Kara Walker's *Excerpt* features four black-and-white vignettes that are a critique of nineteenth-century womanhood. During the nineteenth century, "the cult of domesticity," also called "the cult of true womanhood," framed the notion of womanhood within two main beliefs. The first was that women's piety, submissiveness, devotion, and dutiful nature signaled their virtue. The second was that women ruled the private and domestic sphere (the home, essentially), while men ruled the public sphere, where business and politics took place. Walker uses the stereotypes that produced white womanhood during the nineteenth century to underscore her representation of the era's racialized and gendered tropes.

The vignettes include a nude woman, unkempt and easily impregnable, with babies in tow. Another scene illustrates a man attacking a nude woman from behind. This alludes to the way that Black and white men, as well as white women, sexually violated Black women because of the presumption of their inherent lasciviousness. In each segment, Walker uses the negative space in the image to draw attention to how Blackness makes the inability to meet the standards of womanhood stand out even more. Her use of symmetry and balance, as well as negative and positive space, signals the ways that Black womanhood had no way of fitting into the white ideal. Some of the underlying controlling images of Black women, such as the mammy and jezebel, continue to elide Black women from access to definitions of womanhood.

—JASMINE DARIA CANNON

LITERATURE: Hill Collins 2014, Welter

Notes

1. Carrie Mae Weems, "Aperture: 40 Years." *Aperture*, no. 129 (Fall 1992): 47.

2. Emma Amos, "Measuring Content," in *Looking Forward, Looking Black*, ed. Jo Anna Issak (Hobart and William Smith Colleges Press, 1999), 38.

3. Martin Luther King Jr., "Letter from a Birmingham Jail," April 16, 1963, African Studies Center, University of Pennsylvania, https://www.africa.upenn.edu/Articles_Gen/Letter_Birmingham.html.

4. Jason R. Young, "All God's Children Had Wings: The Flying African in History, Literature, and Lore." *Journal of Africana Religions* 5, no. 1 (2017): 51.

5. Martin Luther King Jr., Interview on "Meet the Press." April 17, 1960, https://kinginstitute.stanford.edu /king-papers/documents/interview-meet-press.

6. "White Clergymen Urge Local Negroes to Withdraw from Demonstrations," *Birmingham News*, April 13, 1963, https://bplonline.contentdm.oclc.org/digital/collection/p4017coll2/id/746/.

7. Martin Luther King Jr., "Letter from a Birmingham Jail."

8. Martin Luther King Jr., "Letter from a Birmingham Jail."

9. Ringgold, quoted by Tanya Sheehan in "Faith Ringgold: Forging Freedom and Declaring Independence," in Judith K Brodsky, Ferris Olin, Tanya Sheehan, and Michele Wallace, *Declaration of Independence: Fifty Years of Art by Faith Ringgold* (Institute for Women and Art, Rutgers, the State University of New Jersey, 2009), 11.

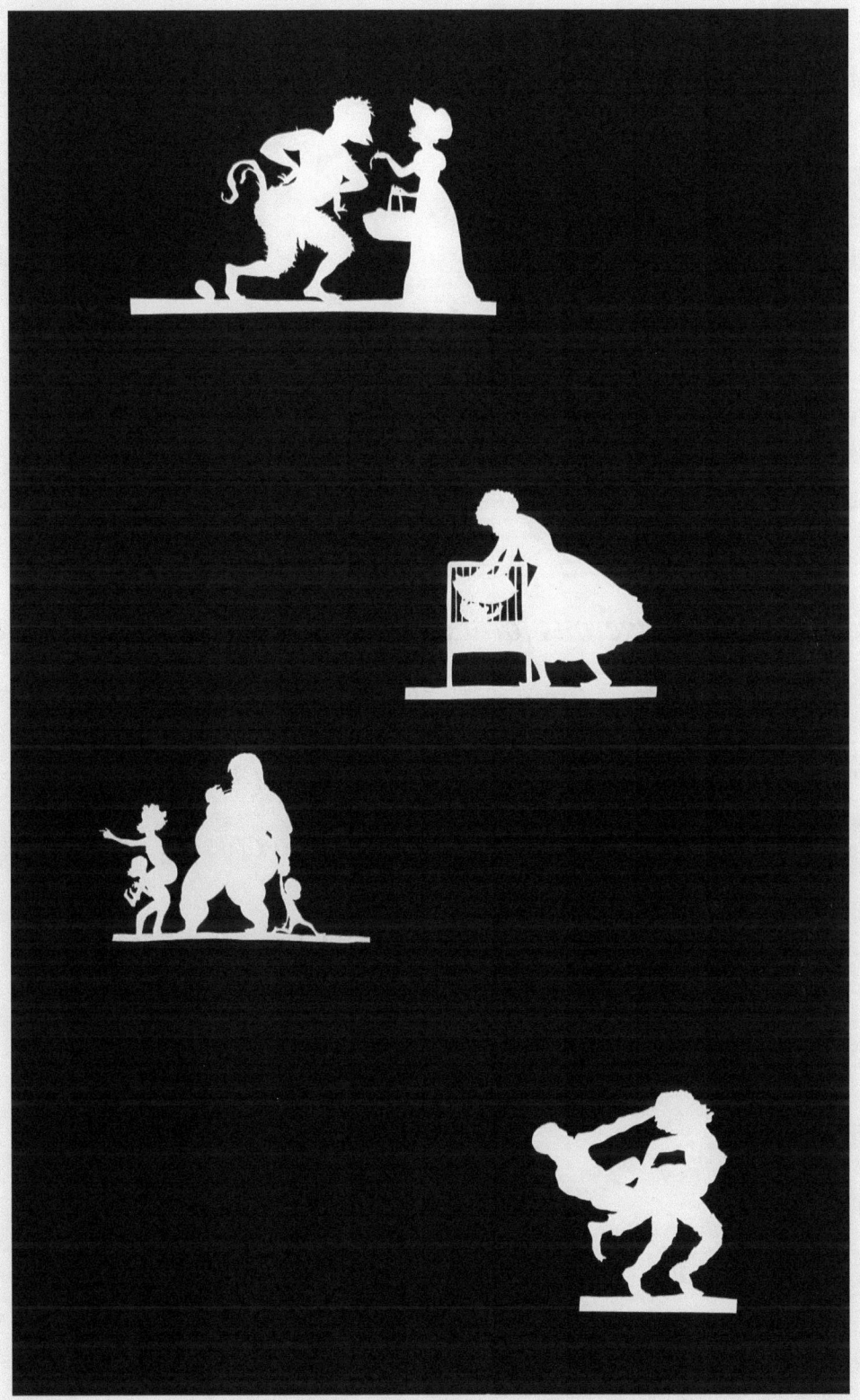

Fig. 7.21. Kara Walker, *Excerpt*, 2014. Lithograph on Somerset Satin paper. 3713/16×243/16 in. (96×61.4 cm). Collection Zimmerli Art Museum at Rutgers University. Gift of Maurice Sánchez, Derrière L'Étoile Studio. TR9406.022. Artwork © Kara Walker.

It is dangerous for a woman to defy the gods;

To taunt them with the tongue's thin tip,

Or strut in the weakness of mere humanity,

Or draw a line daring them to cross . . .

— ANNE SPENCER,
1 9 2 7

8

Alchemy and Spirituality

KYLE B. CO., JASMINE DARIA CANNON,
GRACE LYNNE HAYNES, GRACE KIM, MICHAEL RANDALL,
AND AUDREY ROCLORE

MANY OF THE ARTISTS IN the exhibition explore religion, astrology, numerology, and folklore as part of their practice. They also view womanhood as inherently spiritual in nature and build a decolonized understanding of their own power, implementing conjuring symbols from global spiritual practices, including Afro-Haitian Vodou, ancient Egyptian mythology, Paganism, Vedism, and Christianity. Spirituality is rooted in this process of self-discovery. Not only do these Black women reclaim their identity and heritage, but they also rewrite and redefine narratives of power. This re-creation is a type of alchemy in and of itself.

While alchemy has its early roots as a form of chemistry and science, over the years it began to represent notions of myth, magic, and spiritualism. Material transfiguration and the strengthening of the human body and spirit functioned as primary tenets of the alchemic practice. Indeed, the process of artistic creation is alchemical. Taking materials such as paper, canvas, ink, and paint and turning them into objects of new meaning *is* transfiguration. In expressing human thought and feeling through the creative process in search of catharsis, enlightenment, or wisdom, these artists embark on the path of the alchemist.

—MICHAEL RANDALL AND AUDREY ROCLORE

RENÉE STOUT (1958-)

A Vision I Can't Forget, 1999

This self-portrait depicts the artist in distress, gazing off into space. Stout draws herself against a background of symbols and iconographies that reflect ancestral lineage stripped away during the transatlantic slave trade. Hanging just above her head is an African tribal mask that stands for spiritual ideology highly influential in the diaspora. The mask's placement signifies its importance and relevance in Stout's own spiritual journey. Her work does not fetishize diasporic religious practices; instead, it highlights their importance through detailed renderings that accurately capture the visual language of these objects.

The sketch-like numbers in the background appear frantic, a stream of consciousness or cypher. Stout juxtaposes this with the vivid foreground subject matter. She uses neutral earth tones of sepia, as well as black and white. Deep shadows give the image dimensionality and relate contrasting identities of the physical and spiritual self.

–GRACE LYNNE HAYNES

LITERATURE: Minneapolis Institute of Arts, Ogunleye

Fig. 8.1. Renée Stout, A Vision I Can't Forget, 1999. Lithograph on paper. 301/2 × 211/8 in. (77.5 × 53.7 cm). Collection Zimmerli Art Museum at Rutgers University. Gift of Maurice Sánchez, Derrière L'Étoile Studio. 2008.012.238. © Renée Stout.

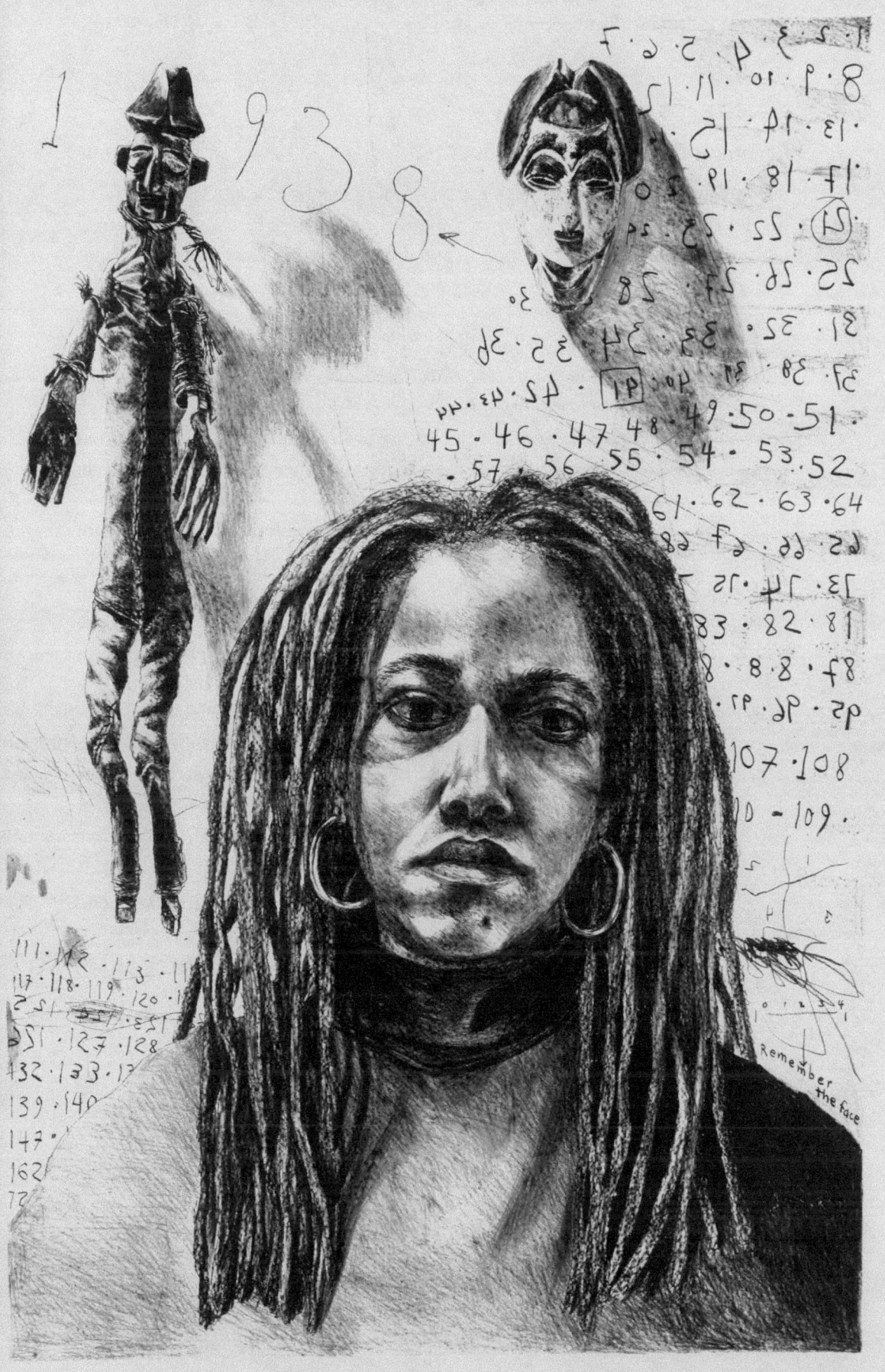

RENÉE STOUT (1958-)

Recurring Damballah Dream, 1999

The woman in *Recurring Damballah Dream* is Stout's alter ego, Fatima Mayfield, whom she describes as "a woman who owns a spiritual supply store here in [Washington,] DC," where "she sells herbs, roots, oils, and dream books, so you can play the numbers based on your dreams; everything you can think of she has in this shop."[1] It is in this very setting that Mayfield receives two unidentified male guests in bowler hats, who are no more than mere shadows in the background.

Stout often draws inspiration and motifs from Haitian Vodou. The phrase "In the dream they always told her to listen to the snake" refers to Damballah, a snake sky god who created the earth with its body and gave birth to life, representing peace and harmony, as well as fertility. Mayfield also has a heart-shaped tattoo on her stomach, which in Vodou stands for Erzulie-Freda, a fertility goddess who wears the rings of Damballah. Thus, the Damballah dream that Mayfield sees is recorded in her dream books.

Through the command to listen to the snake, she explores the distinct gendered potentiality that women harness in their own process of creation. Stout gives birth to worlds through her body's ability to (pro)create with art, in the same way that Damballah created this world. As her hand lightly presses over her womb, this dream physically connects to her body's fertile nature.

As Haitian Vodou syncretized with Christian beliefs, the snake became a reference to Satan from the story of Adam and Eve. The snake successfully tempts Eve to eat the fruit on the tree of knowledge of good and evil. Because of her actions, humanity learns evil, and God banishes them from the Garden of Eden. Listening to the snake is thus an act of harmony, an act of rebellion, and the act of a Black woman artist.

—GRACE KIM

LITERATURE: Collins, Dayan, Thomas and Alanamu

Fig. 8.2. Renée Stout, *Recurring Damballah Dream,* 1999. Lithograph on paper. 323/16×237/16 in. (81.7×59.5 cm). Collection Zimmerli Art Museum at Rutgers University. Gift of Maurice Sánchez, Derrière L'Étoile Studios. 2008.012.239. © Renée Stout.

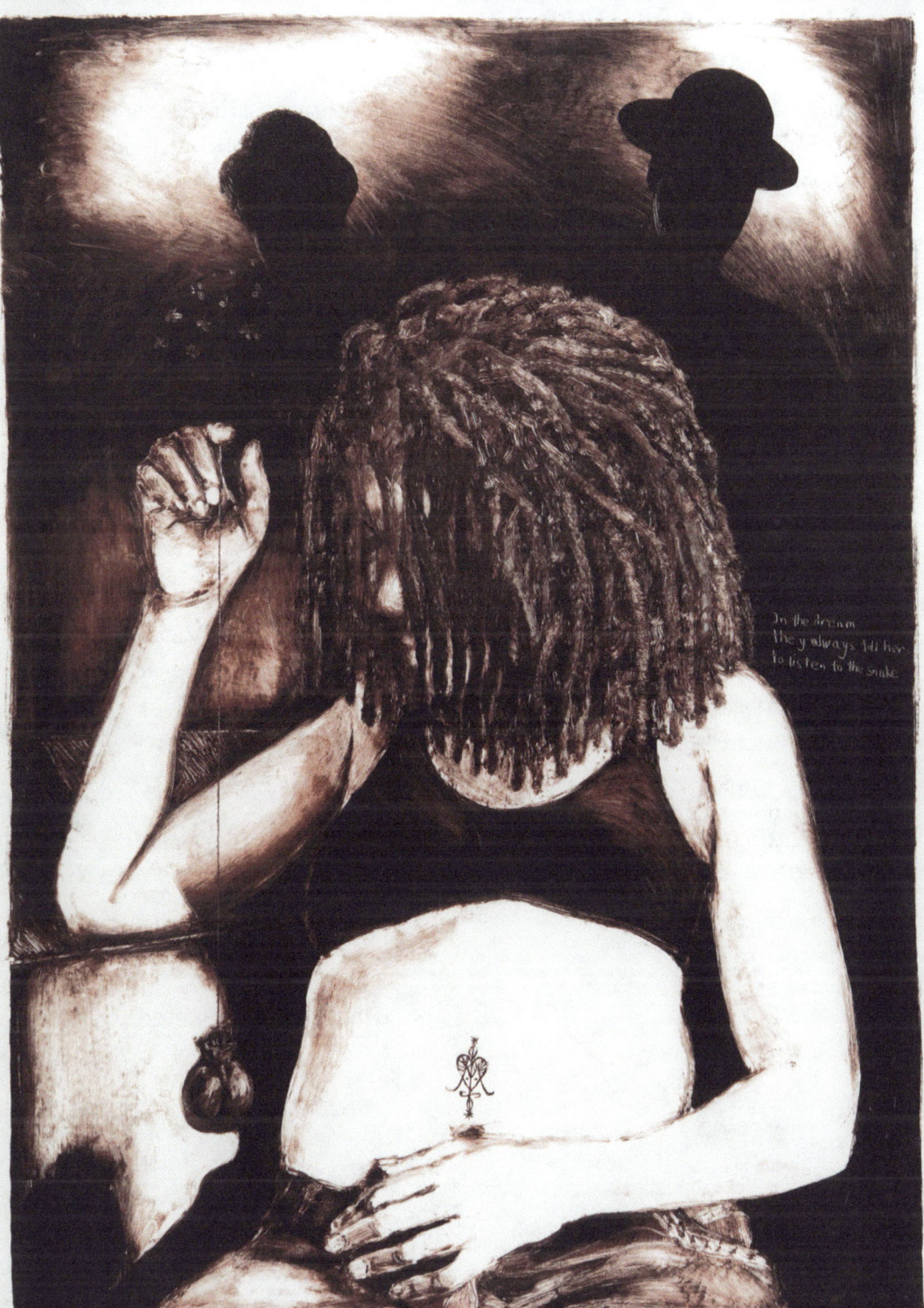

In the dream
they always tell her
to listen to the snake.

KARA WALKER (1969-)

Boo Hoo, 2000

Reminiscent of a minstrel show poster, Walker's *Boo Hoo* considers the complicated relationships between race, gender, slavery, and Christianity. This black-and-white print features a topless afro-donning Black woman adorned with hoop earrings and possessing stereotypically enlarged lips. She cries while holding a snake and a whip.

The snake, which holds biblical references, has multiple meanings when considered with the whip. The first is that Black women hold, and continue to account for two original sins—being Black and being a woman. Additionally, the Black woman is the portal through which the Black past is accessible—the snake and the whip embody common images from the nineteenth century related to religiosity and chattel slavery. The depiction of the woman in Black silhouette and white lips connects this piece to the popularity of Black face and the minstrel show. Thus, Walker illuminates the ubiquity of degrading and stereotypical depictions of Black women.

Walker's childhood in both California and Georgia deeply influenced her work. In her transition from integrated California to segregated Atlanta, she gained a new understanding of how the world can be just black and white. While exploring the disturbing, the melancholic, and the unmentionable of chattel slavery, Walker has made a career despite—or perhaps because of—critique, exploring and re-creating the unimaginable in American history.

—JASMINE DARIA CANNON

LITERATURE: Oh

Fig. 8.3. Kara Walker, *Boo Hoo*, 2000. Linoleum cut on Arches Cover paper. 393/4×205/8 in. (101×52.4 cm). Collection Zimmerli Art Museum at Rutgers University. Gift of Maurice Sánchez, Derrière L'Étoile Studio. 2008.012.252. Artwork © Kara Walker.

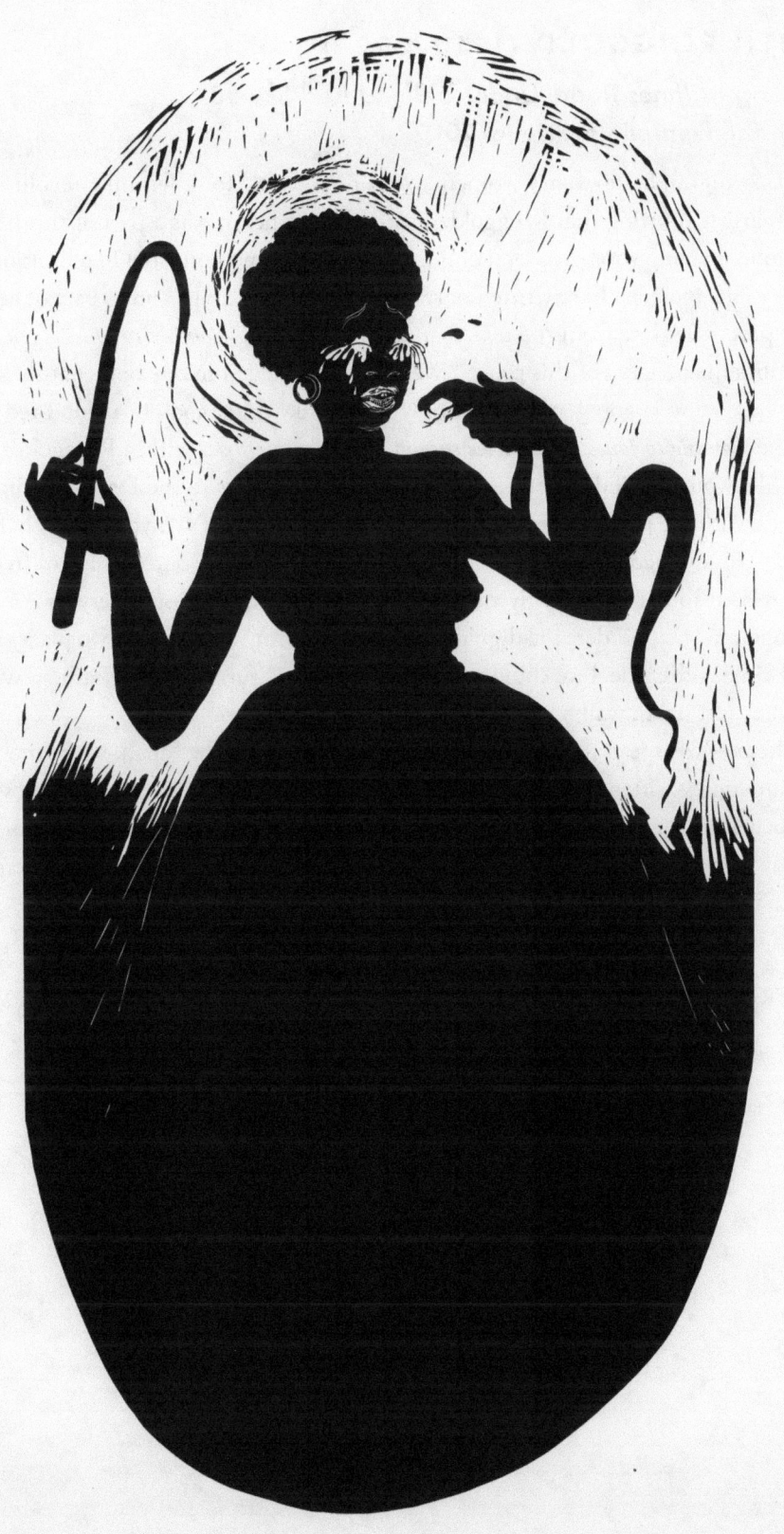

FAITH RINGGOLD (1930-2024)

Coming to Jones Road: Under a Blood Red Sky #8, from the *Femfolio* portfolio, 2007

Femfolio highlighted twenty women artists responsible for a feminist revolution in 1970s art. It is fitting that Ringgold, a storyteller at heart, was a part of this historic portfolio. Having written several children's books, she was invested in education and history. She included handwritten narratives in her story quilts and as part of her creative process. A line from the text that accompanies the *Coming to Jones Road* series describes the imagery of this print: "We moved along as if in one body hardly knowing where we were going, our way lit only by a chalk-white moon in a blood-red sky."[2]

The *Coming to Jones Road* series served multiple purposes within Ringgold's practice. She would periodically release images from the series in the form of prints and images, with the proceeds from the sales benefiting the artist's Anyone Can Fly Foundation. Simultaneously, the series served to grapple with the journey toward freedom as it related to her own family history and the larger history of slavery in America. Lithographic text borders the digital print: "Aunt Emmy could be in two places at the same time and Uncle Tate could vanish in a flash and turn up in the same way. One day they just up an walk to freedom an nobody see 'em go."

These words speak to the character of the forms under the "chalk-white moon"—they are quick-witted disappearing shadows among the trees, like the countless self-emancipators who traveled at night via the Underground Railroad. The figure of Aunt Emmy is inspired by the history of Ringgold's real-life, quilt making Great Grandma Bingham, who started her life in slavery.

–KYLE B. CO.

LITERATURE: Brodsky Center at PAFA, Roth

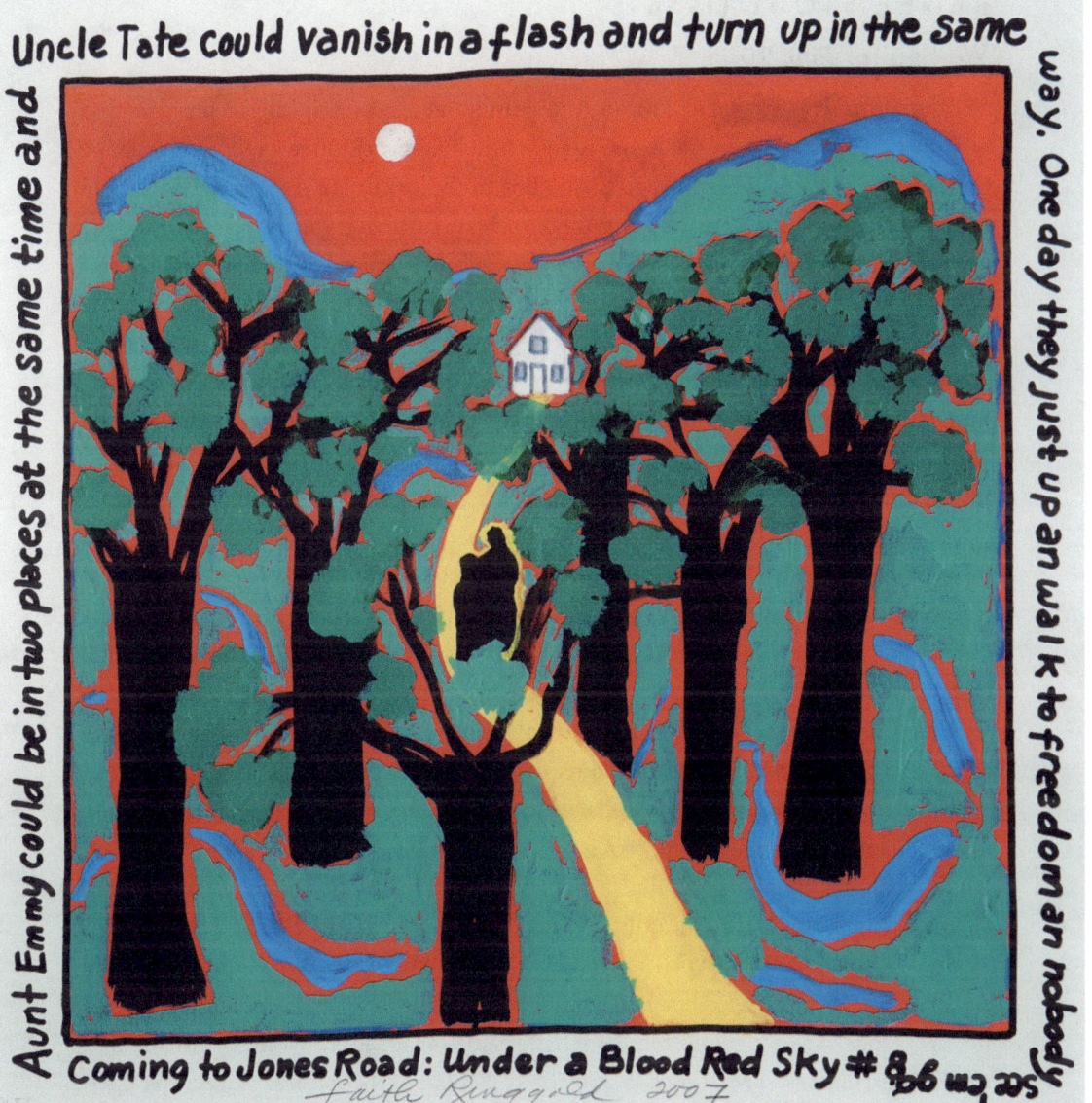

Fig. 8.4. Faith Ringgold, *Coming to Jones Road: Under a Blood Red Sky #8*, from the *Femfolio* portfolio, 2007. Color digital print with hand lithography on Somerset enhanced velvet paper. 11 15/16 × 12 in. (30.4 × 30.5 cm). Collection Zimmerli Art Museum at Rutgers University. Gift of the Brodsky Center at Rutgers, The State University of New Jersey. 2010.006.001.10. © 2026 Faith Ringgold / Artists Rights Society (ARS), New York. Courtesy ACA Galleries, New York.

RENÉE STOUT (1958-)

Waiting for Jimi, 2006

Waiting for Jimi is a tribute to African American music, and specifically to Jimi Hendrix and his influences. The central figure is an ornate house with three windows projecting bright light outward like stained glass, alluding to the sanctity of the space. To the right of the doorway is the heart-shaped symbol in Haitian Vodou for the goddess Erzulie-Freda, a motif found in several of Stout's works. A bright yellow eye, the third eye, stares out directly at the viewer, signifying a space for introspection. Text covers the house's outer walls, identifying the building as the "House of Obeah." The word *obeah* has a complicated history but generally refers to a religious doctor in the Caribbean antebellum context who can control supernatural forces and can heal using spells, divination, dream interpretation, and herbal medicine. Stout thus brings a main aspect of her art practice, healing, into the context of African American music and history.

The year 1916 etched above a skull shows the approximate start date of the first wave of the Great Migration. It is during this period that many African Americans left the Southern states for Northern cities, especially because of Jim Crow laws and segregation. The Great Migration spurred the evolution and dissemination of Black American musical culture, particular the blues and jazz, to northern and western destinations. The skull stands for the historical human cost of southern lynching and abuse and signifies that this place is a requiem for the deceased.

Other texts are written on the walls, including the phrase "Where Jimi Hendrix met a Vodou chile," referencing Hendrix's song "Voodoo Chile" (1968), which was based on Muddy Waters's blues song "Rollin' Stone" (1950). Stout lists the names of famous African American musicians, including Waters, Robert Johnson, Sam Cooke, Phyllis Hyman, Tina Turner, Betty Davis, Tina B., Howlin' Wolf, Sly Stone, and Bobby Womack, many of whom traveled north and brought their soulful sounds with them. Through her art, Stout explores the history of African American music, with a focus on jazz, rhythm and blues, soul, and rock 'n' roll artists. Several of the musical pioneers had personal relationships with and connections to Hendrix. Stout honors these artists with a safe place to come and practice traditional African medicine and spiritual beliefs, allowing them to heal themselves both in body and in soul. She also hints at the healing power of music that has built this house of spiritual worship.

—GRACE KIM

LITERATURE: Handler and Bilby, "African American Song"

Fig. 8.5. Renée Stout, *Waiting for Jimi*, 2006. Color screen print. 2615/16 × 217/16 in. (68.4 × 54.5 cm). Collection Zimmerli Art Museum at Rutgers University. Gift of Pyramid Atlantic, Inc. 2007.0094. © Renée Stout.

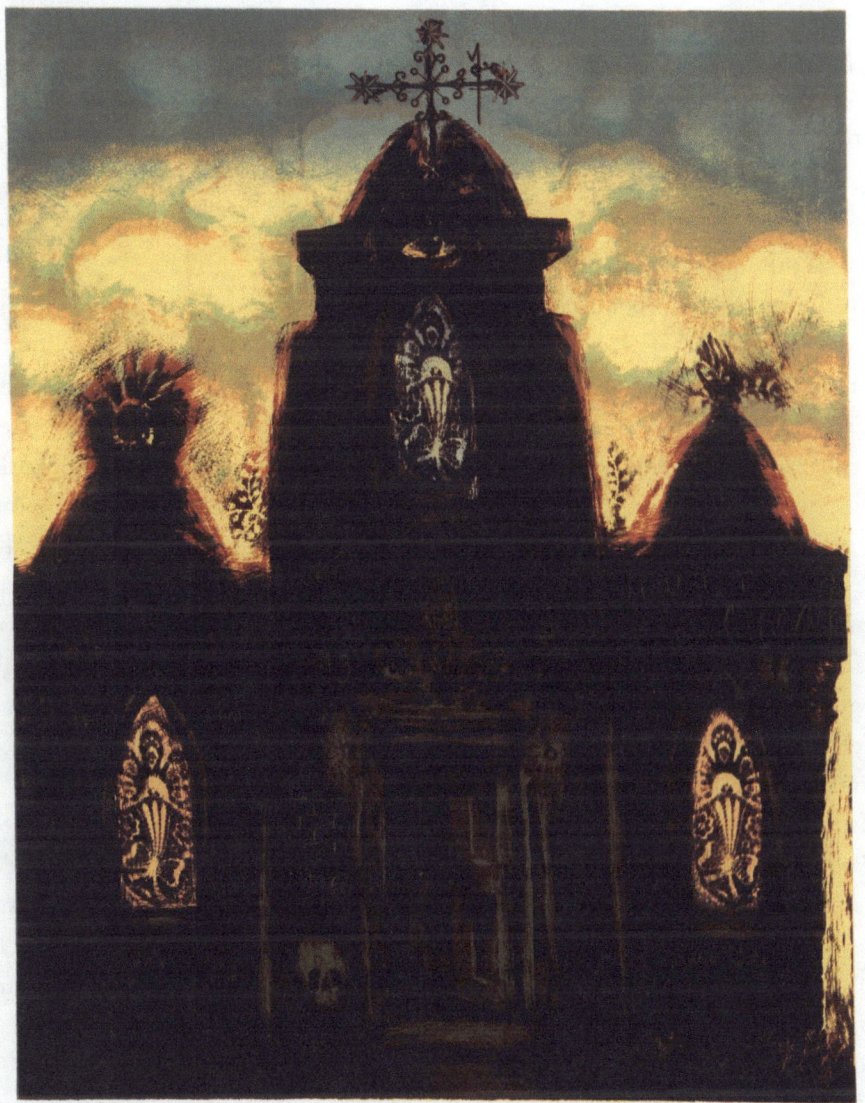

"Waiting for Jesus"   18/30   Denis Stone 2000

BISA WASHINGTON (1952-)

Never Forget, 1999

The central figure of this print resembles a weathervane, while radial elements compose the cardinal directions of a compass. Grounding this imagery is the handwritten, lithographic layer of text spiraling out from the center. Written in cursive, the text is partially obstructed but repeats the following phrase: "The power of love in the face of senseless cruelty and violence."

The text is a chant, or incantation—the markings all together appearing as character forms filling the body of this site of navigation. The words exist in every direction of the weathervane and compass form. "The power of love" is the only force to orient us through this tragic history.

At the crest of each point of the weathervane are enslaved figures fitted with iron masks and pronged iron collars. These pieces of ironwork hold historically cruel meanings. Enslavers commonly attached the pronged or spiked collar to enslaved people who had previously tried to escape. As a form of punishment and deterrent, the collar would prevent the captive from moving inconspicuously or resting. Enslavers also used the iron mask as a means of punishment and a method against escape. The mask prevented suicidal enslaved people from consuming poison or dirt to otherwise end their life. Their captors also used this restriction of the ability to eat as a form of punishment.

The weathervane additionally resembles the Haitian Vodou symbol for Papa Legba, the guardian of the crossroads, boundaries, and paths. Papa Legba is the entity from which one must seek permission to commune with the ancestral plane; he is a representation of communication. Here, we commune with a cruel history.

Investigating other symbols in the print reveals the hamsa (also known as the Hand of Fatima and the Hand of Miriam), a symbol commonly found throughout the Middle East and North Africa and within Jewish faiths. The hamsa is a charm meant to ward off evil or dispel negative energy, in addition to more specific faith-based uses. The heart in hand is an alternative type of hamsa or a symbol associated with the Christian reformist John Calvin and the Shakers. As an icon of the Shakers, it portrays the figurative giving of one's heart to God.

The rough silhouette of a rooster and the filigree above the heads of the slaves visually call on the language of the original ironwork form of the weathervane. We are to view the violence of these forms within the Americana kitsch. We are to never forget that this was America.

–KYLE B. CO.

LITERATURE: Morris, Washington 2010 and 2016, Zimmer

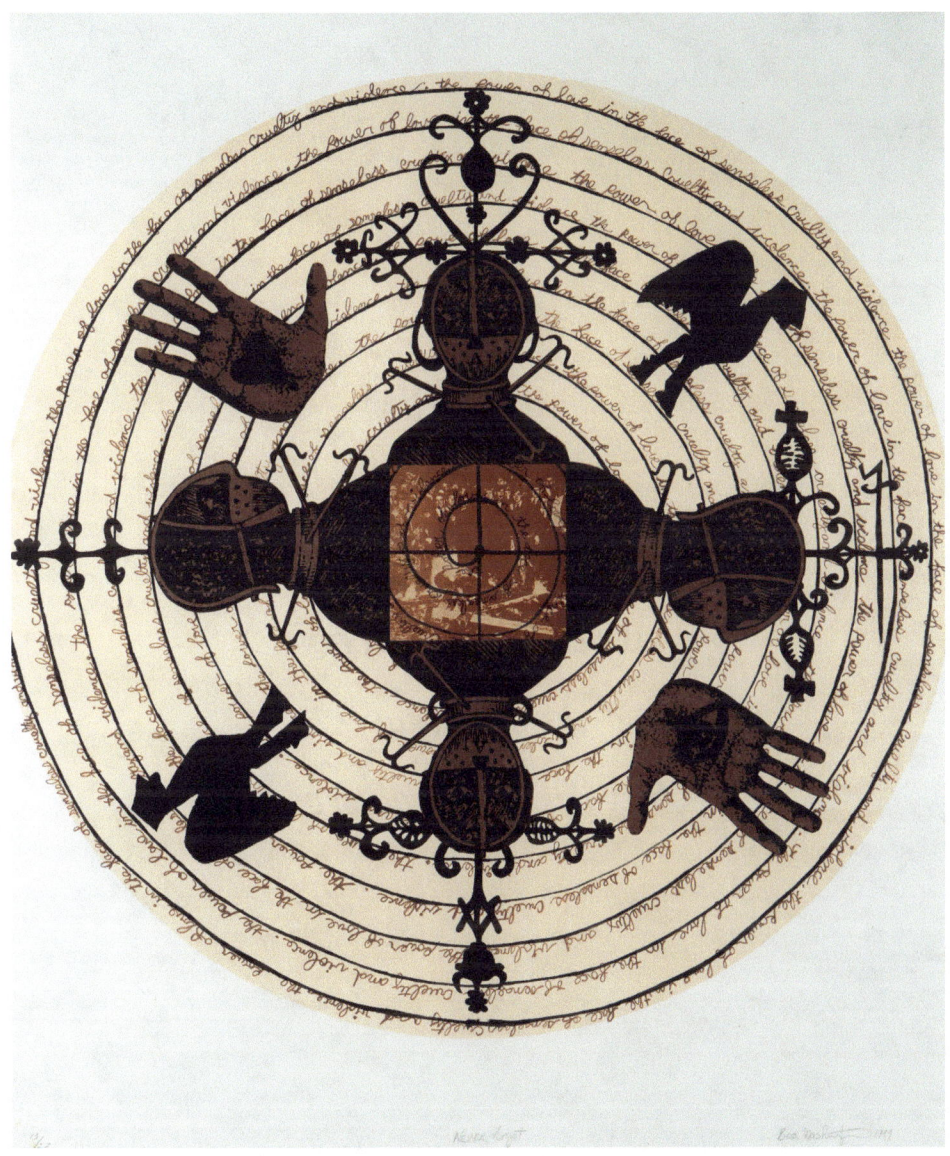

Fig. 8.6. Bisa Washington, *Never Forget*, 1999. Color relief, lithograph, and chine collé. 383/16 × 311/2 in. (97 × 80 cm). Collection Zimmerli Art Museum at Rutgers University. Gift of the Brodsky Center at Rutgers, The State University of New Jersey. 2010.006.003.

Notes

1. Lisa Gail Collins, "The Evidence of the Process," *Transition*, no. 109 (2012): 50.
2. Moira Roth, "Faith Ringgold: Putting Jones Road on the Map," *Nka: Journal of Contemporary African Art*, no. 13–14 (Spring/Summer 2001): 21–22.

We can give students

the education

they desire and deserve.

—b e l l h o o k s ,
1 9 9 4

Conclusion
Seeing Ourselves

AMBER N. WILEY

WE GATHERED TOGETHER, WRAPPED IN a sea of sapphire blue. The beckoning pull of the sublime atmosphere was a welcome feeling after years of social isolation and physical restrictions. We laughed. We gasped. We leaned forward to closely examine. We furrowed our brows and stroked our chins. We truly became a "we." A collective. That thing for which we yearned, finally came to fruition.

It was an early evening in late fall, and the sun hung low in the sky. Rutgers faculty and staff, New Brunswick–area residents, the student curators from the Exhibition Seminar, as well as my current students in the African American Art survey and Curatorial Training seminar, friends, and family circulated through the two galleries of the Mary H. Dana Women Artist Series (DWAS). People commented on the arresting yet calming blue walls, the breadth of the pieces, the vivacity, the details. It was the opening reception for *Collective Yearning: Black Women Artists from the Zimmerli Art Museum.*

Staff at the Mabel Smith Douglass Library directed visitors to the lecture hall, where I had assembled an expert panel of presenters who were forging a new path in the art world through curation, education, and activism. The panel consisted of three Black women Rutgers alumnae: Key Jo Lee, who had received her bachelor's in art history from Douglass College; Stephanie Johnson-Cunningham, who received her master's in

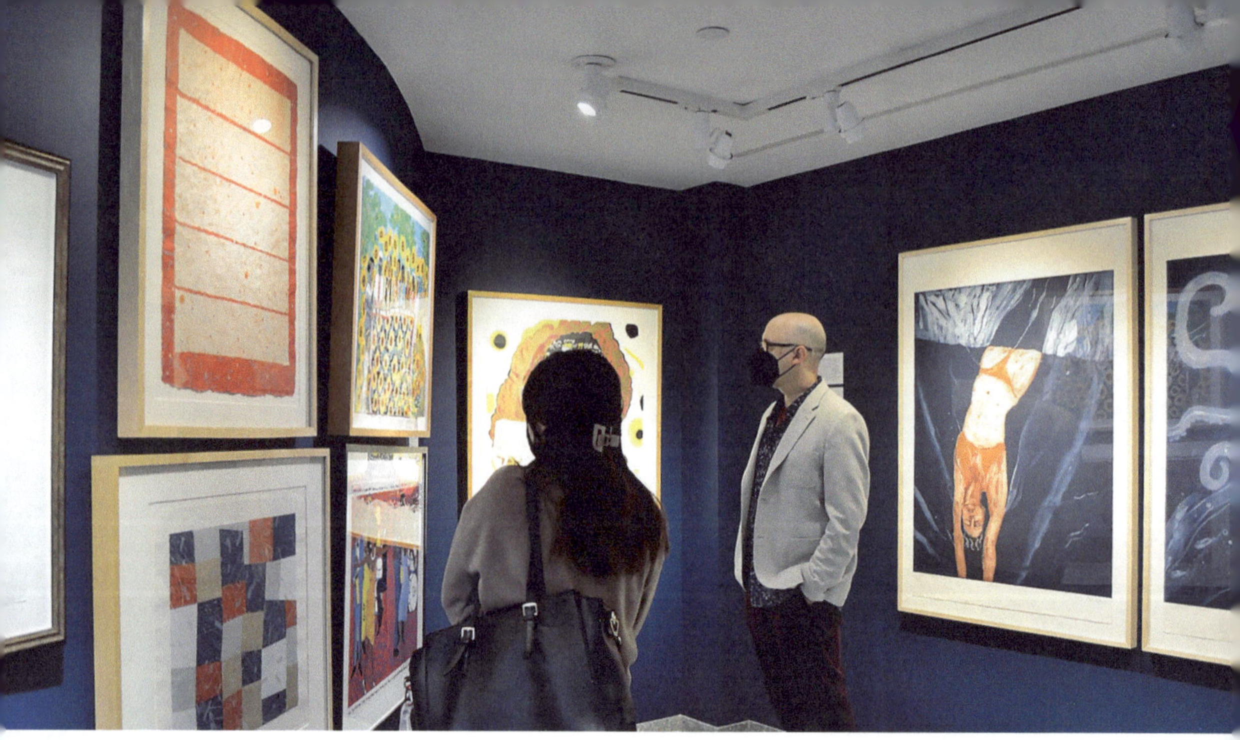

Fig. C.1. Guest and the student curator Helen Gao (back to camera) viewing artwork at exhibition launch in Gallery 104B of the Mary H. Dana Women Artists Series (DWAS) at the Douglass Library. 2022. Nicole Ianuzelli, photographer.

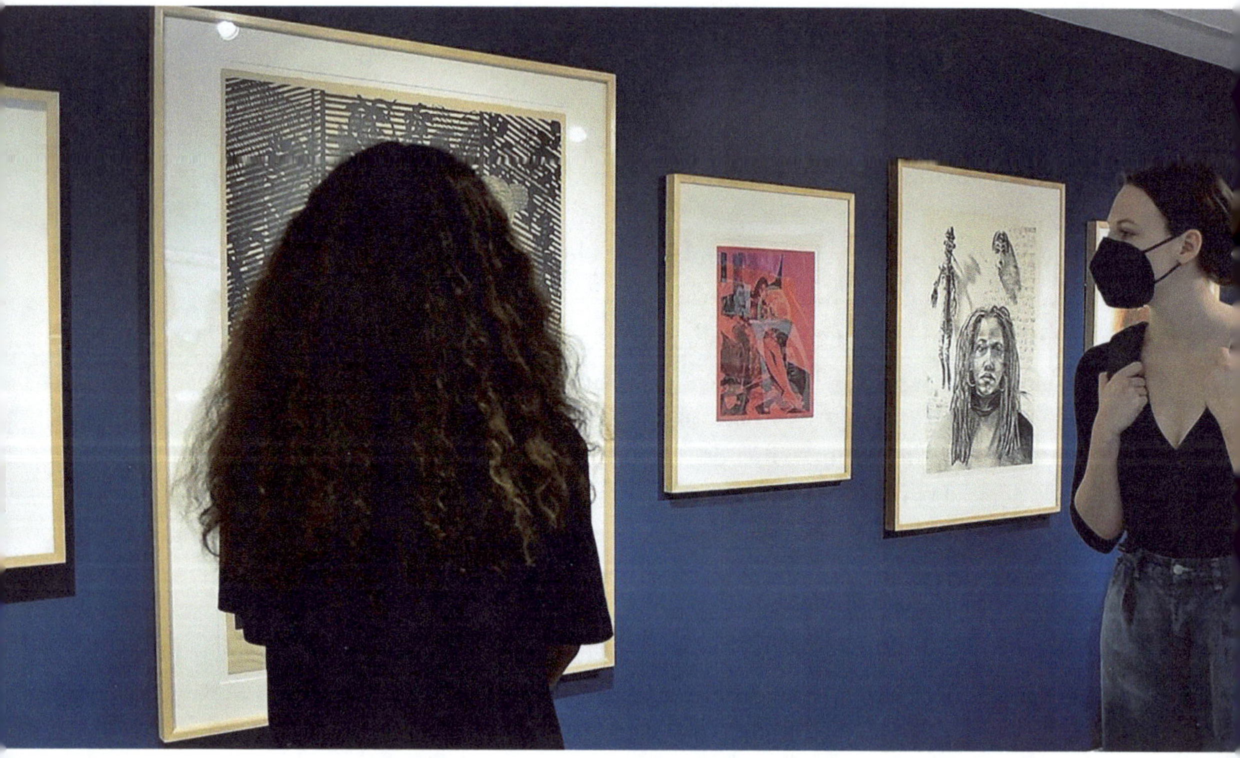

Fig. C.2. Rutgers student and guest Joo-Yung Wiley (back to camera) viewing artwork at exhibition launch in Gallery 104A of the DWAS. 2022. Nicole Ianuzelli, photographer.

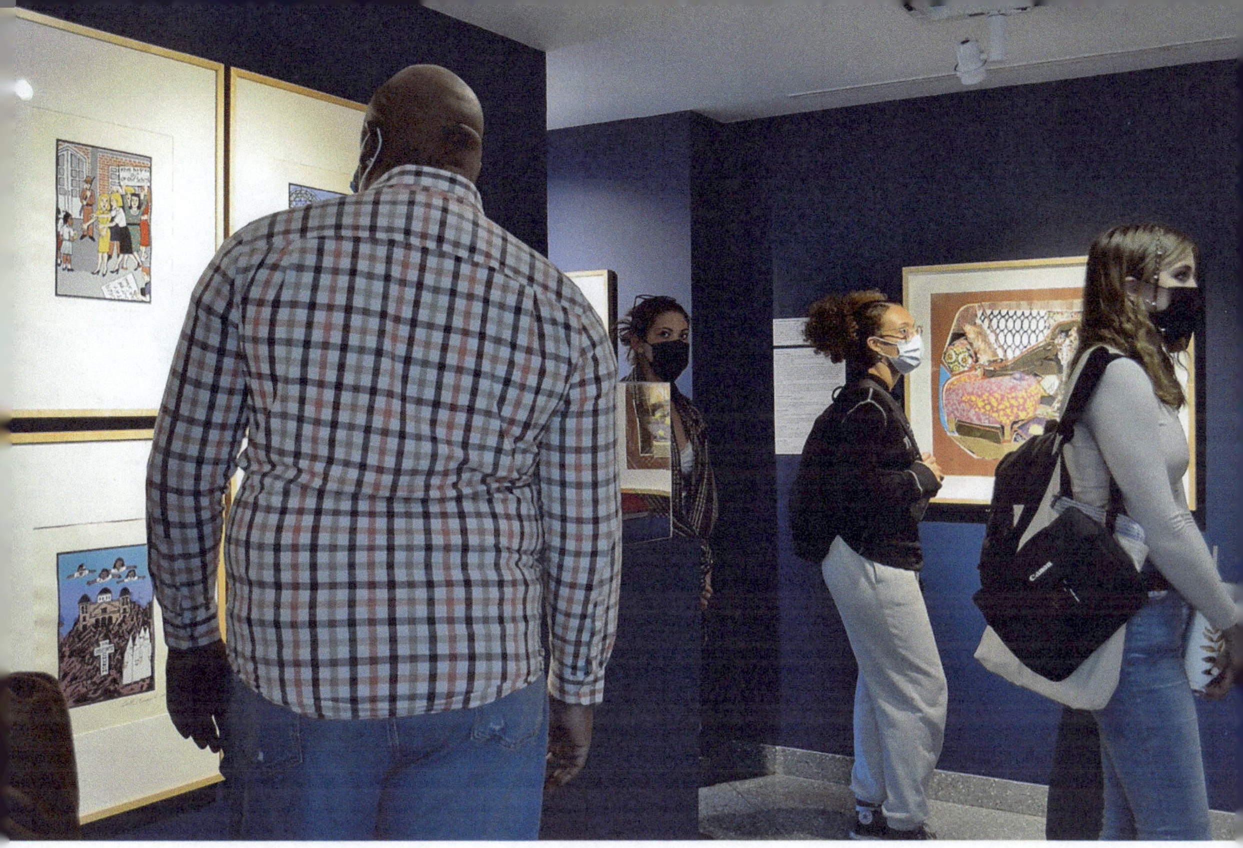

Fig. C.3. Guests viewing artwork at exhibition launch in Gallery 104A of the DWAS. 2022. Nicole Ianuzelli, photographer.

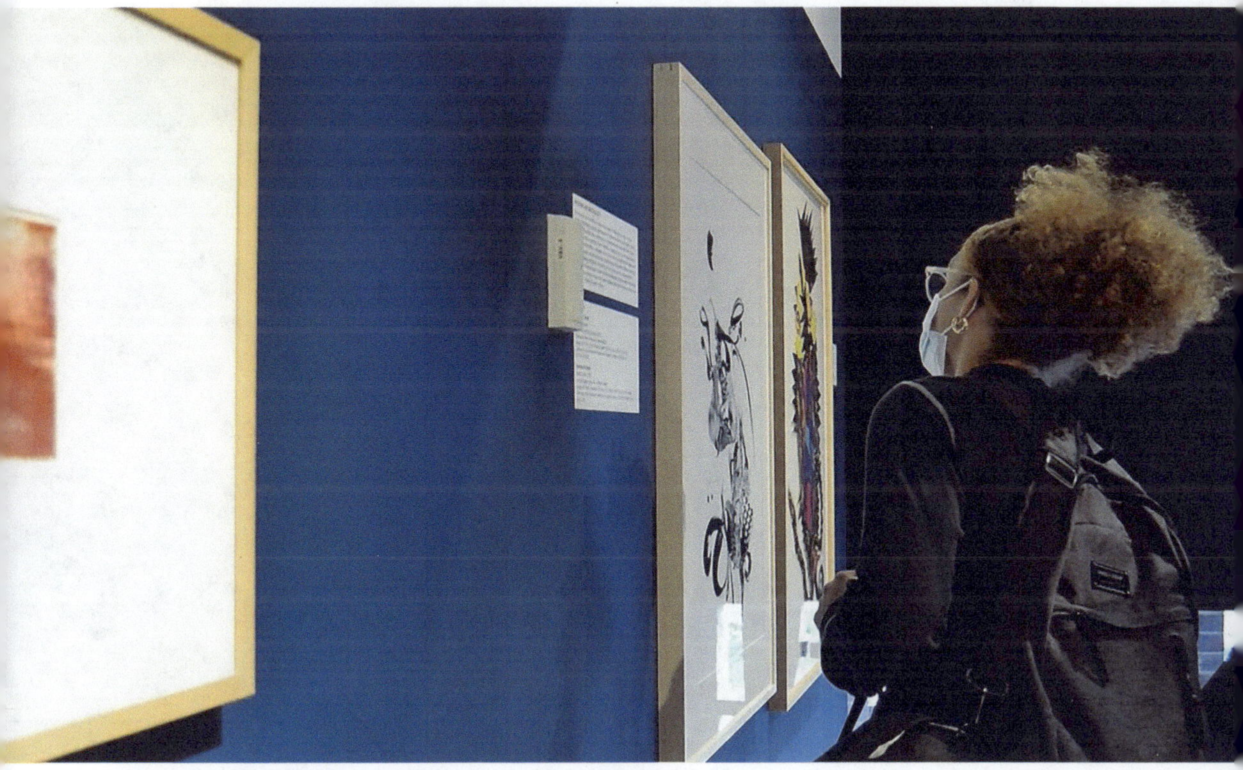

Fig. C.4. Rutgers student examining artwork in Gallery 104A of the DWAS. 2022. Nicole Ianuzelli, photographer.

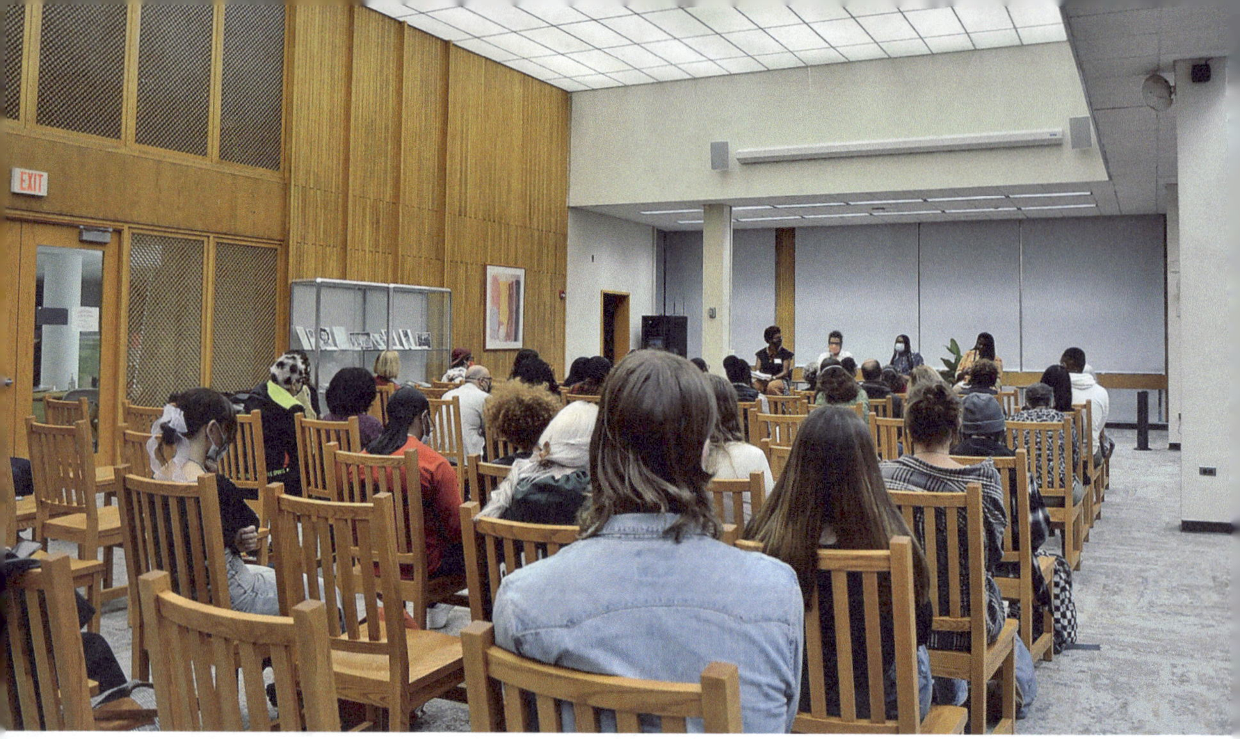

Fig. C.5. Exhibition launch panel discussion at Douglass Library. 2022. Nicole Ianuzelli, photographer.

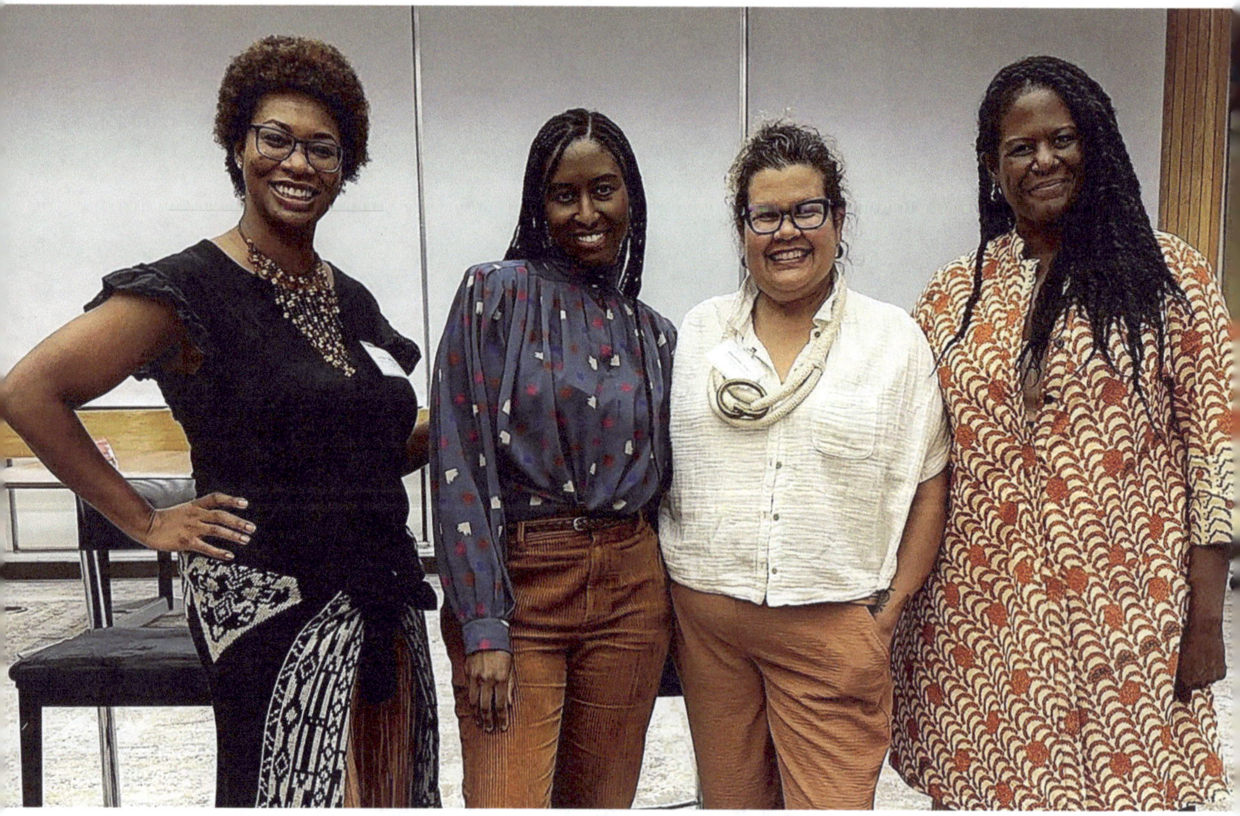

Fig. C.6. Pictured from left to right: Amber N. Wiley and panelists Stephanie Johnson-Cunningham, Heather Hart, and Key Jo Lee. 2022. Nicole Ianuzelli, photographer.

cultural heritage and preservation studies; and Heather Hart, who received her master's in fine arts from the Mason Gross School of the Arts. Combined, these three graduates stood for the different divisional units of the university that had worked in tandem to bring the exhibition to life. The curation of the panel was no small gesture.

In addition to their connections to Rutgers as alumnae, they were engaged in various aspects of the art world. Lee is a curator—at the time, she was the associate curator of American art at the Cleveland Museum of Art, now she serves as chief of curatorial affairs and public programs at the Museum of the African Diaspora in San Francisco.[1] Johnson-Cunningham is an arts advocate and co-founder and executive director of Museum Hue, a nonprofit organization that supports and recognizes Black, Indigenous, and all people of color in museum spaces.[2] And finally Hart, who contributed chapter 2 of this publication, is a practicing artist, Rutgers faculty member, and co-founder of the Black Lunch Table, a radical archiving project.[3] Having these women representing overlapping spheres of influence in the art world demonstrated to my students the possibilities of their own future trajectories as artists, advocates, curators, and historians. I hoped that my students could see themselves in the work of the panelists. Moreover, I wanted Rutgers as an institution to see the social and cultural capital that these women, like those artists in the *Collective Yearning* exhibition, bring to the places they enter.

THE FRUITS OF OUR COLLECTIVE LABOR

The exhibition and its accompanying programming were direct manifestations of the collaborative work of my students and myself during a semester of virtual learning in the spring of 2021. It was also a response to student demand to see and experience more art by Black woman at Rutgers. My survey students made the call, and my seminar students responded. We challenged ourselves in this process, and the greater Rutgers community was rewarded.

The obstacles we faced were multitudinous. First, there was the issue of finding Black women artists in a collection that used a cataloging system that did not include the artist's race, a common convention in the museum world. Second, the collection was physically off-limits to us during the pandemic. Information on some of our artists was extremely sparse (and still is). Third, and finally, our detractors thought basing an exhibition solely on the work of Black women was simplistic, even passé. They expressed doubt about whether there were enough "good" works by Black women in the collection. Aside from the added hurdle of the pandemic, none of these challenges were new.

Indeed, the notion that the work by Black women artists might not be good enough to display was reflective of age-old value frameworks in art historiography. As the cultural critic Michele Wallace has argued, "There has not been nearly the focus on reconceptualizing aesthetic criteria that there has been on refuting scientific rationalizations of racism."[4] After the exhibition launched, the overwhelmingly positive response from students, staff, faculty, and New Jersey residents refuted the assumptions of aesthetic inferiority that have long plagued non-white and non-male artists. As Wallace contends: "These people—black visual artists—make things and make visions. Their job, their goal is to re-envision vision. What have they ever done to deserve our contempt? I think we need to begin to understand how regimes of visuality enforce racism, how they literally hold it in place."[5] Certainly, *Collective Yearning* did the work. Within the first week of its launch, I received an excited note from Nicole Ianuzelli, then senior program manager at the Center for Women in the Arts and Humanities (now Center for Women in the Arts at Douglass): "Someone at the circ[ulation] desk told me that people are loving the exhibit so much, they are coming up to the library staff to tell them!"[6] A colleague in the history department who visited the Focus Gallery shortly after the exhibition opened declared she was "taken aback by the collection, including pieces by Saar, Ringgold and Walker that [she] hadn't seen or known that [the Zimmerli] had."[7] So much for the hierarchy of racist regimes of visuality. As the critical theorist Lindsey Stewart has noted, "Forging [a] Black feminist approach mean[s], in part, canon building."[8] While I would not call what we were doing canon building, per se, we were indeed forging a critical intervention in how the artworks by Black women artists in the Zimmerli collection were valued.

ARTISTS IN CONVERSATION WITH COLLECTIVE YEARNING

By itself, the exhibition was a statement against all those assumptions. We could have left it at that. But my students and I, with the great assistance of Ianuzelli and Alice Hernandez of the Office of the Executive Vice-President for Academic Affairs, presented a series of events to engage various publics with the work. The first was a virtual talk that I delivered as a part of the Scarlet Speakers series organized by the School of Arts and Sciences Alumni Relations and Engagement Office. The second was the hybrid (in-person and virtual) panel and opening reception for the exhibition. We followed those events with an artists' conversation and a student curator roundtable, both virtual. Like all aspects of the exhibition, the programming reflected classroom conversations and student desires. Our internal conversations in class were the basis of the external conversations and engagement with the broader public.

The purpose of offering the virtual artists' talk was twofold. The first reason was to get another perspective on the exhibition artworks from contemporary Black women artists whose work had synchronicities with the major themes in the show. The second point was to highlight the amazing work of artists who very much deserved to be collected or considered for potential inclusion in the Zimmerli collection (and others) at some point in the future. Thus, I invited the artists Rashayla Marie Brown and Ebony Iman Dallas to talk about their reactions to the show and to respond to the following prompts:

1. In what ways are the notions of "Self-Making and Identity" related to the work you do as a curator/artist/activist?

2. Another major theme of the exhibition is "The Art of Storytelling." Student curators describe it as a lens into the radical imagination that invites us to create our own alternate universe through complex narratives that redefine our realities and shape our existence. How has storytelling impacted your practice—in the archive, and as an interpreter of the past/present/future of the field?[9]

Brown is a self-described "undisciplinary" artist-scholar who explores how aesthetics can enact radical thought beyond mere representation. She creates "visually poetic and emotionally engaging artworks with a deeply critical eye toward knowledge, medium and audience," by blending "installation design, photography, performance, writing, video, and filmmaking with the implementation and critique of power structures."[10] The two pieces from *Collective Yearning* that immediately resonated with Brown were Carrie Mae Weems's *Hush of Our Silence* and Renée Stout's *Marie Laveau*. These prints spoke directly to Brown's interests in "the idea of looking" and "seeing and believing"—in particular, what it means to see and "to report what you see in a way that reflects your integrity as a human being."[11] Weems's use of interior language like *you* and *I* in her narrative and Stout's playing with light and shadow to add mystery but also reveal tidbits of truth were two tactics that Brown brought to the fore in her analysis of the works.

In Brown's own piece, *You Can't See Me, Fool*, she tinkers with some of these same motifs. In this photograph, Brown is depicting her grandmother, who spent part of her life passing for white. The piece is a play on the adage that a leopard cannot change its spots. Brown often presents the photograph with an artist contract that includes a clause guaranteeing Brown 50 percent of the resale profits for the artwork. This move, which is completely atypical in the art world, is a rejection of the exploitative nature of the art market and is a direct way to combat the historical trend of misrepresenting Black women in the public sphere.

Students from my African American Art survey who watched Brown's talk connected it with topics they had learned in that course, such as Sojourner Truth's copyright ownership and her selling of her carte de visite for her own profit. *You Can't See Me, Fool*, like many of Brown's installation and performance pieces, "create[s] counternarratives to oppressive stories" in powerful ways. The rhetorical drama in Brown's art and narrative voice, as well as the pieces in *Collective Yearning*, answer bell hooks's desire for "intellectual work that connects with habits of being, forms of artistic expression and aesthetics, that inform the daily life of a mass population as well as writers and scholars."[12] Art becomes the idiom for what has been left unsaid or unwritten.

Dallas, a fifth-generation Oklahoman and second-generation Somali American, is a multimedia artist, arts educator, and writer. She founded Afrikanation Artists Organization, based in Hargeisa, Somaliland, and Oklahoma City, to unify African American, Afro-Caribbean, and continental African populations through art and design for community activism. As she contends, "Art is the most powerful tool I have to fight injustice."[13] Part of her artistic practice is the healing process in reckoning with her father's death. Thus, much of her work is autobiographical. Dallas found resonance with Margo Humphrey's *The History of Her Life Written Across Her Face* and the artist's attempts to fit an entire memoir into one piece. She also found parallels in Emma Amos's *Identity*, its depiction of a singular woman divided by race and the symbolism that spoke to her heritage. Dallas's contention was that the latter piece reflected the diasporic diversity in her own family.

Dallas's multimedia artwork *The Way You Frame It* incorporates textiles from places of ancestral importance to her: Somalia, Kenya, Ghana, and Nigeria. The piece depicts Dallas's family—her two brothers, her sister, the adoptive father who raised her, and

Fig. C.7. Rashayla Marie Brown, *You Can't See Me, Fool/Keïta and Sherman Had a Baby/ Near Threatened/Endangered Species/Passing for a Leopard/Imitation of Life/Equal Opportunist/The Domestication Effect/True Beast Dionysius, the Dying God/For My Grandma Who Passed for White, then Stopped/Living a Lie is a Poor Substitute/Fuck you, I like leopard/50 Shades of Slay/Jeremiah 13:23: Can the Ethiopian change his skin, or the leopard his spots? then may ye also do good, that are accustomed to do evil*, 2014. Courtesy of the artist.

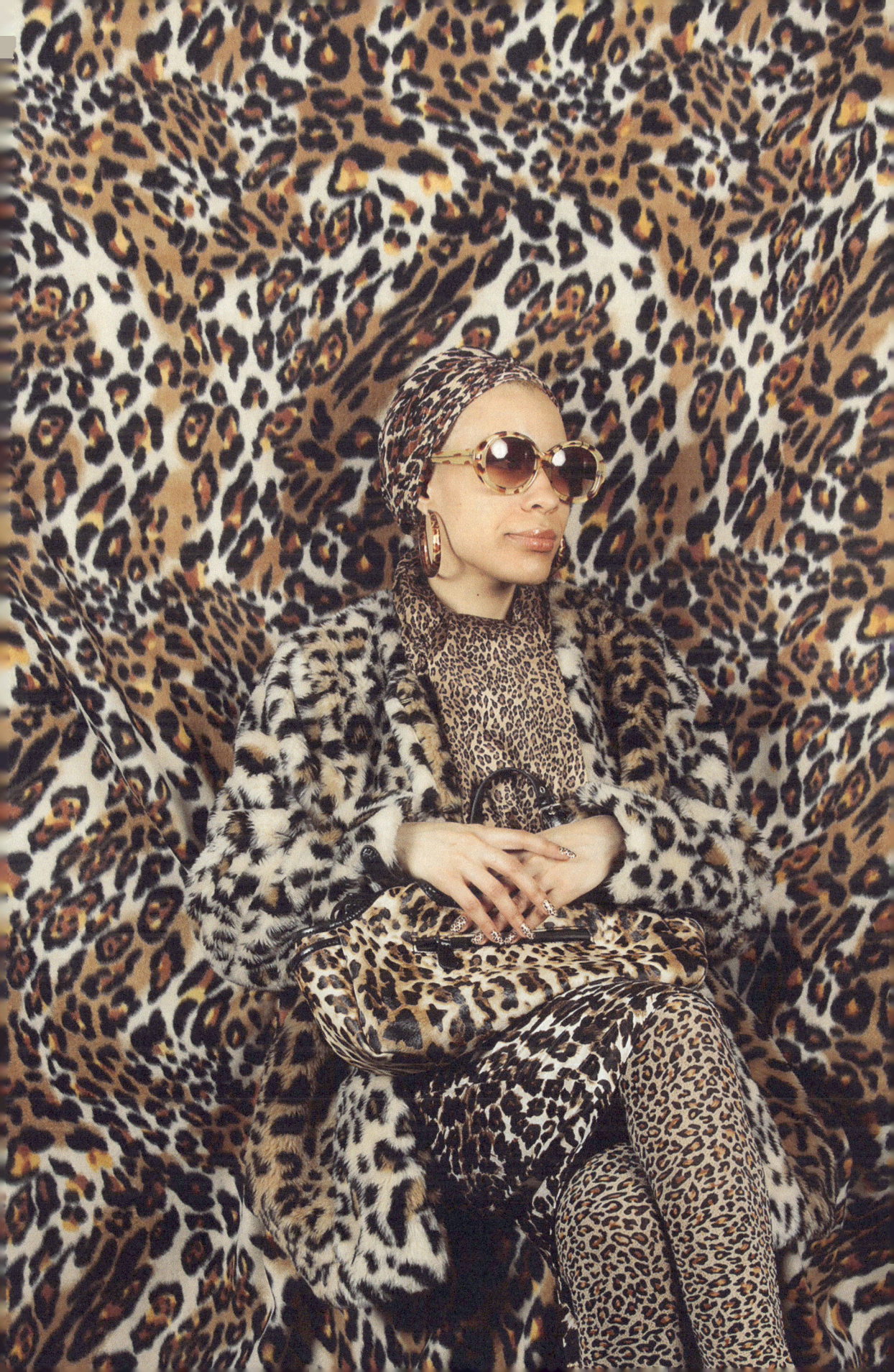

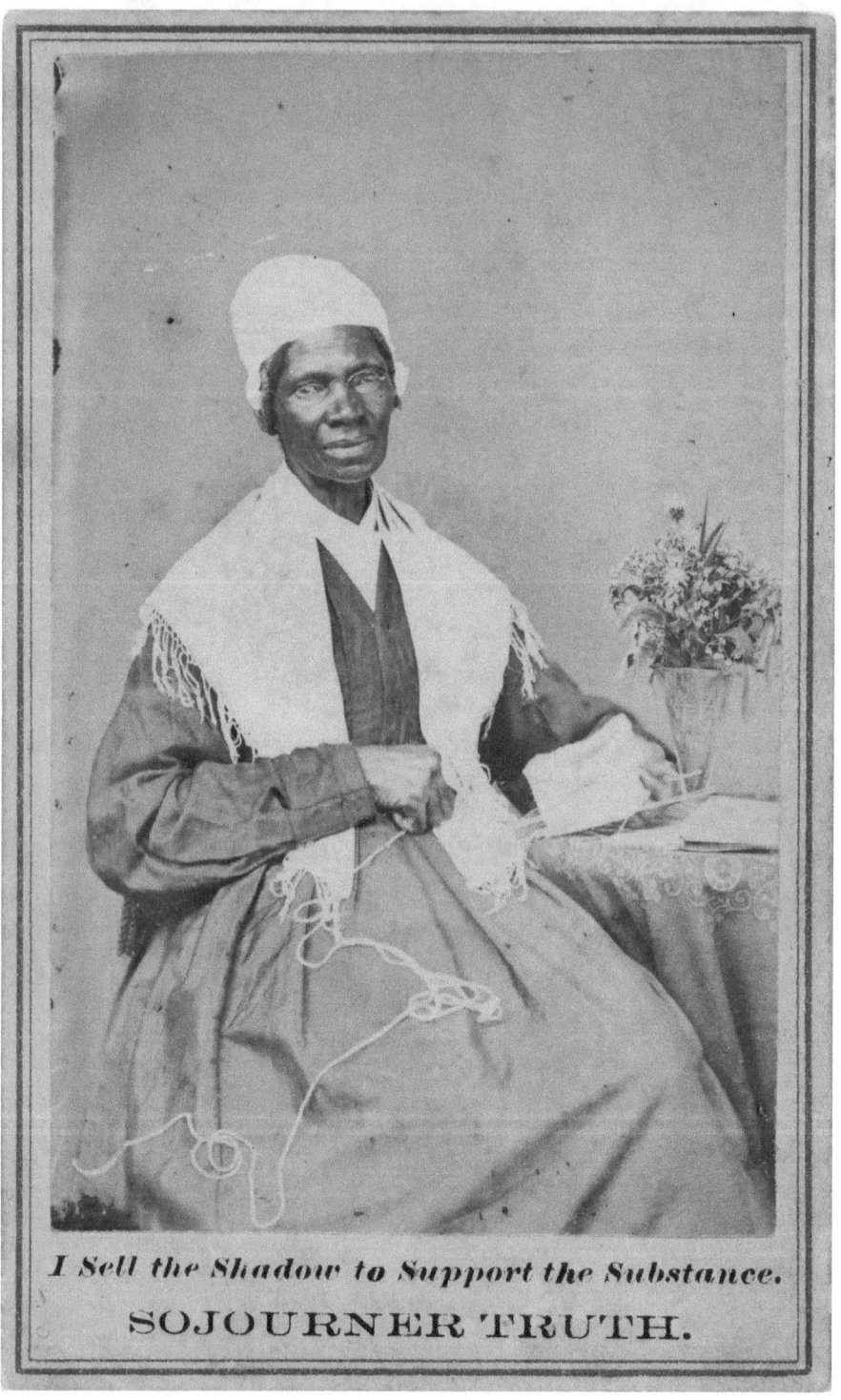

Fig. C.8. Unknown photogapher, *Sojourner Truth*, *"I Sell the Shadow to Support the Substance,"* ca. 1864. Albumen print on carte de visite mount. 3.94×2.4 in. (10×6 cm). Library of Congress.

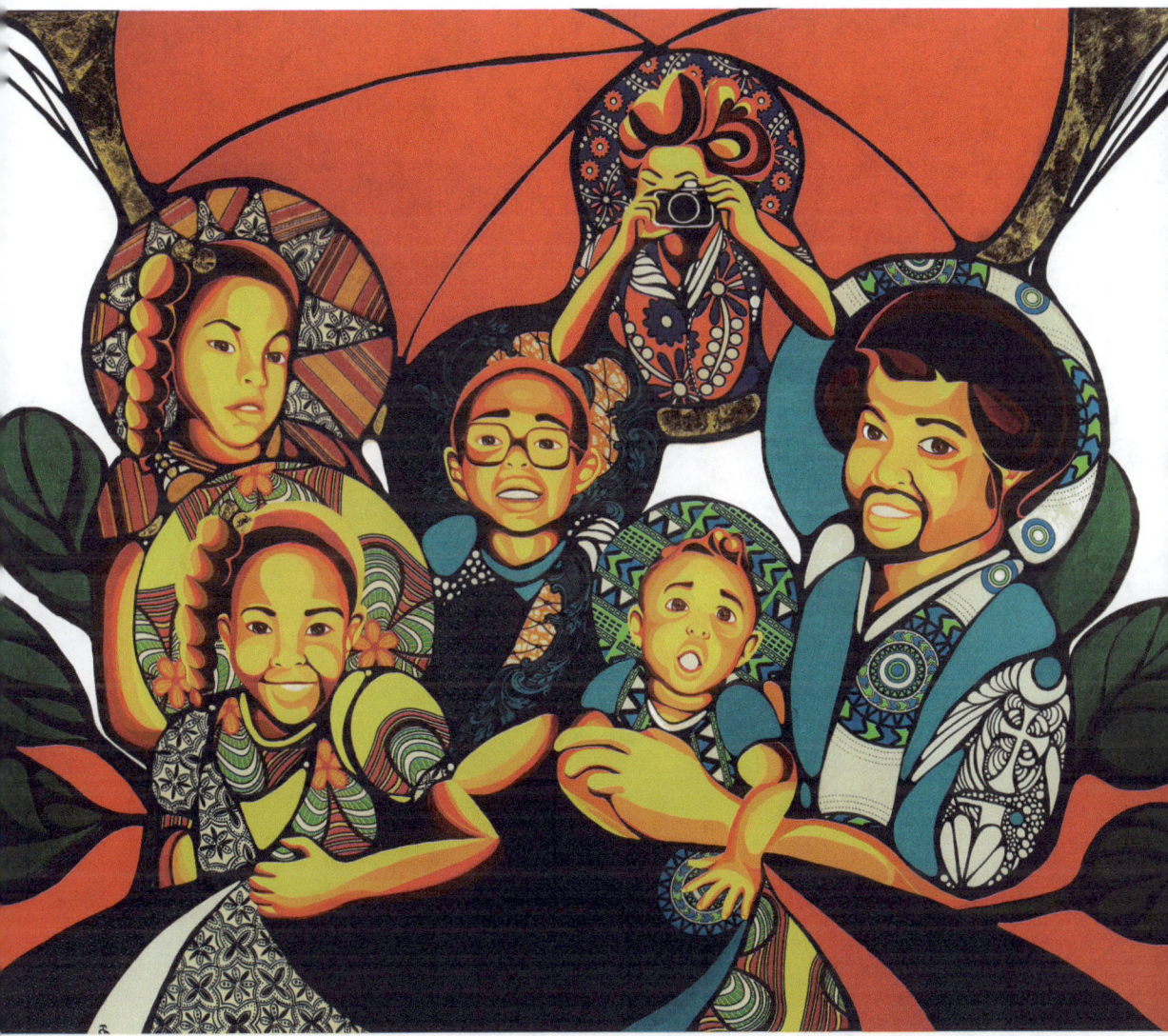

Fig. C.9. Ebony Iman Dallas, *The Way You Frame It*, from the series *Through Abahay's Eyes*, 2020. Acrylic, gold leafing, and Ghanaian, Kenyan, Nigerian, and Somali textiles on canvas. 50×40 in. (127×101.6 cm). © Ebony Iman Dallas.

her mother. Somali henna design inspired the line work that encapsulates and connects her family members. The artwork is alluring in its vibrancy, but also in how Dallas shows us that family is based on blood as well as love. The original photographic reference for the painting does not include her mother, as her mother was the one behind the camera taking the picture. In Dallas's multimedia painting, however, her mother is incorporated and is the central figure. By providing multiple lenses from which to approach the concept of family, Dallas affords us the flexibility to find mean-

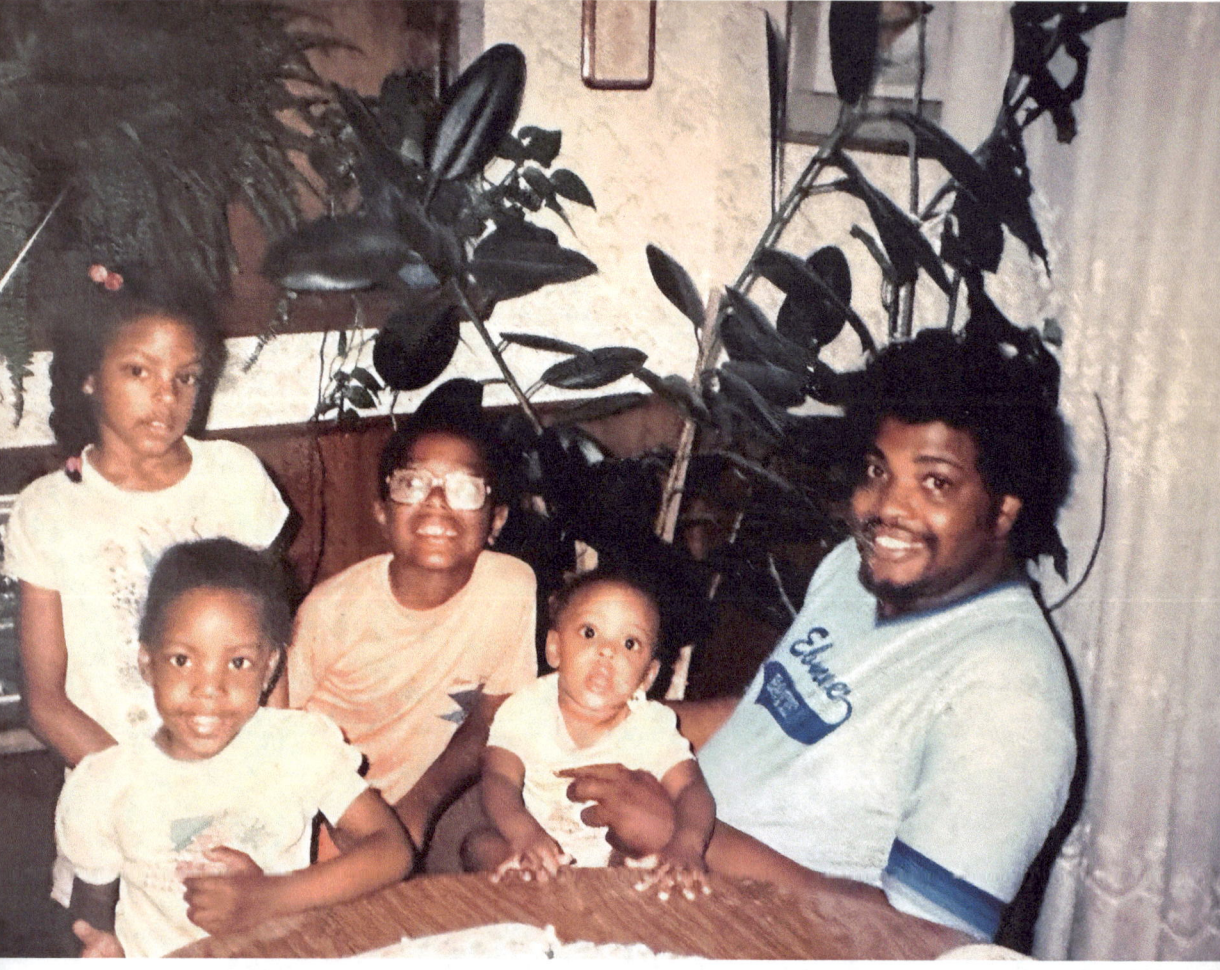

Fig. C.10. Dallas family seated around a table. Viola Dallas, photographer. ca. 1986. Courtesy of the artist.

ing in crafting our own definitions and telling our own stories. This strategy allows for "change that can renew spirits and reconstruct grounds for collective Black liberation struggle," in the domestic interior as well as in the Afrodiasporic world.[14]

The artists' talk and the exhibition revealed conversations between our artists—those spoken and unspoken. Faith Ringgold's *The Sunflower Quilting Bee at Arles* reflects this kind of intergenerational discourse. In that print, Ringgold depicts Black women figures, from the past and present, some whose lives crossed in both time and space, and others who lived in completely different eras. By bringing them all together in one place, Ringgold not only showed how they laid the foundation for her own existence—she paid homage to that inheritance.

Ringgold's print reminds me of a point that writer Alice Walker makes in her essay "In Search of Our Mothers' Gardens." In this essay, Walker is struggling to come to terms with society's subjugation of the latent creativity that existed within Black women—including our mothers and grandmothers—in the oppressive eras of generations past. Walker argues, "[Black women] waited for a day when the unknown thing that was in them would be made known; but guessed, somehow in their darkness, that on the day of their revelation they would be long dead."[15] This sentiment is also in line with what the artist Hart describes as "echoes" in her manifesto in chapter 2. Perhaps this is why the student curators describe the artworks in the exhibition as compressing, re-creating, and even rebuking time. Time is immaterial, really, when dealing with the creative reimaginings of oneself.

THE HUMAN DIMENSION IN STUDENT LEARNING

The student curators took the lessons learned in class, through the exhibition design process, to creatively reimagine what was possible. Thus, the final program for the exhibition was an ode to their work. The virtual roundtable featured three student curators who discussed their research findings—artist biographies, catalog entries, wall texts—as well as the ways they applied their lessons to reach beyond the limits of the semester and academic calendar.

In the months after the Exhibition Seminar, student curator Helen Gao took the time to interrogate her experience in the course. In a period of intense stress, while stuck inside the house because of the pandemic, she picked up a paintbrush. Starting in summer 2021, she created portraits of the twenty-four artists included in *Collective Yearning*. The act of painting was an extension of the joy she found in the learning process. She was also able to create a space for relaxation in a time of great uncertainty. Just as her classmates found it difficult to research some of the lesser-known artists, Gao found obstacles securing good reference photographs for the artists. Nadine DeLawrence Maine, for example, passed away from cancer in 1992 at age thirty-nine, before the advent of the contemporary digital age and the proliferation of artist promotion through social media. Ever cognizant of the need to increase the visibility of our artists who were often on the margins of the art historical canon, Gao's bold lime green backdrop was a conscious aesthetic choice to keep the artists from "fading into the background" of her painting.[16]

Kyle b. co. served as a Faculty Fellow in the Douglass Residential College, leading the Black Women Printmakers project, a direct outgrowth of programming that they conceived of in their exhibition proposal assignment in the Exhibition Seminar.

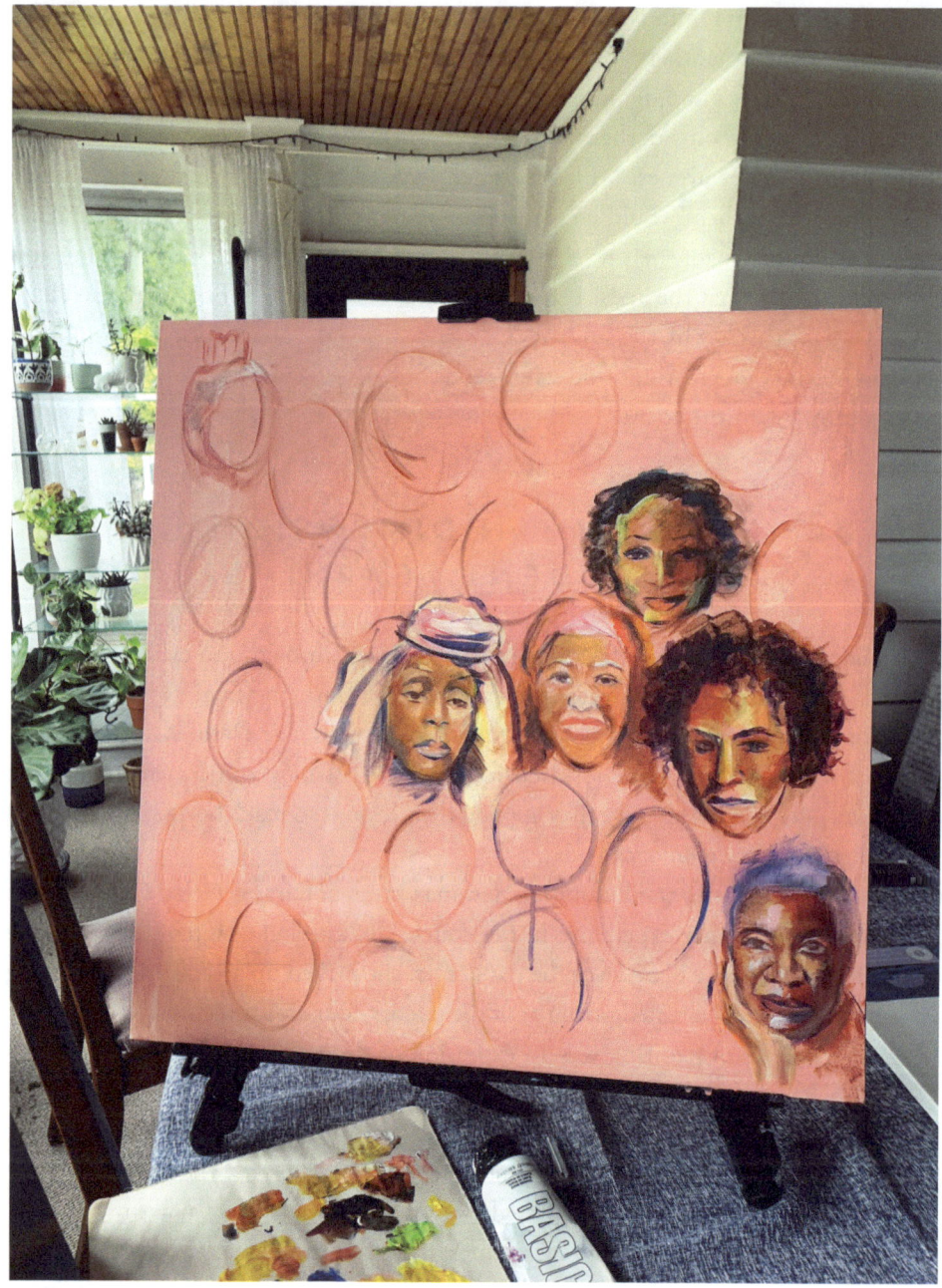

Fig. C.11. Process shot of Helen Gao's *The Faces of Collective Yearning*, 2021. Courtesy of the artist.

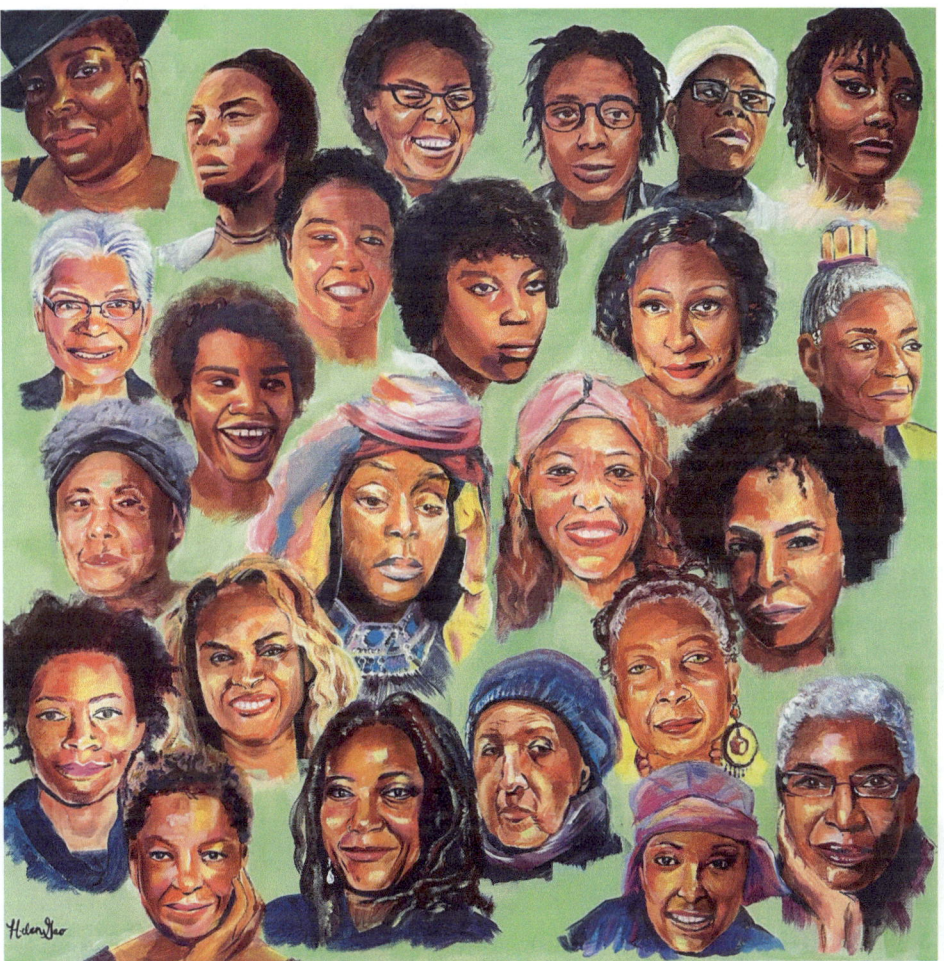

Fig. C.12. Helen Gao, *The Faces of Collective Yearning*, 2022. Acrylic on canvas. 24×24 in. (60.9×60.9 cm). From top to bottom, left to right: Nona Faustine, Nefertiti Goodman, Elizabeth Catlett, Mickalene Thomas, Bisa Washington, Atisha Fordyce, Sharon E. Sutton, Daonne Huff, Carmen Cartiness Johnson, Nadine DeLawrence Maine, Shinique Smith, Faith Ringgold, Betye Saar, Chakaia Booker, Stefanie Jackson, Lorna Simpson, Kara Walker, Emma Amos, Howardena Pindell, Barbara Bullock, Carrie Mae Weems, Renée Stout, Margo Humphrey, and Nell Irvin Painter. Courtesy of the artist.

Jacquelyn Litt, then-Dean of Douglass College, had audited the Exhibition Seminar and recommended that b. co. develop a proposal for the Faculty Fellow program after observing the richness and strength in the student work. Participants in the Black Women Printmakers project gained firsthand experience examining the artworks, learning about the printmaking process, producing their own prints, and developing docent scripts for exhibition tours. The student tour guides were available in the DWAS galleries from Monday through Friday at select times during the exhibition and interacted with numerous visiting class groups and library patrons.

Jasmine Daria Cannon applied her curatorial experience to research she conducted over summer 2022 in Raleigh, North Carolina, where she lived. That year, she organized a special Juneteenth display at the Pope House Museum, the former residence of one of the first Black physicians in the state. The exhibition featured aspects of twentieth-century Black social life through a careful selection of pins, jewelry, and ephemera that revealed aspects of the Pope family members' careers, politics, and community.

Thinking back to chapter 1 and my course development goals, the Exhibition Seminar assignments measured how students fulfilled the first three aspects of L. Dee Fink's taxonomy of significant learning—building foundational knowledge, application of critical thinking and problem solving, and integration of those lessons with other ideas and application within and outside the course. The subsequent engagement of student curators after the seminar ended reflects two other aspects of significant learning: the human dimension and caring.[17] The student curator roundtable and conversations I have had with students during and after the exhibition highlight what students learned about themselves in fulfilling our classroom tasks and also the strong association of their personal feelings and values with the subject matter and related topics.

As Rutgers French professor Mary Shaw has contended, "Long experience had taught me that students could accomplish wonderful things on their own, when allowed to choose what they wish to focus on and provided with strong examples, flexible guidelines, and the resources they need."[18] That notion rang true for the *Poetries— Politics* project she was involved with, as well as with the classwork that led up to the *Collective Yearning* exhibition. By taking the efforts of the classroom to the world, these student curators benefited from the exertions of applied learning. As the art historian and education specialist Jenevieve DeLosSantos maintains, project-based learning, such as the Exhibition Seminar, facilitates "research, analysis, collaboration, creativity, and even project management skills—through the act of doing."[19] It is heartening to see over the course of eight years, from the initial student assignment in African American Art to the publication of this book, the way students charted their own learning paths through expansive empathy and self-empowerment.

NEXT STEPS

It is my hope that this publication is not the end of these efforts for engaged learning and knowledge production, but a turning point. As Rutgers approaches its 260th anniversary, it should continue to examine and promote the relationship of Black women and femme artists from the area—New Jersey, New York City, and Philadelphia—to the university. There remain untapped resources and stories yet to be told. Rutgers Libraries Special Collections and University Archives hold the Miriam Schapiro Papers, which include the DWAS archives and the Faith Ringgold collection, among others. These resources can serve as the focus of new classes, as can the growing collection of Black women artists held by the Zimmerli due to the Jersey City Museum gift.

Furthermore, this project can push forward the dialogue around inequality and reparative justice. Many pieces in the exhibition spoke to enslavement, violence against Black men and women, discrimination, segregation, and the mental and physical toll these conditions have had on the Black community. As the poet Audre Lorde argued, racism, sexism, heterosexism, and homophobia are "forms of human blindness [that] stem from the same root—an inability to recognize the notion of difference as a dynamic human force, one which is enriching rather than threatening to the defined self, when there are shared goals."[20] Students, in their own way, can address these concerns, talk about them, see how they intersect with and compound other forms of oppression, and bring that knowledge with them to their respective corners of the world. Understanding difference while illuminating our shared humanity continues the process of historical reckoning at Rutgers and within and outside the United States.

I went into academia to teach—not to just be an intellectual, or to have high-level conversations with other intellectuals (although I do that too). I came specifically to make a difference in someone's educational journey the way other teachers have done for me. But there is an aspect of teaching that does not get much publicity, and something I only realized when I stepped into the classroom with the responsibility to lead. There exists a reciprocity of ideas that happens within the classroom. My students do not just learn from me—I learn from them. I learn so much. Any professor who cannot say that about their students is not actually paying attention. They are not actually listening. The mutual sharing of ideas is at the heart of our learning process. Being challenged with new insights, being shown something you did not know before, adding it to your intellectual tool belt to create something novel—that is what the learning process is about. And while teaching is hard, and academia is also hard, the reward is there to be had.

The heuristic journey of the course assignment that turned into a seminar that turned into an exhibition with programming that turned into a publication—that is the epitome of engaged pedagogy and resistant knowledge projects. It takes effort for academics to let go. To unleash control to see what comes from the work itself. This process was a creative act that I accepted with students over many years and across time and (virtual) space. While we worked within certain parameters and built upon a foundation I created, the end results were in the hands of my student curators. They were the team; I was the coach. I hope they see themselves on every page in this book.

Notes

1. Key Jo Lee, Erica Moiah James, Robin Coste Lewis, and Christina Sharpe, *Perceptual Drift: Black Art and an Ethics of Looking* (Yale University Press, 2022); Key Jo Lee, "Fragile Intimacies in the Portrait Miniature of Rose Tufts," Recent Acquisitions, *Yale University Art Gallery Bulletin*, 2017, 56–61.

2. Stephanie Johnson-Cunningham, "Culturally Responsive Museums Are Leading the Way," Museum Hue (blog), June 8, 2020, https://www.museumhue.org/2020/06/08/2020-6-8-culturally-responsive-museums -leading-the-way/.

3. Heather Hart and jina valentine, "Black Lunch Table," in *Out of Place: Artists, Pedagogy, and Purpose*, ed. Tim Doud and Zoë Charlton (Punctum Books, 2021), 223–234; jina valentine, Eliza Myrie, and Heather Hart, "The Myth of the Comprehensive Historical Archive," in *Wikipedia @ 20: Stories of an Incomplete Revolution*, ed. Joseph Reagle and Jackie Koerner (MIT Press, 2020), 259–272.

4. Michele Wallace, "Why Are There No Great Black Artists? The Problem of Visuality in African American Culture," in *Dark Designs and Visual Culture* (Duke University Press, 2004), 190.

5. Wallace, "Why Are There No Great Black Artists?," 191.

6. Nicole Ianuzelli, e-mail message to author, September 15, 2022.

7. Marisa J. Fuentes, e-mail message to author, September 29, 2022.

8. Lindsey Stewart, "Black Feminist Figures: Interventions and Inheritances," *Southern Journal of Philosophy* 59, no. 1 (March 2021): 10.

9. It was a virtual event, so I gave the guest artists access to an art checklist and digital reproductions of the pieces ahead of time.

10. Biography provided by Rashayla Marie Brown.

11. Rashayla Marie Brown, "Collective Yearning: Discussion with Artists Ebony Iman Dallas and Rashayla Marie Brown," lecture (virtual), Rutgers University, October 26, 2022.

12. Brown, "Collective Yearning: Discussion with Artists"; bell hooks, "Postmodern Blackness," *Postmodern Culture* 1, no. 1 (September 1990), https://dx.doi.org/10.1353/pmc.1990.0004.

13. Ebony Iman Dallas, "Collective Yearning: Discussion with artists Ebony Iman Dallas and Rashayla Marie Brown," lecture (virtual), Rutgers University, October 26, 2022.

14. hooks, "Postmodern Blackness."

15. Alice Walker, *In Search of Our Mothers' Gardens: Womanist Prose* (Amistad Press, 2023), 241.

16. Helen Gao, "Collective Yearning: Student Curator Roundtable with Jasmine Daria Cannon, Kyle b. co, and Helen Gao," lecture (virtual), Rutgers University, November 9, 2022.

17. L. Dee Fink, *Creating Significant Learning Experiences: An Integrated Approach to Designing College Courses* (Wiley, 2013).

18. Mary Shaw, "Why *Poetries—Politics*?," in *Poetries—Politics: A Celebration of Language, Art, and Learning*, ed. Jenevieve DeLosSantos (Rutgers University Press, 2023), 17.

19. Jenevieve DeLosSantos, "The Pedagogy of *Poetries—Politics*: How to Craft Your Own Project-Based Learning Course," in DeLosSantos, *Poetries—Politics*, 70.

20. Audre Lorde, *Sister Outsider: Essays and Speeches* (Crossing Press, 2007), 45.

Artist Biographies

EMMA AMOS was a critically acclaimed figurative painter and printmaker whose work interrogated racism, sexism, white hegemony, and the Black female body. She had notable involvement in the African American art collective Spiral and the feminist art collectives Heresies and the Guerilla Girls. She spent twenty-eight years as a professor and chair at the Mason Gross School of the Arts, while continuing her artistic practice. *Emily Hu*

CHAKAIA BOOKER is an American sculptor from Newark, New Jersey, based in New York City. Her work is open to the possibilities of imagination, and frequently meditates on the interactions between urban environments, abstractionism, Black politics, and culture. After thirty years of exceptional work with rubber, she is most well known for her robust tire sculptures. Booker's mediums have also spanned from ceramics to painting, photography, and printmaking. *Jasmine Daria Cannon*

BARBARA BULLOCK was born in Philadelphia and studied at the Hussein School of Art. She has held exhibitions at Howard University and the African American Museum in Philadelphia. Her studies of the culture and religion of the African diaspora inspired her exploration of spirituality and mythology in her art. Bullock often uses collage, color, texture, and sculpture to build three-dimensional, lifelike figures that walk the line between reality and myth. *Audrey Roclore*

ELIZABETH CATLETT was an American artist who spent the pivotal moments of her career as a citizen in Mexico, where she resided for over sixty years. Mexico's sociopolitical and postrevolutionary idealism, often expressed through printmaking, inspired Catlett. She tackled topics such as Black motherhood, femininity, and systematic racism through a dignified and regal lens. Throughout her career, Catlett produced a wide variety of work ranging from graphic prints to drawings, sculpture, and paintings. *Grace Lynne Haynes*

NONA FAUSTINE was a visual artist and photographer. Her work focused on history, identity, representation, and the evocation of a critical and emotional understanding of the past. Faustine exhibited at the Studio Museum of Harlem, the International Center of Photography, and Harvard University, among other institutions. *Desiree Morales*

NEFERTITI GOODMAN, born Cynthia Freeman, is known for her exquisitely detailed and expansive black and white relief prints that she embellishes with colorful, jewel-like tones in gouache and watercolor. While her practice began in Boston, a printmaking fellowship from the New Jersey Council on the Arts brought her to New Jersey, where she currently resides. *Emily Hu*

DAONNE HUFF is an arts administrator, performance artist, and poet. Huff's practice is rooted in observation, vulnerability, process, and synchronicity. She has performed at BLDG 92 at the Brooklyn Navy Yard, Rutgers University, and the Whitney Museum of American Art. *Desiree Morales*

MARGO HUMPHREY creates a spiritual realm that is vividly colorful and uniquely autobiographical. A native of Oakland, California, Humphrey designs celebrated illustrative work layered with meaning and identity. Using a bright "sophisticated naïve" style, she tells multiple stories of Blackness, womanhood, and cultural heritage. *Michael Randall*

STEFANIE JACKSON makes paintings that are concerned with African American history and contemporary U.S. politics. Pulling from assorted styles of painting, such as surrealism and expressionism, Jackson often brings the focus of her brush to major historical events, like the 1906 Atlanta race riots and Hurricane Katrina's devastation in New Orleans. *Kyle b. co.*

CARMEN CARTINESS JOHNSON is a self-taught artist based in San Antonio, Texas, and Bordentown, New Jersey. She was a resident artist at the Brodsky Center in 2005. Working primarily in acrylic, her prints and paintings show the intimacy of everyday life and are meant to resonate with a wide audience. *Emily Hu*

NELL IRVIN PAINTER is a historian and artist. In addition to her research on race in the nineteenth century, she uses found images, drawing, and digital manipulation to create art. Her works produce discourse around freedom and discrimination. They also reflect her personal experiences during her distinguished academic career at Princeton University, followed by her journey earning bachelor and master of fine arts degrees in her second career as an artist. *Helen Gao*

HOWARDENA PINDELL is a mixed-media artist and professor, whose works combine a variety of techniques, including deconstructing and reconstructing canvases, magazines, and drawings. Her art addresses major historical events, like the AIDS crisis and apartheid, as well as issues of racism, feminism, and xenophobia. As an avid activist, she frequently interviews with curators and lectures in university seminars. *Helen Gao*

FAITH RINGGOLD was an artist, activist, and educator revered for an expansive social practice and her bold statements in art. Ringgold's visual work often employed various sewing and quilting techniques and narrative and text to produce radical imaginings of the past, present, and future. Her work is protest in practice and form. *Kyle b. co.*

BETYE SAAR uniquely blends elements of the past, present, and speculative future in the construction of her altars, boxes, and collages. Born in Los Angeles, Saar spent several decades redefining visual storytelling methods by reconstructing found objects inspired by race, gender, spirituality, and personal and political history. *Michael Randall*

LORNA SIMPSON is a Brooklyn native who reinvented the mediums of photography, film, and sculpture to explore history, identity, place, and materiality. Simpson has shown at the Whitney Museum of American Art, CCA Kitakyushu Project Gallery in Japan, and the Museum of Modern Art, among other institutions. *Michael Randall*

SHINIQUE SMITH is a sculptor and painter who combines a wide variety of fine art media to interrogate consumerism. She often uses found materials, such as clothing and stuffed animals, to create free-flowing, complex, and visually poetic pieces. The graffiti scene in her hometown of Baltimore and her studies of Japanese calligraphy and abstraction in college influenced much of her work. *Helen Gao*

RENÉE STOUT is a contemporary sculptor and visual artist known for creating reimagined fictional narratives that derive from her personal history and African

American lineage. Stout explores themes of spirituality, urban life, and ancient African traditions through mediums of photorealism, drawing, and three-dimensional works. She conveys history by employing her radical imagination, resulting in a network of rich imagery and creativity with no bounds. *Grace Lynne Haynes*

SHARON E. SUTTON, FAIA, is an architectural activist, educator, and artist. In 1984, at the University of Michigan, Sutton became the first African American woman in the United States promoted to full professor of architecture. Her scholarship addresses urban architectural inequalities and advocates for inclusion of underrepresented groups in the profession. Her art explores abstractions of experiences at the intersection of art, music, and architecture through geometric shapes, line, color, and rhythm in her mixed-media paper works. *Grace Kim*

MICKALENE THOMAS is a Brooklyn-based mixed-media painter from New Jersey. Having painted the likes of Eartha Kitt and Oprah Winfrey, Thomas is best known for her ability to capture Black women's self-confidence and beauty, by exploring themes of race, gender, and sexuality. Her professional experiences as a model and actress influenced her evolution as an artist, and this has shifted with her curiosities in photography, collage, and printmaking. *Jasmine Daria Cannon*

KARA WALKER is a New York–based, internationally renowned artist, born in Stockton, California. Her works reflect her own internal dialogue with the thin lines between the horrible and comedic, playful and terrible, and childlike and perverse. In her artistic practice, she turned to forms historically considered feminine and unsophisticated, like drawing and silhouetting. Her career-long study of the evils of nineteenth-century social constructions of race and gender are full of her own reimaginings. *Jasmine Daria Cannon*

BISA WASHINGTON constructs multimedia works from fiber and found materials. Centering the familial and the historical, she calls forth African sculptural traditions and ritual practices in her work. Raised in Newark, New Jersey, in the 1960s, Washington credits the era's wealth of African American thought during the Black Power and Black Arts movements as the foundation of her practice. *Kyle b. co.*

CARRIE MAE WEEMS creates complex bodies of work from a variety of media such as installation, audio, photography, fabric, and text. Weems explores the mundane in contemporary Black life, familial dynamics, male-female interactions, sexism, and beauty through a defined feminist perspective. Weems is an award-winning image maker and storyteller whose works stimulate dialogues on timeless subject matter and serious political issues facing contemporary African American life. *Grace Lynne Haynes*

Appendix
Art Analysis Worksheet

IDENTIFYING INFORMATION

- Think carefully about the title—why would the artist choose to name this piece in this manner?

- Talk about the subject matter: who or what is being represented?

FORMAL ANALYSIS

- What colors are used in the work? Bright? Dull? Complementary?

- Describe the use of texture. Is the piece smooth and polished or rough?

- What about the size of the piece? How does that impact your perception of it?

- What stands out? Is there a focal point (an area to which your eye is drawn)?

- Explain any symbols (people, objects, colors, words, phrases). What do you think those symbols represent, or how did the artist intend for us to read them?

CREATOR'S INTENT

- Who made the art?
- Why do you think the creator made this source?

CONTENT OF THE SOURCE

- What is the main idea of the artwork? Describe what you see.
- What biases or other cultural factors might have shaped the message of this source?
- What questions are left unanswered by this source?

AUDIENCE/MESSAGE

- Who is the intended audience?
- How might the intended audience shape the perspective of this source?
- What is the tone of the source?

HISTORICAL CONTEXT

- What was going on in the world, country, region, or locality when this was created?
- What other primary or secondary sources might help provide answers to this question?
- What else do we need to know to better understand this source?

RELEVANCE OF THE SOURCE

- What contributions does this make to our understanding of art history, the present art world, and/or the future of art?
- Connect the piece to contemporary, popular, and everyday culture. Does it conjure up a song, theory, historical event?
- Does your piece convey a social or political message?

Note: This worksheet combined methods, questions, and resources from Lisa E. Farrington, "The Art of Perception: How Art Communicates," in *African-American Art: A Visual and Cultural History* (Oxford University Press, 2016, 3–13; Anne D'Alleva, *How to Write Art History*, 2nd ed. (Laurence King Publishing, 2010); National Archives and Records Administration, Education Resources, "Document Analysis," 2023, https://www.archives.gov/education/lessons/worksheets; Library of Congress, "Primary Source Analysis Tool for Students," Teacher's Guides and Analysis Tool, accessed November 18, 2025, https://www.loc.gov/programs/teachers/getting-started-with -primary-sources/guides/.

Acknowledgments

THIS BOOK IS INDEBTED FIRST and foremost to my Rutgers students, to those undergraduates and graduate students who took African American Art between 2018 and 2022, to those who enrolled in the Curatorial Training seminar in 2019 and 2022, and, most especially, to the intrepid students who took a chance on the Exhibition Seminar in the spring of 2021. It is your collective vision, your desire to push beyond what was offered to you as students of art history, as museum visitors, as art critics, who made this exhibition and publication a reality.

I would also like to thank my Rutgers colleagues from across disciplines and departments, who supported the class, exhibition, public programs, and finally, this publication, in particular Donna Gustafson, Maura Reilly, Nicole Simpson, Christine Giviskos, and Claire D'Amato of the Zimmerli Art Museum and Jenevieve DeLos-Santos, Tatiana Flores, Susan Sidlauskus, Tamara Sears, Laura Weigert, Carla Yanni, and Andrés Mario Zervigón of the Department of Art History. Carla especially has encouraged my growth in numerous areas of my personal and professional life, and for that I am eternally grateful. I also thank Jacquelyn Litt of Douglass Residential College, Alice Hernandez of the Office of the Executive Vice-President for Academic Affairs, Michelle Stephens of the Institute for the Study of Global Racial Justice, and an anonymous donor. Thanks go to the Institute for Women in Leadership at Douglass, which allowed us to transcribe and screen a student interview by Karin Zahavi with Faith Ringgold for the exhibition and book. An incredibly special shout out to Nicole Ianuzelli senior program coordinator for the Center for Women in the Arts at Douglass (formerly the Center for Women in the Arts and Humanities, CWAH). In her previous role at the CWAH she wore countless hats, securing the space for the exhibition and securing the artwork loans, working on set-up and installation, running the programming for the length of the exhibition, facilitating class visits, and de-installing the art pieces as well. This fabulous production would not have happened if she were not the integral touchpoint for the CWAH.

I have sincere appreciation for the Black women artists, activists, and curators who participated in exhibition programming: Rashayla Marie Brown, Ebony Iman Dallas, Heather Hart, Stephanie Johnson-Cunningham, and Key Jo Lee. Thanks also to student curators Kyle b. co., Jasmine Daria Cannon, and Helen Gao for partaking in a panel for our program series.

Gratitude to greats in the art world—Judith Brodsky for allowing us to borrow some prints from her personal collection, Ferris Olin for bringing an engaged and energetic group of Douglass alumnae to see the exhibition, and Rhinold Ponder for his support and promotion of the show.

Thanks also to Lini Radakrishnan, who proofread and edited most of the manuscript, and valiantly and thoroughly tracked down image permissions for the publication; Kimberly Rosen at Artists Rights Society for facilitation of the majority of the permissions for this publication; Micah Kleit and Peter Mickulas at Rutgers University Press for believing in and supporting this publication, and press interns Isabel Holland and Sofiya Tkach for their diligent administrative support. Finally, my gratitude to Randy Jones, a board member of the Zimmerli Art Museum, promoter of the exhibition and advocate of the student curators.

To my family and friends who came to see the exhibition (some visiting the galleries multiple times), supported our programming, and otherwise promoted the show throughout the course of its run—it means so much to have you all show up for me, time and again. Sincere thanks to Christopher Boraski, Duane Dudley, Kelly Garnes Pages, Ghislaine Sabiti, Christopher Wiley, Joo-Yung Wiley, and the mothers of Central New Jersey chapter of Jack and Jill, Incorporated.

Bibliography

"African American Song." Library of Congress. Accessed November 18, 2025. https://www.loc.gov/item/ihas .200197451/.

Akigbogun, Sarah. "In Conversation . . . Sharon Egretta Sutton." Parlour: Gender, Equity, Architecture, October 6, 2019. https://archiparlour.org/in-conversation-with-sharon-egretta-sutton/.

Amos, Emma. *My Mother, My Sisters*. Emma Amos, January 1, 1992. https://emmaamos.com/wordpress/1992/01 /01/my-mothers-my-sisters/.

Andersen, Margaret L., and Patricia Hill Collins. *Race, Class, and Gender: An Anthology*. 9th ed. Cengage Learning, 2016.

Angeleti, Gabriella, and Margaret Carrigan. "Three Exhibitions to See in New York This Weekend." *Art Newspaper*, September 3, 2020. https://www.theartnewspaper.com/review/three-exhibitions-to-see-in-new -york-this-weekend-4-september.

Armand, Claudine. "Visual, Aural, and Temporal Traces in Lorna Simpson's Phototexts and Installations." *KronoScope: Journal for the Study of Time* 14, no. 2 (2014): 163–179.

Ater, Renée. Review of *Creating Their Own Image: A History of African-American Women Artists* and *African Queen*. *African Arts* 38, no. 2 (Summer 2005): 82–83.

Baldwin, James. *The Fire Next Time*. Vintage International, 1993.

Banks, Ingrid. *Hair Matters: Beauty, Power, and Black Women's Consciousness*. New York University Press, 2000.

Bates, Albert. "Octopodal Pictoriality: The Self-Reflexivity of the Octopus in Graeco-Roman Art." *Art History* 47, no. 1 (February 2024): 154–186.

Belisle, Brooke. "Felt Surface, Visible Image: Lorna Simpson's Photography and the Embodiment of Appearance." *Photography & Culture* 4, no. 2 (2011): 157–178.

Bell, David. *Ukiyo-e Explained*. Global Oriental, 2004.

Booker, Chakaia. "Chakaia Booker Biography." Chakaia Booker—International Artist. Accessed November 18, 2025. https://chakaiabooker.com/chakaia-booker-biography/.

Boone, Emilie. "An Ode to James Van Der Zee: Lorna Simpson's 9 Props." *Metropolitan Museum Journal* 55, no. 1 (2020): 76–90.

Brenson, Michael. "Form That Achieves Sympathy: A Conversation with Elizabeth Catlett." *Sculpture*, April 1, 2003. https://sculpturemagazine.art/form-that-achieves-sympathy-a-conversation-with-elizabeth-catlett/.

Breton, André. "Manifesto of Surrealism" (1924). In *Manifestoes of Surrealism*, translated by Richard Seaver and Helen R. Lane, 1–48. University of Michigan Press, 1972.

Brodsky Center at PAFA (Pennsylvania Academy of the Fine Arts). *Femfolio*. Brodsky Center at PAFA, 2025. https://brodskycenter.com/artists/femfolio/.

Brodsky, Judith K., Ferris Olin, Tanya Sheehan, and Michele Wallace, *Declaration of Independence: Fifty Years of Art by Faith Ringgold*. Institute for Women and Art, Rutgers, the State University of New Jersey, 2009.

Brown, Kay. "The Emergence of Black Women Artists: The Founding of 'Where We At.'" *Nka: Journal of Contemporary African Art*, no. 29 (Fall 2011): 118–127.

Cahan, Susan E. *Mounting Frustration: The Art Museum in the Age of Black Power*. Duke University Press, 2016.

Camp, Stephanie M. H. "Black Is Beautiful: An American History." *Journal of Southern History* 81, no. 3 (August 2015): 675–690.

Childs, Adrienne L. "Humphrey, Margo." Grove Art Online, February 24, 2010. https://www.oxfordartonline.com/groveart/.

Cole, Karl. "African American History Month: Henry Taylor and Carmen Cartiness Johnson." *Curator's Corner* (blog), Davis Publications, February 26, 2018. https://www.davisart.com/blogs/curators-corner/henry-taylor-carmen-cartiness-johnson/.

Collins, Lisa Gail. "The Evidence of the Process." *Transition*, no. 109 (2012): 45–61.

Columbia University GSAPP (Graduate School of Architecture, Planning and Preservation). "Sharon Sutton." Accessed December 1, 2025. https://www.arch.columbia.edu/events/2028-sharon-sutton/.

Corbett, Rachel. "Exit Art Closes Its Doors After 30 Years." *Artnet*, March 23, 2012. http://www.artnet.com/magazineus/features/corbett/exit-art-3-23-12.asp.

Cotter, Holland. "Chakaia Booker—'Not That Daughter.'" Art in Review, *New York Times*, July 10, 1998. https://www.nytimes.com/1998/07/10/arts/art-in-review-chakaia-booker-not-that-daughter.html

Cotter, Holland. "Emma Amos, Painter Who Challenged Racism and Sexism, Dies at 83." *New York Times*, May 29, 2020. https://www.nytimes.com/2020/05/29/arts/emma-amos-dead.html.

Crenshaw, Kimberlé. "Mapping the Margins: Intersectionality, Identity Politics, and Violence Against Women of Color." *Stanford Law Review* 43, no. 6 (1991): 1241–1299.

Dawson, John. *The Complete Guide to Prints and Printmaking: Techniques and Materials*. Excalibur Books, 1981.

Dayan, Joan. "Erzulie: A Women's History of Haiti." In "Caribbean Literature," special issue, *Research in African Literatures* 25, no. 2 (Summer 1994): 5–31.

D'Alleva, Anne. *How to Write Art History*. 2nd ed. Laurence King Publishing, 2010.

D'Alleva, Anne. *Methods & Theories of Art History*. 2nd ed. Laurence King Publishing, 2012.

DeLosSantos, Jenevieve, ed. *Poetries—Politics: A Celebration of Language, Art, and Learning*. Rutgers University Press, 2023.

Deveney, Grace. "Interrupting the Broadcast: Howardena Pindell's Video Drawings." In *Howardena Pindell: What Remains to Be Seen*, edited by Naomi Beckwith and Valeri Cassel Oliver, 151–168. DelMonico Books / Prestel and Museum of Contemporary Art Chicago, 2018.

Devlin, Rachel. *A Girl Stands at the Door: The Generation of Young Women Who Desegregated America's Schools*. Basic Books, 2018.

Donoghue, Katy. "Nona Faustine Captures Our Nation's Monuments, Both Historic and Temporary." *Whitewall*, December 4, 2019. https://whitewall.art/art/nona-faustine-captures-nations-monuments-historic-temporary/.

Drew, Kimberly. "The Lenny Interview: Carrie Mae Weems." *Lenny Letter*, August 26, 2016. https://www.lennyletter.com/story/the-lenny-interview-carrie-mae-weems.

Edwards, Stassa. "Nona Faustine's Nude Self Portraits Expose New York's History of Slavery." *Vice*, August 5, 2015. https://www.vice.com/en/article/nona-faustines-nude-self-portraits-expose-new-yorks-history-of -slavery/.

Exit Art Archive. "Guide to the Exit Art Archive, 1982–2014." Fales Library and Special Collections, New York University Libraries. Accessed December 1, 2025. http://dlib.nyu.edu/findingaids/html/fales/exitart/index .html.

Farrington, Lisa E. *African-American Art: A Visual and Cultural History*. Oxford University Press, 2016.

Farrington, Lisa E. *Art on Fire: The Politics of Race and Sex in the Paintings of Faith Ringgold*. Millennium Fine Arts Publishing, 1999.

Farrington, Lisa E. "Emma Amos: Art as Legacy." *Woman's Art Journal* 28, no. 1 (Spring–Summer 2007): 3–11.

Farrington, Lisa. "Emma Amos: Bodies in Motion." *The International Review of African American Art* 21, no. 2 (2007): 32–44.

Farrington, Lisa E. and Faith Ringgold. *Faith Ringgold*. Pomegranate, 2004.

Fink, L. Dee. *Creating Significant Learning Experiences: An Integrated Approach to Designing College Courses*. Wiley, 2013.

Flint Institute of Arts. "Renée Stout, *Maria Laveau*, 2009/2013." Accessed November 18, 2025. https:// collections.flintarts.org/objects/8163/marie-laveau?ctx=bfaaee2c1109872107b9d80c3e6a58f174b841f6&idx =0.

Franks, Pamela, and Robert Emanuel Steele. *Embodied: Black Identities in American Art from the Yale University Art Gallery*. Yale University Art Gallery, 2010.

Fuentes, Marisa J., and Deborah Gray White, eds. *Slavery and Dispossession in Rutgers History*. Vol. 1 of *Scarlet and Black*. Rutgers University Press, 2016.

Genocchio, Benjamin. "Where the Rubber Meets the Sublime." Art Review, *New York Times*, February 15, 2004. https://www.nytimes.com/2004/02/15/nyregion/art-review-where-the-rubber-meets-the-sublime.html.

Gopnik, Blake. "Shinique Smith's Street Art, Taking the High Road." *Washington Post*, March 16, 2008.

Greene, Nikki A. *Grime, Glitter, and Glass: The Body and the Sonic in Contemporary Black Art*. Duke University Press, 2024.

Greenwald, Diana. "What Can Data Teach Us About Museum Collections?" *Alliance Blog*, American Alliance of Museums, April 27, 2020. https://www.aam-us.org/2020/04/27/what-can-data-teach-us-about-museum -collections/.

Handler, Jerome S., and Kenneth M. Bilby. "Obeah: Healing and Protection in West Indian Slave Life." *Journal of Caribbean History* 38, no. 2 (2004): 153–183.

Hart, Heather, and jina valentine. "Another Country." *Art21 Magazine*, September 14, 2018.

Hartman, Saidiya. "Venus in Two Acts." *Small Axe* 12, no. 2 (June 2008): 1–14.

Hayes, Shannan L. "Wanting More." *differences* 31, no. 1 (2020): 64–97.

Herzog, Melanie Anne. *Elizabeth Catlett: An American Artist in Mexico*. University of Washington Press, 2000.

Herzog, Melanie Anne. *Elizabeth Catlett: In the Image of the People*. Art Institute of Chicago; distributed by Yale University Press, 2005.

Hill Collins, Patricia. *Black Feminist Thought: Knowledge, Consciousness, and the Politics of Empowerment*. 2nd ed. New York: Routledge, 2014.

Hill Collins, Patricia. *Intersectionality as Critical Social Theory*. Duke University Press, 2019.

Holloway, Camara Dia. "Critical Race Art History." *Art Journal* 75, no. 1 (2016): 89–92.

Holmes, Jessica. "Nona Faustin *White Shoes*." ArtSeen, *Brooklyn Rail*, March 2016. https://brooklynrail.org/2016 /03/artseen/nona-faustine-white-shoes.

hooks, bell. *Art on My Mind: Visual Politics*. New Press, 1995.

hooks, bell. "Postmodern Blackness." *Postmodern Culture* 1, no. 1 (September 1990). https://dx.doi.org/10.1353 /pmc.1990.0004.

hooks, bell. *Teaching to Transgress: Education as the Practice of Freedom*. Routledge, 1994.

Huff, Daonne. "About." Daonne Huff, 2020. https://www.daonnehuff.com/about.

Huff, Daonne. Conversation with Desiree Morales, April 1, 2021.

Hurston, Zora Neale. *Their Eyes Were Watching God*. Perennial Library, 1990.

J. Paul Getty Museum. *Complete Guide to Adult Audience Interpretive Materials: Gallery Texts and Graphics*. J. Paul Getty Trust, 2011.

Jenkins, Melissa. "'The Next Thing You Know You're Flying Among the Stars': Nostalgia, Heterotopia, and Mapping the City in African American Picture Books." *Children's Literature Association Quarterly* 41, no. 4 (Winter 2016): 343–364.

Johnson, Carmen Cartiness. "About Carmen Cartiness Johnson." Carmen Cartiness Johnson, 2025. https://carmencartinessjohnson.crevado.com/about.

Johnson-Cunningham, Stephanie. "Beyond Gallery Walls and Performance Halls." *Museums & Social Issues* 13, no. 1 (2018): 2–7.

Johnson-Cunningham, Stephanie. "Culturally Responsive Museums Are Leading the Way." Museum Hue (blog), June 8, 2020. https://www.museumhue.org/2020/06/08/2020-6-8-culturally-responsive-museums-leading-the-way/.

Kent, Sarah. "Kara Walker, Camden Arts Centre." *Arts Desk*, October 13, 2013. https://theartsdesk.com/visual-arts/kara-walker-camden-arts-centre.

Kierulf, Caroline. "Printmaking and Multiple Temporalities." *Journal of Visual Art Practice* 14, no. 3 (November 2015): 179–191.

King, Martin Luther, Jr. Interview on "Meet the Press." April 17, 1960. https://kinginstitute.stanford.edu/king-papers/documents/interview-meet-press.

King, Martin Luther, Jr. "Letter from a Birmingham Jail." April 16, 1963. African Studies Center, University of Pennsylvania. http://www.africa.upenn.edu/Articles_Gen/Letter_Birmingham.html.

King, Martin Luther, Jr. *Letter from Birmingham City Jail*. With serigraph prints by Faith Ringgold. Limited Editions Club, 2008. Rhode Island School of Design Museum. https://risdmuseum.org/art-design/collection/letter-birmingham-city-jail-200985.

Kino, Carol. "A Confidence Highlighted in Rhinestones." *New York Times*, April 7, 2009. https://www.nytimes.com/2009/04/12/arts/design/12kino.html.

Lancaster, Lex Morgan. "Feeling the Grid: Lorna Simpson's Concrete Abstraction." *ASAP/Journal* 2, no. 1 (January 2017): 131–155.

Landers, Sean. "Interview: Mickalene Thomas." *BOMB*, no. 116 (Summer 2011). https://bombmagazine.org/articles/mickalene-thomas-1/.

Leaf, Ruth. *Intaglio Printmaking Techniques*. Watson-Guptill Publications, 1976.

Lehrer, Erica, and Shelley Ruth Butler. "Curatorial Dreaming in the Age of COVID-19." Museums and Equity in Times of Crisis. *Alliance Blog*, American Alliance of Museums, May 4, 2020. https://www.aam-us.org/2020/05/04/curatorial-dreaming-in-the-age-of-covid-19/.

Lewis, Samella S. *African American Art and Artists*. University of California Press, 2003.

Litt, Steven. "Akron Art Museum Debuts 'Pattern ID' Exhibit That Marries Patterns, Cultural Themes." *Plain Dealer*, January 30, 2010. https://www.cleveland.com/arts/2010/01/akron_art_museum_debuts_patter.html.

Loos, Ted. "Mickalene Thomas Shares Everything. Even a New Show." *New York Times*, November 20, 2019. https://www.nytimes.com/2019/11/20/arts/design/mickalene-thomas-baltimore.html.

Lorde, Audre. *Sister Outsider: Essays and Speeches*. Crossing Press, 2007.

Lunde, Karl. Introduction to *American Portfolio*. Joseph Kleinman Fine Arts Printing, 1980.

Marter, Joan M. *Women Artists on the Leading Edge: Visual Arts at Douglass College*. Rutgers University Press, 2019.

McCabe, Jennifer. "Review of *Betye Saar: Still Tickin'*." *Panorama: Journal of the Association of Historians of American Art* 2, no. 1 (Summer 2016). https://journalpanorama.org/article/betye-saar-still-tickin/.

McKenna-Cress, Polly, and Janet Kamien. "Advocacy for the Subject Matter." In *Creating Exhibitions: Collaboration in the Planning, Development, and Design of Innovative Experiences*, 69–87. Wiley, 2013.

MICA (Maryland Institute College of Art). "A Conversation with Shinique Smith." *Commotion*, no. 2 (Spring 2016). https://www.mica.edu/art-articles/details/a-conversation-with-shinique-smith/.

Miller, Nicholas. "The History of the Group Exhibition from the Harmon Foundation to *Black Male*." In *The Routledge Companion to African American Art History*, edited by Eddie Chambers, 301–310. Routledge, 2020.

Minneapolis Institute of Arts. Renée Stout, *A Vision I Can't Forget*, 1999. https://collections.artsmia.org/art/13298/a-vision-i-cant-forget-renee-stout.

Morris, Brian. "Vodou in Haiti." In *Religion and Anthropology: A Critical Introduction*, 191–198. Cambridge University Press, 2006.

Morrison, Toni. "Playing in the Dark: Whiteness and the Literary Imagination." In *Racism in America: A Reader*, 1–9. Harvard University Press, 2020.

Murrell, Denise. *Posing Modernity: The Black Model from Manet and Matisse to Today*. Yale University Press, 2018.

National Museum of African Art. "Introduction." *Mami Wata: Arts for Water Spirits in Africa and Its Diasporas*. Accessed November 18, 2025. https://africa.si.edu/exhibits/mamiwata/intro.html.

Nochlin, Linda. "From 1971: Why Have There Been No Great Women Artists?" *ARTnews*, January 1971, reposted May 30, 2015. https://www.artnews.com/art-news/retrospective/why-have-there-been-no-great-women-artists-4201/.

Ode, Kim. "No Bones About It, Breaking the Wishbone Is a Family Tradition." *Minneapolis Star Tribune*, November 26, 2014. https://www.startribune.com/no-bones-about-it-breaking-the-wishbone-is-a-family-tradition/283837301/.

O'Grady, Megan. "How Carrie Mae Weems Rewrote the Rules of Image-Making." *New York Times*, October 15, 2018. https://www.nytimes.com/2018/10/15/t-magazine/carrie-mae-weems-interview.html.

Ogunleye, Tolagbe. "African American Folklore: Its Role in Reconstructing African American History." *Journal of Black Studies* 27, no. 4 (1997): 435–455.

Oh, Janet. "Kara Walker." *Art Story*, April 4, 2021, https://www.theartstory.org/artist/walker-kara/.

Painter, Nell. *Old in Art School: A Memoir of Starting Over*. Counterpoint Press, 2018.

Painter, Nell, and Paola Morsiani. "Nell Painter: Working in the Year 2017." *Art in Print* 7, no. 3 (2017): 13–16.

Patton, Sharon F. *African American Art*. Oxford University Press, 1998.

Patton, Sharon F. "Emma Amos: Art Matters." *Nka: Journal of Contemporary African Art* 16–17 (Fall/Winter 2002): 40–47.

Petrucci Family Foundation Collection of African American Art. "Barbara Bullock." Works in the Collection. Accessed December 1, 2025. https://www.petruccifamilyfoundation.org/artists/48-barbara-bullock/overview/.

Pindell, Howardena. Oral history interview with Howardena Pindell, December 1–4, 2012. Conducted by Judith Olch Richards. Archives of American Art, Smithsonian Institution. https://www.aaa.si.edu/collections/interviews/oral-history-interview-howardena-pindell-1611.

Pinder, Kymberly N. "Black Representation and Western Survey Textbooks." *Art Bulletin* 81, no. 3 (September 1999): 533–538.

Pinder, Kymberly N. "Unbaled: An Interview with Shinique Smith." *Art Journal* 67, no. 2 (2008): 6–17.

Powell, Richard J. *Interview of Margo Humphrey by Rick Powell*. Hatch-Billops Collection, 1987.

Rao, Anita, and Frank Stasio. "Fact Meets Fiction in 'La Sombra y el Espiritu IV.'" WUNC North Carolina Public Radio, February 11, 2016. https://www.wunc.org/arts-culture/2016-02-11/fact-meets-fiction-in-la-sombra-y-el-espiritu-iv.

Ringgold, Faith. *Dancing at the Louvre: Faith Ringgold's French Collection and Other Story Quilts*. University of California Press, 1998.

Ringgold, Faith. *Taking Flight: An Interview with Faith Ringgold*. Interview by Karin Zahavi, Institute for Women's Leadership, Rutgers University, 2008.

Rosenberg, Karen. "Elizabeth Catlett, Sculptor with Eye on Social Issues, Is Dead at 96." *New York Times*, April 3, 2012. https://www.nytimes.com/2012/04/04/arts/design/elizabeth-catlett-sculptor-with-eye-on-social-issues-dies-at-96.html.

Roth, Moira. "Faith Ringgold: Putting Jones Road on the Map." *Nka: Journal of Contemporary African Art*, no. 13–14 (Spring/Summer 2001): 18–25.

Rowe, Kristen Denise. "'Nothing Else Mattered After That Wig Came Off': Black Women, Unstyled Hair, and Scenes of Interiority." *Journal of American Culture* 42, no. 1 (2019): 21–36.

Rowell, Charles Henry. "Elizabeth Catlett." *Callaloo* 39, no. 5 (2016): 999–1080.

Saggese, Jordana Moore, Camara Dia Holloway, T'ai. Smith, Tina Takemoto, and Tobias Wofford. "Beyond the Numbers Game: Diversity in Theory and Practice." *Art Journal* 75, no. 1 (Spring 2016): 98–109.

San Antonio Art League and Museum. "2019 Invitational." 2019. https://www.saalm.org/2019-invitational.html.

Schneede, Uwe M. *Surrealism*. Translated by Maria Pelikan. H. N. Abrams, 1974.

Schnier, Jacques. "Morphology of a Symbol: The Octopus." *American Imago* 13, no. 1 (Spring 1956): 3–31.

Schor, Mira, Emma Amos, Susan Bee, Johanna Drucker, María Fernández, Amelia Jones, Shirley Kaneda, Helen Molesworth, Howardena Pindell, Collier Schorr, and Faith Wilding. "Contemporary Feminism: Art Practice, Theory, and Activism—an Intergenerational Perspective." *Art Journal* 58, no. 4 (Winter 1999): 8–29.

Schwob, Olivia. "Painter, Anew." *Harvard Magazine*, September–October 2018.

Shaw, Gwendolyn DuBois. *The Art of Remembering: Essays on African American Art and History*. Duke University Press, 2024.

Smith, Beryl K. "The Mary H. Dana Women Artists Series: From Idea to Institution." *Journal of the Rutgers University Libraries* 54, no. 1 (1992): 4–16.

Smith, Sarah Stefana. 2018. "Surface Play: Rewriting Black Interiorities Through Camouflage and Abstraction in Mickalene Thomas's Oeuvre." *Women & Performance: A Journal of Feminist Theory* 28, no. 1 (2018): 46–64.

Smith, Valerie. "Abundant Evidence: Black Women Artists of the 1960s and 1970s." In *Entering the Picture: Judy Chicago, the Fresno Feminist Art Program, and the Collective Visions of Women Artists*, edited by Jill Fields, 119–131. Routledge, 2012.

Spencer, Anne. "Sybil Warns Her Sister." In *Ebony and Topaz: A Collectanea,* edited by Charles S. Johnson. Opportunity, 1927.

Steinhauer, Jillian. "At 77, Howardena Pindell Exorcises a Chilling Memory from Childhood." *New York Times*, October 16, 2020, https://www.nytimes.com/2020/10/16/arts/design/howardena-pindell-shed-video.html.

Stewart, Lindsey. "Black Feminist Figures: Interventions and Inheritances." *Southern Journal of Philosophy* 59, no. 1 (March 2021): 5–15.

Suzuki, Harunobu. Color woodblock print, 1765–1770. Museum no. 1937,0710,0.11. British Museum. https://www.britishmuseum.org/collection/object/A_1937-0710-0-11.

Swain, Rhea. "Art History Professor Highlights Iconic Black Artists." *Daily Targum*, February 19, 2020. https://dailytargum.com/article/2020/02/honoring-black-artists-zimmerli.

Tani, Ellen Y. "Keeping Time in the Hands of Betye Saar: *Betye Saar: Still Tickin'*." *American Quarterly* 68, no. 4 (December 2016): 1081–1109.

Taylor, Paul C. "Post-Black, Old Black." In "Post-Soul Aesthetic," special issue, *African American Review* 41, no. 4 (Winter 2007): 625–640.

Tempini, Niccolò. "Visual Metaphors: Howardena Pindell, Video Drawings, 1975." In *Data Journeys in the Sciences* edited by Sabina Leonelli and Niccolò Tempini, 401–404. Springer, 2020.

Thomas, Douglas, and Temilola Alanamu, eds. *African Religions: Beliefs and Practices Through History*. ABC-CLIO, 2018.

Thomas, Mickalene. "About." Mickalene Thomas. Accessed November 18, 2025. https://mickalene.herokuapp.com/about/.

Topaz, Chad M., Bernhard Klingenberg, Daniel Turek, Brianna Heggeseth, Pamela E. Harris, Julie C. Blackwood, C. Ondine Chavoya, Steven Nelson, and Kevin M. Murphy. "Diversity of Artists in Major U.S. Museums." *PLoS One* 14, no. 3 (2019): e0212852. https://doi.org/10.1371/journal.pone.0212852.

University of Washington. "Sharon E. Sutton, PhD, FAIA." University of Washington Faculty. Accessed November 18, 2025. http://faculty.washington.edu/sesut/index.html.

Valentine, Victoria L. "Artist Emma Amos on Her Falling Series: I Liked the Idea Somebody Was 'Trying to Catch You' or 'Holding onto You.'" *Culture Type*, November 6, 2020. https://www.culturetype.com/2020/11/06/artist-emma-amos-on-her-falling-series-i-liked-the-idea-somebody-was-trying-to-catch-you-or-holding-onto-you/.

Valentine, Victoria L. "Culture Talk: Courtney Willis Blair on Ryan Lee Gallery's Representation of Emma Amos." *Culture Type*, April 6, 2016. https://www.culturetype.com/2016/04/06/culture-talk-courtney-willis -blair-on-ryan-lee-gallerys-representation-of-emma-amos/.

Walker, Alice. *In Search of Our Mothers' Gardens: Womanist Prose*. Amistad Press, 2023.

Walker, Kara. "Kara Walker at the MAC: 24 Jan–27 Apr 2014." The MAC Belfast, January 14, 2014. YouTube. https://youtu.be/5QbXdPv-O1g?si=rw96iDCTG-INoH7I.

Walker, Kara. "Kara Walker Speaks About Her Art." Talk at the Risible Visual: Humor and Art Biennial, the Menil Collection and the Department of Art History, Rice University, Houston, TX, March 14, 2011. YouTube, https://www.youtube.com/watch?v=clvQRQO5x7E.

Walker, Kara. "Mickalene Thomas." *BOMB*, no. 107 (Spring 2009). https://bombmagazine.org/articles/2009/04 /01/mickalene-thomas/.

Wallace, Caroline V. "Exhibiting Authenticity: The Black Emergency Cultural Coalition's Protests of the Whitney Museum of American Art, 1968–71." *Art Journal* 74, no. 2 (2015): 5–23.

Wallace, Michele. "Why Are There No Great Black Artists? The Problem of Visuality in African American Culture." In *Dark Designs and Visual Culture*, 184–194. Duke University Press, 2004.

Washington, Bisa. "The Artist Recreates the World with Bisa Washington." The Artist Recreates the World, September 26, 2016. YouTube, https://www.youtube.com/watch?v=PIbRJP6Q5Vk.

Washington, Bisa. "Bisa Washington." *Black Renaissance / Renaissance Noire* 10, no. 1 (Spring 2010): 58–65.

Weems, Carrie Mae. "Aperture: 40 Years." *Aperture*, no. 129 (Fall 1992): 47.

Weems, Carrie Mae. "Artist Talk: Carrie Mae Weems." Guggenheim Museum, 2019. YouTube. https://www .youtube.com/watch?v=mCp9X3VTo0s.

Weems, Carrie Mae. "Women Behind the Camera: Carrie Mae Weems." National Gallery of Art, September 12, 2015. YouTube. https://www.youtube.com/watch?v=_jIwiBgSNtk.

Welch, Sherri. "Detroit Institute of Arts Acquires Works from 2 Contemporary African- American Artists." *Crain's Detroit Business*, May 20, 2016. https://www.crainsdetroit.com/article/20160520/NEWS/160529972 /detroit-institute-of-arts-acquires-works-from-2-contemporary.

Welter, Barbara. "The Cult of True Womanhood: 1820–1860." *American Quarterly* 18, no. 2, pt. 1 (Summer 1966): 151–174.

"White Clergymen Urge Local Negroes to Withdraw from Demonstrations." *Birmingham News*, April 13, 1963. https://bplonline.contentdm.oclc.org/digital/collection/p4017coll2/id/746/.

Wiley, Amber N. "Amber N. Wiley on Teaching with the Tang Collection." In *Accelerate: Access and Inclusion at the Tang Teaching Museum*, edited by Ian Berry and Rebecca McNamara, 8–9. Frances Young Tang Teaching Museum and Art Gallery, Skidmore College, 2017, vol. 1.

Wiley, Amber N. "Carrie Mae Weems, *When and Where I Enter the British Museum*." In *Accelerate: Access and Inclusion at the Tang Teaching Museum*, edited by Ian Berry and Rebecca McNamara, 10–13. Frances Young Tang Teaching Museum and Art Gallery, Skidmore College, 2017, vol. 1.

Wiley, Amber N. "Integrating Architecture into Digital and Public Humanities: Sites and Sounds + MediaNOLA." *Journal of Digital Humanities* 2, no. 2 (Spring 2013). https://journalofdigitalhumanities.org /2-2/integrating-architecture-into-digital-and-public-humanities-by-amber-wiley/.

Wiley, Amber N. *Model Schools in the Model City: Race, Planning, and Education in the Nation's Capital*. University of Pittsburgh Press, 2025.

Wolfskill, Phoebe. "Love and Theft in the Art of Emma Amos." *Archives of American Art Journal* 55, no. 2 (Fall 2016): 47–65.

Wolfskill, Phoebe. "Old and New Negroes, Continued: Betye Saar and Kara Walker." In *Archibald Motley Jr. and Racial Reinvention*, 146–173. University of Illinois Press, 2017.

Yasha, Ilk. "Studio Check In with Daonne Huff." *Studio Magazine*, June 29, 2019. https://www.studiomuseum .org/article/studio-check-daonne-huff.

Young, Jason R. "All God's Children Had Wings: The Flying African in History, Literature, and Lore." *Journal of Africana Religions* 5, no. 1 (2017): 50–70.

Zimmer, William. "Inspired by a Different Set of Saints." Art Review, *New York Times*, August 30, 1998. https://www.nytimes.com/1998/08/30/nyregion/art-review-inspired-by-a-different-set-of-saints.html.

Notes on Contributors

JASMINE DARIA CANNON, a Black feminist curator, writer, and researcher, focuses on late nineteenth- to early twentieth-century African American women's history. Her curatorial work celebrates the richness of historic Black communities nationwide. A first-generation college graduate, she previously served as the women's history predoctoral fellow at the National Women's History Museum. She holds an MA in women's, gender, and sexuality studies from Rutgers University and an MA in American studies from George Washington University, where she was recognized as a Columbian College of Arts and Sciences' 2019 Distinguished Master's Scholar. Cannon earned her BA in women's and gender studies from North Carolina State University. She is a Paulsboro, New Jersey, native, descendant of Southern migrants from Georgia and North Carolina, and a daughter, sister, and friend.

KYLE B. CO. is a transdisciplinary artist, performer, educator, and baker. Their work explores collage making through practices of printmaking, sculpture, installation, poetry, dance, and set design. In their work they seek to congeal transient realities, and to envision quantum positions especially as they relate to Black and queer histories of survival and existence. Kyle b. co. was a Douglass Faculty Fellow who trained and mentored the *Collective Yearning* student tour guides as part of their project, Black

Women Printmakers, and worked with students to create a special print portfolio in celebration of this historical exhibit. They received their MFA in visual arts from Mason Gross School of the Arts at Rutgers University. Their work has found kinship at Hera Gallery (South Kingstown, RI), the Rhode Island School of Design Museum of Art (Providence), Buoy Gallery (Kittery, ME), the Zimmerli Museum of Art (New Brunswick, NJ), and Lucas, Lucas (Brooklyn, NY), among other spaces.

HELEN GAO is a third-year medical student with an emphasis in global health at Robert Wood Johnson Medical School. She is a member of the inaugural class of the Rutgers Honors College–New Brunswick and Robert Wood Johnson Medical School 4 + 4 Program. Gao has conducted extensive research in the Hart Lab at Rutgers and in the Aresty Science Program. She graduated from Rutgers Honor College with a double major in art history and cell biology neuroscience. Her love for science and art drove her undergraduate experience, and she believes that an interdisciplinary education is vital to becoming a well-rounded physician-scientist. She was named an Honors College Changemaker and Rutgers Trustee Scholar and received the Henry Rutgers Scholarship as well as the Patrick Quigley Scholarship for art history majors.

HEATHER HART is an interdisciplinary artist who makes objects that are activated and expanded through collaboration with performers and publics. Hart's work has been exhibited at the Queens Museum, Storm King Art Center, Kohler Art Center, NCMA, Albright-Knox Art Gallery, Eastern Illinois University, Seattle Art Museum, Brooklyn Museum, Newfields Museum, University of Buffalo, and University of Toronto, Scarborough. She was awarded grants from Anonymous Was A Woman, the Graham Foundation, the Joan Mitchell Foundation, the Jerome Foundation, NYFA, and the Harpo Foundation. She co-founded the award-winning Black Lunch Table in 2005. Hart is an assistant professor of Art & Design at Mason Gross School of the Arts at Rutgers University, a member of the Black Trustee Alliance for Art Museums, an external adviser for AUC Art Collective, and a trustee at Storm King Art Center. She studied at Skowhegan, Whitney ISP, Cornish College of the Arts, Princeton University, and Rutgers University, where she received her MFA.

GRACE LYNNE HAYNES is a California native currently based in New Jersey. Her brightly colored, abstracted, and patterned visual art, which has twice graced the cover of the *New Yorker*, primarily consists of gouache paintings and collages that depict dignified Black women. She explores issues of femininity, solitude, and rest in playful scenes of otherworldly environments. She has had solo shows at the Band of Vices in Los Angeles and the Luce Gallery in Turin, Italy. A participant in the inaugural Black Rock artist residency in Senegal, her work has been published in *LA Weekly*, *New American Paintings*, *Creative Quarterly*, and *Culture Type*. Grace received a BFA from the ArtCenter College of Design and an MFA from Rutgers Mason Gross School of the Arts.

EMILY HU is a 2024–2026 Bridge-to-PhD Fellow with the Center for Chemical Currencies of a Microbial Planet at Brown University. Her work focuses on marine microbial communities and the relationship between physical ocean dynamics and biogeochemical fluxes. She was drawn to studying the ocean due to the interdisciplinary nature of the field and a desire to apply her physical science background to better understand the natural world. Her research interests also include community-engaged approaches to science and climate justice. Prior to Brown, she received her BA in chemistry from Rutgers University with a minor in art history. After graduation, she worked for three years as a science book editor at Oxford University Press.

GRACE KIM is an independent scholar who is interested in the ways gender is represented in Japanese Edo period prints, particularly in relation to transformation, costume, and performance in Kabuki prints. She graduated from Rutgers University–New Brunswick with an MA in art history, specializing in Japanese prints, and spent a year in Yokohama, Japan, for the ten-month intensive language program at the Inter-University Center. She is an intern at the Japan Society Gallery, where she is cataloging the gallery's permanent collection. She has helped with the production of the *Bunraku Backstage, Acky Bright: Studio Infinity*, and *Kotobuki: Auspicious Celebrations of Japanese Art* exhibitions.

DESIREE MORALES is an artist based in Harrison, New Jersey. A native of St. Louis, Missouri, she uses photography as a vehicle to navigate representation, personal archive, and photographic history. Morales received a BFA in photography from the Kansas City Art Institute in 2015 and an MFA in interdisciplinary arts from Rutgers University in 2022. She is a previous Charlotte Street resident and was a rotating artist in the Kansas City Collection V. Morales has shown at the H&R Block Artspace, Delaware County Community College, Westbeth Gallery, and Kemper Museum of Contemporary Art.

MICHAEL RANDALL is a graphic designer, visual artist, writer, and art historian with a focus in cultural and historic preservation. Born and raised in Detroit, Michigan, and a current resident of New Jersey, he earned his master's degree in cultural heritage and preservation studies from Rutgers University. He completed his thesis, "Black American Culture and the Digital Landscape: Modern Heritage Challenges in the 21st Century," in May 2023. He currently works at Rutgers as an environmental graphic designer and historic preservation coordinator. His hobbies include video games, film, television, comics, anime, and reading and writing both fiction and nonfiction.

AUDREY ROCLORE is a curatorial assistant at the Montclair Art Museum. She has a passion for understanding the intersections of art, contemporary life, social change, and digital culture. She received her master's in art history / curatorial studies from Rutgers University, concentrating on Iranian modern art. Her time at the Zimmerli Art Museum and within the Department of Art History at Rutgers were instrumental in shaping her commitment to improving accessibility in the arts through community engagement and programming. She is dedicated to redefining art institutions as facilitators of structural change within their respective communities.

NICOLE SIMPSON is the associate curator of prints and drawings at the Zimmerli Art Museum. She previously worked in the print departments at the New York Public Library, Christie's, and the Baltimore Museum of Art and as an adjunct instructor at Cooper Union. She received her MA from the Institute of Fine Arts, New York University, and PhD from the City of New York Graduate Center.

AMBER N. WILEY is the Wick Cary Director of the Institute for Quality Communities and an associate professor of planning, landscape architecture and design in the Christopher C. Gibbs College of Architecture at the University of Oklahoma. Her publications include *Model Schools in the Model City*, and numerous articles, book chapters, and essays on African American and African diasporic cultural heritage, public history, urbanism in New Orleans, urban renewal, and preservation. She received her PhD in American Studies from George Washington University, master's in architectural history and Certificate in Historic Preservation from the University of Virginia School of Architecture, and BA in Architecture from Yale University. She is a native of Oklahoma City with roots in Washington, DC, Maryland, North Carolina, and Arkansas.